HERE THERE ARE
TIGERS

The Stackpole Military History Series

THE AMERICAN CIVIL WAR

Cavalry Raids of the Civil War
Ghost, Thunderbolt, and Wizard
Pickett's Charge
Witness to Gettysburg

WORLD WAR II

Armor Battles of the Waffen-SS,
    1943–45
Army of the West
Australian Commandos
The B-24 in China
Backwater War
The Battle of Sicily
Beyond the Beachhead
The Brandenburger Commandos
The Brigade
Bringing the Thunder
Coast Watching in World War II
Colossal Cracks
D-Day to Berlin
Dive Bomber!
Eagles of the Third Reich
Exit Rommel
Fist from the Sky
Flying American Combat Aircraft of
    World War II
Forging the Thunderbolt
Fortress France
The German Defeat in the East,
    1944–45
German Order of Battle, Vol. 1
German Order of Battle, Vol. 2
German Order of Battle, Vol. 3
Germany's Panzer Arm in World War II
GI Ingenuity
Grenadiers
Infantry Aces
Iron Arm
Iron Knights
Kampfgruppe Peiper at the Battle
    of the Bulge
Luftwaffe Aces

Massacre at Tobruk
Messerschmitts over Sicily
Michael Wittmann, Vol. 1
Michael Wittmann, Vol. 2
Mountain Warriors
The Nazi Rocketeers
On the Canal
Packs On!
Panzer Aces
Panzer Aces II
The Panzer Legions
Panzers in Winter
The Path to Blitzkrieg
Retreat to the Reich
Rommel's Desert War
The Savage Sky
A Soldier in the Cockpit
Soviet Blitzkrieg
Stalin's Keys to Victory
Surviving Bataan and Beyond
T-34 in Action
Tigers in the Mud
The 12th SS, Vol. 1
The 12th SS, Vol. 2
The War against Rommel's Supply Lines

THE COLD WAR / VIETNAM

Flying American Combat Aircraft:
    The Cold War
Here There Are Tigers
Land with No Sun
Street without Joy

WARS OF THE MIDDLE EAST

Never-Ending Conflict

GENERAL MILITARY HISTORY

Carriers in Combat
Desert Battles

HERE THERE ARE TIGERS

TIGERS

The Secret Air War in Laos, 1968–69

Reginald Hathorn

STACKPOLE
BOOKS

Published by
STACKPOLE BOOKS
5067 Ritter Road
Mechanicsburg, PA 17055
www.stackpolebooks.com

Printed in the United States of America

10 9 8 7 6 5 4 3 2 1

FIRST EDITION

Library of Congress Cataloging-in-Publication Data

Hathorn, Reginald.
  Here there are tigers : the secret air war in Laos, 1968–69 / Reginald Hathorn. — 1st ed.
     p. cm. — (Stackpole Military history series)
  Includes index.
  ISBN-13: 978-0-8117-3469-1
  ISBN-10: 0-8117-3469-2
  1. Vietnam War, 1961–1975—Aerial operations, American. 2. Vietnam War, 1961–1975—Personal narratives, American. 3. Vietnam War, 1961–1975—Campaigns—Laos. 4. Hathorn, Reginald. I. Title.
  DS558.8.H386 2008
  959.704'348—dc22
                                                       2007037711

In memory of the unknown trooper who wrote these words on a scrap of paper at a premission briefing before his LRRP team's insertion into Laos, from which he never returned:

I see as the eagle, clear and all
I listen as the deer, alert, head cocked
I think as the snake, unblinking, silent
I walk as the panther, soft and sinuous
I crouch as the lion, ready and muscled
I kill as the mongoose, swift and sure
I die like a man
I am Mike Force

NKP/CCN
5th SPF

This book is humbly dedicated to all FACs who flew the skies of Southeast Asia during the war in Vietnam, Laos, and Cambodia—especially to those of the 23rd TASS stationed at Nakon Phanom Royal Thai Air Base, Thailand, and to our groundcrews who kept us in the air.

It is also dedicated to the pilots and groundcrews of the Nimrods, Sandys, Candlesticks, Hobos, Knives, and Jollys, who, under the most difficult of conditions, assisted me in our mutual service to our country.

Last, but not least, it is dedicated to those who will remain in Southeast Asia forever. May God always look after these heroes' souls who did not come home.

I give thanks to the guardian angel who rode with me through the terror, chaos, and hell of Southeast Asia on The Trail.

Table of Contents

Preface

Webster's *International Dictionary*, 2nd edition, defines the word narration as "an act of telling or relating the particulars of an occurrence, or course of events. That which is related: a story."

This is my story, a story of becoming an Air Force forward air controller (FAC). The events I recount are but a few of the combat missions I flew in the skies over Laos, North Vietnam, and South Vietnam in support of U.S. and allied military forces against the North Vietnamese, the Viet Cong, and the Pathet Lao during 1968 and 1969. I flew 229 sorties: 42 in South Vietnam, 21 in North Vietnam, and 166 in Laos. The missions in North Vietnam were flown in support of the 5th Special Forces, MACV-SOG. They, as well as all the missions in Laos, were top secret.

Laos was a land of inhospitable factions, political turmoil, armed insurrection, and invasion by another country. It was an extremely dangerous place to be. Like the tigers that walked its green jungles and misty karst mountains, it would consume the careless and unwary without so much as a hiccup. I unwittingly threw myself into this arena of mystery, secrecy, and danger when I volunteered to become a SCAR FAC. If I were young again, I'd do it all over.

I freely admit that I found myself as I flew the skies of Southeast Asia. I found my limitations, my abilities, my weaknesses, my strengths, and I found a belief in God I had never had before. As missions and events unfolded, I became strongly convinced that a guardian angel had attached herself to me to guide and protect me—from myself perhaps—to whisper to me as I flew, to keep me right-side-up.

I also freely admit that, flying my O-2 under the call sign of Nail 31, I came to believe I had a hunting license for an unlimited bag limit. I grew hard, and harder, as I witnessed what the enemy did to our people and their own people. I eventually reached the point where I relished the arrival of fighter-bombers who expended their munitions on the enemy at my call. I grew cold as stone and saw what I did the same way a guy back home might view catching the bus and going to work. Many of us had business cards printed up. At first it was a joke, but after three of my buddies—FAC Captains Bob Rex and Don Luna and my Special Forces covey rider, Sgt. Timothy Walters— were killed, I passed my cards out freely.

Having trouble with hostile neighbors? Need a change? Call Nail 31, 23rd TASS.
Killing is my Business. Business is good.
Have O-2. Will travel.

Business had been good—too good—and each day saw me and the enemy's AAA guns in a pissing contest with each other. I won each match, but I came to realize that, like in the Old West, sooner or later a faster gun comes along. My guardian angel began to whisper to me more and more, and one day, as I headed out on a MACV-SOG mission, I stopped in the little chapel set up there in the intelligence building. I knelt in my tiger stripes, laid my Swedish K submachine gun down beside me, and spoke to my angel. I promised that if I came back from this one, I'd quit the insanity.

The missions were very dangerous. It had gotten to the point where the NVA knew where our LZs were. Some 70,000 NVA troops were positioned along the Ho Chi Minh Trail. If they caught us, there was no doubt that they'd kill us. I'd been in Southeast Asia since 1968; it was now April 1969, and I felt as though my luck was wearing thin. We had lost eighty-six aircraft in six months, and with two months to go on my tour, I took myself off day flights and became a night fighter until my last flight on June 22, 1969.

When I first came to Thailand and began flying into Laos and North Vietnam, I saw several very old maps of Indochina. Great expanses of territory were labeled "Here There Are Tigers." To the Orientals, a tiger was a demon, both feared and revered. That described Laos for me—beautiful as well as deadly.

The names in this book—except for those of Capt. Bob Rex, Capt. Don Luna, Sgt. Timothy Walters, and several photo subjects—are fictional and have no real-life connection to the events described. Call signs have also been changed, except the author's.

Introduction

Any man who goes to war and says he is not afraid is a liar. Any man who goes to war and doesn't realize why he is there is a fool. And any man who goes to war wanting to is an idiot. Those of us who flew and fought in the unpopular war in Southeast Asia were not there by choice. We would certainly much rather have been at home with our loved ones. But it was our duty to go—our duty to our country, to ourselves, to freedom.

We were trying to halt the spreading of the cancer of communism across Indochina. None of us was a mercenary or had a particular axe to grind. We were simply professional airmen serving our nation the best we knew how. Our job was to fly in a hostile environment and kill the enemy, though sometimes it was difficult to tell who the enemy was. There were no legions lined up on opposite sides of a field. Often, there weren't even uniforms on either side. My own "uniform" carried no name, patches, or country markings; my planes had no markings except for the last three digits of its serial number.

The war in Southeast Asia was weird and unorthodox. It was a war of shadows, of confused rules, of political bickerings, of secrecy. Decisions about its conduct were often made far removed from the people it affected the most: the peoples of North and South Vietnam, of Laos and Cambodia. They knew nothing of communism. They wanted only to be left alone to live their lives as they had done for thousands of years. The communist masterminds saw them as putty to be molded to suit their needs, starting in South Vietnam and spreading to Laos and Cambodia and beyond. Many of these people resisted the communists and joined the efforts of the U.S. in fighting them.

Laos was supposed to be a neutral country, but in reality, it was dominated by the Pathet Lao guerrilla forces, assisted by the regular North Vietnamese Army and the Viet Minh, who were using Laos as a supply route to transport war materiel from North Vietnam to South Vietnam. They accomplished this using the Ho Chi Minh Trail, a network of trails and roads that paralleled the border of both Vietnams. Those of us who flew in Laos were tasked with preventing these supplies from reaching South Vietnam.

Had we pilots been left alone by Washington—specifically Lyndon Johnson and Robert McNamara—we could have ended the entire war in one week, but the rules of the game prevented us from doing so. We saw the ships in the harbors, the trucks coming into North Vietnam, the boats streaming into the ports of Cambodia through the Gulf of Thailand. But we could not strike. Instead, we poked and probed. We shot at the enemy here, burned him there, and then retreated, allowing him to regain his strength so we could fight him again the next day.

Under the rules of engagement in Southeast Asia, we were permitted to use our guns and rockets on uniformed NVA troops and to drop fragmentation bombs on them day or night, provided they were not in a village. Napalm could not be used during the day unless friendlies were engaged in direct battle with the enemy. At night, however, napalm could be used to burn the world down, except villages. Villages were off limits to air strikes unless you were taking fire from it—in which case you could annihilate the entire village. We could not bomb or strafe boats unless the boat was at least thirty feet long and ten feet wide and was in the war zone.

The war zone in Laos was the entire country except for a 200-mile stretch along the Mekong River that extended inland for another twenty miles. However, in order to attack in Laos inside the 200 by 20 mile area called "Free Laos", a Royal Lao Army officer had to be on board the aircraft. U.S. Air Force forward air controllers regularly flew in this area with Royal Lao observers as part of the Cricket West Program. Highly experienced FACs from the 23rd Tactical Air Support Squadron (TASS), based at Nakhon Phanom Royal Thai Air Base (NKP) in

Thailand, flew these missions. In addition to the FACs, the CIA also carried out missions inside Laos from NKP. According to the official position of the U.S., there were no American personnel in Laos.

NKP and Udorn Air Base to its northwest were the bases from which Heavy Hook and Prairie Fire missions were launched. Heavy Hook was conducted by the U.S. Army's 5th Special Forces, part of MACV-SOG, and involved inserting teams and individual intelligence agents into North Vietnam. Prairie Fire missions began after the bombing halt imposed by President Johnson in autumn of 1968. These missions involved the insertion of five- to eight-member teams of Cambodian mercenaries into Laos to gather intelligence.

It was a known fact among squadron pilots of the 23rd TASS that there were 5th Special Forces road-watch teams being inserted into Laos on a frequent basis. Sabotage of enemy forces was commonplace. The capture and acquisition of enemy personnel and equipment was forever on somebody's mind. An array of NVA equipment showed up at NKP with regularity— Chinese and Russian AK-47 assault rifles, SKSs, Russian trucks, Red Chinese equipment, and other Com-Bloc countries' gear. Then it would disappear. Unmarked and strange green and black C-130 transports would come and go, showing up near dusk and rarely remaining overnight.

The International Control Commission would fly over Laos from time to time. Word would filter down to us, and we would simply stand down for the day. The "war" that was going on inside of Laos was supposed to be between the North Vietnamese and the Pathet Lao and the free Lao people, with the Royal Lao Army and Air Force led by Lao General Vang Pao and his Meo tribesmen. The real truth was that the CIA was Mr. Money Bags behind all of that activity, along with Air America and USAF pilots in civilian clothes and gear in unmarked aircraft. Those of us FACs who flew the unmarked Cessna O-1 and O-2 spotter aircraft in Laos were the eyes and ears of everything that was happening inside Laos.

The mission of the 23rd TASS at NKP—under call signs Raven and Nail—had many facets. The TASS did many things in its endeavors in the secret war inside of Laos. As attested to by its three Presidential Unit Citation awards for extraordinary gallantry in connection with military operations, such as controlling and directing ordinary strike and aerial reconnaissance missions using USAF, USN, USM, and Australian combat aircraft supporting the U.S. Army's 5th Special Forces under MACV-SOG, and the Royal Laotion Army under Gen. Vang Pao, and CIA forces. The 23rd TASS's FAC pilots personally controlled and directed all search and rescue missions that went on inside Laos and often in North Vietnam.

Pilots of the 23rd were personally involved in the flying of 5th Special Forces personnel into North Vietnam as part of the Heavy Hook and Prairie Fire operations. These very dangerous missions were directly under sanction by Supreme U.S. Headquarters, Pentagon, through MACV-SOG, Saigon, and Da Nang, and involved "intelligence gathering" teams inserted into North Vietnam and Laos. Personnel used on these insertion teams were South Vietnamese and Cambodians, sometimes Thai, sometimes Meo or Montanyard. Pay—per man, per mission—was $50 American. Throughout SEA at the time, $50 was equal to about one year's wage. Therefore, if a team member could survive the normal insertion time of four to seven days on the ground inside North Vietnam or Laos, and return to Thailand, he would be a rich man.

The U.S. 5th Special Forces, the "Green Berets," had their own compound located at NKP. It was manned and guarded by 5th Special Forces personnel, and unless you were "one of them," or were personally known to them, or showed official orders that you had a need to visit that compound, nobody got inside. The personnel were part of an A Team and were commanded by a Special Forces major. These Special Forces personnel operated and functioned totally on their own except for aerial support from the 23rd TASS and six specially selected FAC pilots.

Strange looking black and green USAF MC-130 aircraft that were equipped with the Fulton Skyhook system and assigned to the 15th, then 90th SOS, 1st Flight Detachment, Nha Trang, also came and went at will from NKP, on 5th Special Forces "business." These birds resupplied the A Team and brought insert team members in and out of NKP.

When it came time for a team insertion into North Vietnam or Laos, a black and green MC-130 would arrive at NKP on a straight-in single approach, land, and taxi off the runway to an isolated spot on the airfield. A black Ford van would zip out from the sidelines and back right up to the side rear door of the bird. The insert team members would be escorted directly into that black van and driven straight into the 5th's compound at NKP. The main building of the compound was built in such a fashion that it was four-sided and had a large open-air patio-like area in the middle, designed so that insert team members could enjoy fresh air and sun without being seen. Nor could they escape if so desiring. The insert team members were equipped with whatever variety of clothing and armament, food, and necessities that were needed for the programmed length stay of the team on the ground—assuming, of course, that the team would not make contact with the NVA or Pathet Lao, and could remain undetected.

It was the FAC's job to supervise and direct the missions that put the teams into Laos and North Vietnam, though always with a 5th Special Forces Green Beret person on board with the FAC in a 23rd aircraft. That Special Forces man was known as a "covey rider."

Strike Control and Aerial Reconnaissance (SCAR) missions of the 23rd TASS were the "normal" day and night time missions, aside from the support to the 5th Special Forces and the Royal Lao Cricket West missions. There also were the "specials." These were one-time laid-on missions directed by higher headquarters for pilots of the 23rd. And who was "higher headquarters"? Who the hell knew? Pilots went to intelligence briefings and were told what the mission of the day was then. It was normal procedure for the 23rd TASS to keep a FAC "on station" over the Ho Chi Minh Trail constantly. Day and night, seven days a week. Such "normal" missions were scheduled by the 23rd's squadron scheduling officer one week ahead of flight time.

"Special missions" were scheduled on the flying schedule for specific days and times, but the precise nature of the special missions was never revealed until the FAC walked into TUOC (Tactical Unit Operations and Control). Missions flown in support of the Royal Lao Army and General Vang Pao were, really, "normal" missions since they were flown everyday, Monday through Friday from 0800 to just before dark. Strange as it may seem, these support missions over "free Laos" were flown on a schedule like going to catch a bus. The "war" simply was not fought on Saturday and Sunday by the Lao Army unless under direct attack. And it was a normal routine for the FAC to have to "buzz" the Lao Army barracks in Laos in order to get someone awake to get on the radio and relay to the Royal Lao Army lieutenant on board the 23rd FAC aircraft just what was needed in a mission for that day.

Other FAC missions done by the 23rd TASS were sensor-marking missions, in which the FAC shot smoke rockets, Willie Pete white phosphorous rockets, marking starting and stopping points for F-4 fighter-bomber aircraft to drop receiver/transponder sensor devices at specific latitude and longitude map coordinates throughout Laos so that any movement by man or animal, especially vehicles, could be detected by Task Force Alpha, located at NKP. TFA was a sensor-monitoring unit with 30- and 40-foot parabolic noise receiving dishes mounted on top of a building at NKP where personnel sat day and night listening to movement in Laos. Laos was, like a recording studio, "wired for sound." When specific sounds were detected by the listeners, an airborne FAC was directed to specific map coordinates to check the strange sounds out visually. Air-to-ground visibility, day or night, was an absolute must for FACs. The FAC had to be able to see everything that was going on beneath him and in the air. Strikes amounted to everything from fighter-bomber guns strafing targets to the dropping of bombs and napalm, to rocketing trucks, vehicles, boats, bicycles, animals, people, buildings, to catching enemy personnel and equipment. Air strike aircraft came from South Vietnam and Thailand or from navy aircraft carriers off shore.

None of what was actually happening in Laos was supposed to be happening, at least not on an official basis. Hanoi frequently claimed to have shot down several thousand American aircraft in Southeast Asia. Washington staunchly refuted these figures, claiming that North Vietnam was inflating loss rates. However, the North Vietnamese *were* shooting down the numbers they claimed—but they were doing so in Laos, where the U.S. could not admit that planes had gone down. At NKP alone, we lost eighty-six aircraft between January and June 1969. The Department of Defense would never admit that an aircrew was lost inside Laos. The fate of such a crew was always described as "lost in hostile action in the extreme western DMZ." Of course, the extreme western DMZ was Laos.

The bottom line was that American forces *were* in Laos, from 1966 until the 23rd TASS flew its final FAC mission on August 15, 1973. On July 23, 1962, the United States and other nations had signed an agreement at Geneva prohibiting any military alliance—including the Southeast Asia Treaty Organization (SEATO)—inconsistent with the neutrality of Laos. The U.S. violated that treaty.

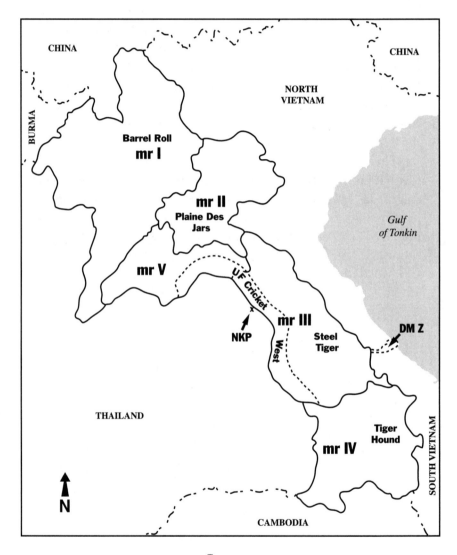

Laos

CHAPTER 1

A Call to Go to War

The Laughlin Air Force Base Officer's Club was always a center of activity on Friday afternoons from four o'clock until at least a shade after six. Happy hour at the club always saw a jam-packed audience. Located at the "Queen City of the Rio Grande," as we called Del Rio, Texas, Laughlin was a very active base under normal circumstances. Formerly a secret base for the U-2s and B-57s, Laughlin was now an Air Force Undergraduate Pilot Training base, full of young pilots and their instructors, and Friday was the day of the week when the Air Force Military Personnel Center (AFMPC) at Randolph AFB in San Antonio informed us who had been picked for an assignment to Southeast Asia.

This particular Friday, the last Friday of January 1968, I'd finished conducting the two academic classes I taught and had gone to the flight line to solo one lieutenant and do a "contact ride" on a second one. Then I hustled my butt via my Cushman Eagle motorscooter up to the O Club. I was sucking suds with fifty-six other jocks in sweat-stained flying suits when the personnel officer, an old lieutenant colonel, rushed in, a bit out of breath. At 5:20 he climbed up on a chair. "Gentlemen," he began, "we have reason to believe the enemy forces in Vietnam will be increasing activity and destruction; therefore, accordingly, AFMPC has decided rather than pick the usual four to five members of you gallant warriors, it will double the number of pilots selected to receive a tour for one year to the Republic of South Vietnam. I have a list of ten names on it." There were grumbles and mumbles: "Ahhh shit!" "Ohhh me!"

There were three names read for F-105s and four for F-4s, then three for FACs in O-2s. A chorus of cheers would erupt

after each name was read. Then, just as I was taking a swig of
Pearl Pop with the Foam on Top, I heard "Hathorn, Reginald
Harris, Major type, Bien Hoa, O-2s, forward air controller." I
almost gagged. A cheer went up, "Yeah, Cajun! Low and slow.
Yeah!" Two other majors were named for the same duty, FAC-
ing. One said, "I think I'll go cut my wrists." The other one
replied, "Hey, man, you get to have a bird's eye view of the
Gomers from treetop level—if you live long enough." My stomach churned. I sure hadn't expected the FAC job. I'd felt confident I'd get a "Thud." I asked the PO how people got picked
for various aircraft jobs in SEA. His answer was, "Damned if I
know. I think they throw darts at a personnel board. . . . Hey!
Shit! They don't tell me anything. They just Twix me a list
every Friday, and I have the most unpleasant job of telling you
guys who has been selected. And you, major, have been here
almost five years. You are ripe, man, to go do your part." I told
him, "Yeah, I know, sir, it is time to go answer the call to go to
war." The PO held out his hand and said, "Good luck to you." I
replied, "Thank you, sir."

So the die was cast. I had a set of orders coming that would
make me an FAC, a forward air controller flying the Cessna O-
2A aircraft.

Meanwhile, the situation in Vietnam left no doubt about the
severity of conditions there. Early on the morning of January 31,
1968, the 6th North Vietnamese Regiment of the 800th and
802nd Battalions launched attacks in Hue on the Old Imperial
Citadel. It was the Tet Offensive. In fact, all over South Vietnam
battles raged with the Viet Cong and NVA. Back on January 5,
the buildup of enemy forces indicated that something big was
coming. And on January 21, 1968, the NVA launched its attack
upon Khe Sanh. Khe Sanh was under siege and Lyndon Johnson was yelling he didn't want another Dien Bien Phu. The shit
had hit the fan.

By mid-February I had orders in hand. There was no fool-
ing around. I was to be in Florida by March 1, 1968, at Hurlburt
Aux No. 9, Eglin AFB, to undergo O-2A transition training and

familiarization. It was to be a concurrent assignment, which meant that my wife and two young daughters could accompany me. The course would take me up through March, April, and most of May. I'd then travel to Travis AFB, California, for departure on June 1 to Clark AFB in the Philippines for Jungle Survival Training ("Snake School"). This meant I'd have to leave my family over the Memorial Day holiday. While everyone else was celebrating and barbecuing, I'd be heading to California aboard an American Airlines 707.

Once in California, I drove to Travis to board a plane for the Philippines. The Flying Tiger Stretch DC-8 was a big mother, lean and long of fuselage, a long-haul bird. We were headed to Guam Island in the Marianas in the middle of the Pacific Ocean. As a co-pilot on a B-36 out of the 95th Bomb Wing, Biggs AFB, at El Paso, Texas, I'd been to Guam several times before. Including me, there were 265 souls on board the Stretch Eight for the long ride.

Once the pilot levelled off and the seat belt sign went off, the hostesses brought out drink and peanut carts and began going up the aisle. Soft drinks or alcohol drinks were offered. The majority of the personnel on board were young "grunts," Army or Marine troops in their late teens or early twenties who probably had not ever been very far from home, and this was all one big adventure for them. Most ordered some sort of an alcoholic beverage, but the hostesses, all experienced ladies, held the young guys to no more than three drinks.

Compared to these young troops, I was an old man, a thirty-four-year-old "senior officer" (a relatively new one, though, but nobody here knew that). I'd made it a point to select a seat near the tail of the bird, more for my safety than anything else. As a pilot, I reasoned that the tail section most usually survived a crash if one happened. I fully realized more fatalities happen from stupidity and carelessness than an actual shooting engagement. I had transitioned from B-36s to B-47s, then on to RB-47s at Forbes, and back to B-47s and EB-47s. The Suez crisis was behind me, as was the Francis Gary Powers crisis, and the

Cuban crisis. So was alert duty to England, Spain, Newfoundland, and North Africa, as well as gathering intelligence on Russian radar sites over the Berents Sea. Gone were months of TDY to Tripoli, Algeria, Sidi Slimaine, Tel Aviv, and a prelude to war between Egypt and Israel. I considered myself an "experienced" pilot with 2,000 hours in the B-47 series alone, with another 1,000 in the Cessna T-37 trainer, and over 1,000 in B-36s, F-84s, and another seven aircraft.

Manila International airport was a very busy place. Airline aircraft from world carriers were in evidence no matter which way one looked. Our aircraft taxied up to a special military unloading dock away from the commercial carriers with non-military personnel and cargo to unload. Gray military buses were lined up for our ride to Clark Air Force Base.

Once at Clark, we were directed to our barracks. Twenty-one other officers were there for Snake School, and to my surprise, all the other candidates were first lieutenants and captains, except for me and one other major, who became my roommate. He was headed to Korat to be a "Thud" jockey.

"Snake School"—or more formally called Pacific Air Force Jungle Survival School—was a basic three-week survival school intended to keep aircrew members alive until being rescued. Experts talked to us about jungle warfare as well as creatures we might encounter there. They showed us snakes of all poisonous and non-poisonous varieties, insects, reptiles, and a wide variety of fish and marine life. We were taught how to find water, make protective cover from vegetation, construct weapons, and hide without leaving traces. We spent a full week in the Philippine jungle, being instructed by the most notorious jungle people of the Southwest Pacific, the Nigritos. The two Nigritos who instructed my group of seven pilots had fought the Japanese during World War II. Their warfare was pure guerrilla: sneak in, be quiet, be deadly, and sneak away.

Overall, the training we received in Snake School was terrific, beneficial, and practical. Some of us would put those skills into practice. To illustrate what we faced, the chief instructor had all twenty-two of us count off. "Gentlemen," he said, "look at the third, sixth, the ninth, and every other third man in your class. I guarantee everyone of you that by the time you complete your one-year tour in Southeast Asia, one third of you won't be going home." I would find out just how right he was.

My arrival in Saigon, at Tan Son Nhut airport, was like I had just landed from a space ship from another planet. The regulated pace and organization at Clark gave way to the chaos that was Vietnam at war. As our C-130 turned off the active runway, the crew chief lowered the aft cargo panel door. The heat and smell of Vietnam popped me like a left to the jaw. Being from Louisiana, I had thought the humidity would be no problem. I was wrong. And the smell of Vietnam was like the smell of a rattlesnake you never forget. The scene out the back was pure pandemonium. Helicopters, C-130s, and fixed-wing aircraft and F-4 and F-100 fighter-bombers could be seen everywhere. Even above the whine of the Herky's four engines, other noises filtered in strange and alien to us. I marveled how aircraft, vehicles, and people did not kill each other in the hustle and bustle of this place.

Into this melee of people and machines, I dragged my two bags off of the 130. I asked someone behind a counter how to get to Bien Hoa. "Sir, you can fly there or drive there. Distance is about forty miles. But I suggest you not go by ground because the VC have been shooting up buses and vehicles on both Route 1 and Route 15. One goes to Bien Hoa. Fifteen branches off. One just short of Thy Duc. The VC just shot up a USO bus yesterday." I flagged an MP going by in a jeep and asked him if he could drive me to an officer's club if he knew of one close by. "Sure thing, major, hop in, just four blocks away."

At the officers' club, I managed to stash my two bags in a cloak room and prayed they'd still be there when I got back from dinner. I managed to get seated in a dining room of sorts and got a reasonable meal, a steak. I shared a table with an Army colonel who'd been in Saigon for three months. We talked, and I told him I was a new bean, had just come in earlier today, was trying to get to Bien Hoa, and at the moment needed a place to bunk. Glory be! He told me he was staying in an open-bay barracks not far away, and if I didn't mind double-bunk beds, he thought there was one available for a night or two. After dinner and a drink, which I treated him to, he helped me with my gear and even had a jeep himself. I was delirious at my luck. The barracks was open-bay, half-screened, same as in the Philippines. I spotted a bottom bunk on a "two-decker" with the mattress rolled up. I took it. I unrolled the cotton G.I. old-type mattress and even found a set of sheets, a pillow with no cover, and an olive-drab blanket. I was set. Despite the orange-colored flares that floated in the skies all night and the *krumppp, krumppp, krumppp* of artillery fire and the *bump, bump, bump* of .50-caliber machine guns shooting at who knew what, I just passed out.

It was bright day when my eyes came open. I was in a sweat, but the noises of firing artillery and heavy machine guns had given way to the *whup, whup, whup* of helicopter blades and the whine and roar of jet engines. People were yelling and talking, vehicles were moving—all of it mixed up and blended together. Then this sing-song voice yelled at me, "You get up, I need clean, you get up." I reared my head back to try and saw this old-looking Vietnamese woman clad in pink shower clogs, black pantaloons, and white short-sleeved blouse. She hollered at me again, "You get up now, I hooch lady, need clean, hokay?" I replied, "Yeahhh, sure, just hold on and I'll get up."

A goose, lost in a snowstorm, would have had an advantage on me as I stood outside the barracks. I had absolutely no idea where anything was except maybe the runways, because of the engine noises. Mess hall? Officers' club? Transportation? Signs? A phone? I spied two young airmen and yelled, "Hey, airmen, hold up a minute. I need to talk with you." They saluted; so did I. I told them of my predicament. They were most courteous and told me not to try to take a bus, or drive, to Bien Hoa. The VC were shooting up any vehicles that tried to drive the highway to Bien Hoa and Long Binh. They said to go by air. "Well," I told them, "that is fine and dandy, but I don't even know where base operations is to try to get a ride." One of the pair said to me, "Major, we have to take this mail over to the Army Helo Operations hut, and they have Hueys that run regular mail runs to Long Binh. Maybe you could bum a ride with the grunts? You may have to wait a few hours, but we think there will be a chopper going that way after lunch, and if you'll get your stuff, we'll be happy to take you there. That's where we gotta go now."

We drove up to a very large olive-drab squad tent that had a huge hand-painted sign on two posts, which read: "The mail goes come the VC, rain, VC, snow, VC, drunkfronts, VC, or any other nuisance." Everyone seemed to be wearing pistols, and I asked one of the airmen about it. "Sir, we never know who is the enemy around here, and which of these dinks is not. Any one of the Vietnamese workers you are seeing here on base could very well be a Viet Cong member and decide to throw a grenade, pull out a pistol themselves and here, for instance, hijack the mail—which contains official orders, maps, and even operational plans. We need to be prepared, and if you'll look around, you'll see we are on the edge of the base, with the civilian countryside just a few hundred yards away. The enemy would love to grab our mail."

About 2 P.M. a Huey came whup-whupping in, landed in a marked-off area on the edge of the concrete ramp, and shut down. Two Army pilots got out of it, as well as a left and right door gunner. All four came to the tent, went inside, and were in and out in less than six minutes. One of the young warrants walked up to me, saluted, and said, "Major, I hear you are looking for a ride up to Long Binh?" I returned his salute and answered him, "Yes, I am, I'm new in town, and I need to report in at the 504th Combat Support Group at Bien Hoa by or before midnight tomorrow and I'm sort of lost around here." He laughed and replied, "New in town, huh? Well, welcome to the war, sir. We'll be happy to give you a ride. Get your stuff and throw it on that bird there and we'll be gone in a cat's hair." He stuck out his hand. I shook it, looked him in the eye, and saw tiredness. He motioned to one of the gunners to help me. My bags and I were strapped in on the rear bench seat of the Huey.

I was in my 1505 Air Force summer uniform with flight cap tucked in under my web belt. The Huey whined to life.

I soon realized that this was no pure "mail run." We'd no sooner gotten airborne than both door gunners jacked a cartridge into the breech of their M60 machine guns. The pilots barely cleared the coconut trees that lined the river, and the Huey twisted and turned as it followed the snake-like course of the river. Once over the river, the door gunners started raking the banana and coconut trees along the river's edge with their M60s. The .308-cal guns deafened me. I watched in silent amazement. They later explained that if there were bad guys below, a firing chopper would make them keep down.

Long Binh had a pierced steel helo pad. In late June, as it was, there was also more than enough red dust as we came in for a "running" landing, hovering at the last minute. The chopper crew walked off into a small Quonset building with their mail bags and left me to my fate. I knew the distance between Bien Hoa and Long Binh was only a few miles—heavily guarded and mostly fenced in—and I decided to try to use one of the Army's phones long enough to call the 504th TASG at Bien Hoa.

After dialing the number, a professional-sounding voice came on the line, saying, "504th Tactical Air Support Group, Senior Master Sergeant Culpepper speaking, how may I help you?"

I informed the senior master sergeant who I was, where I was, and what my orders said.

"Major, welcome aboard. We have been expecting you. You are a little earlier than we had thought, must have had good luck in getting here maybe?"

I replied, "Sergeant Culpepper, you have no idea about the pure confusion I have experienced to get here, and had it not of been for some very cooperative U.S. Army personnel, I would damn sure still be at Tan Son Nhut lost in the crowd there. Ahhh, and while I have you on the phone, can you give me the number for the 604th SOS AT-37 organization? I have an old buddy there and maybe he can come get me. Save you guys a trip. I want to see him anyway."

After I finished my business with the 504th sergeant, who told me to check with him the next day before noon, I phoned the 604th. As fate would have it, my buddy, George Koohman, had just walked in at operations and was scheduling some pilots for a mission on the morrow.

"Hey there, we knew you were headed this way. Where you be right now?" he yammered at me.

"George, I am standing over here in Long Binh at the Army's mail helo office and I need a ride to where you are there at Bien Hoa," I told him.

"No problem," he came back with and instructed me, "Stay where you are. I got a jeep, and I'll be there within the hour to fetch you to the rip roaringest best damn Super Squeak Fighter outfit you ever did see."

"George, I haven't ever seen any AT-37 Fighter outfit, much less a rip roaring one," I reminded him.

George was his usual exuberant self. Tall, a bit stooped, hairline like a monk, bald on top with an otherwise decent mop of dark hair. But this time, when I spotted him behind the wheel of the jeep, he sported a huge "Yosemite Sam" mustache. He grabbed my hand and pumped it up and down. I filled him in on the details of my assignment and explained I had to check in with the 504th Group the next day.

He asked me if I needed a place to stay, and I told him I did. I got invited to share his room for a few days as his roomie was gone on R & R for two weeks. I gladly took him up on that kind offer. "Home" was a one-story white cinderblock building with a tin roof—neat, clean, air conditioned, and with hot and cold running water and indoor facilities. It felt good to relax and know I was with friends.

Two days later, about midnight of my third night as a guest of the Rip Roaringest Squeak Fighter Squadron in 'Nam, the VC launched a rocket attack on the base. Roaring explosions lit the blackness. A 122mm hit shook the building. Sirens blared, whistles screamed, people were yelling. *Whumpp*—a rocket slammed into the far end of the barracks building. Lights went out. It was as black as inside a whale except for the flashes outside. There was a gigantic *karumppp* just outside the sandbags against the side of our room. Glass shattered. I heard, "I'm hit! Oh, my God, I'm hit. I feel my blood running down my neck." I threw back the cotton mattress, under which I had taken refuge instinctively, and grabbed the pen light flashlight I habitually carried and used when in strange quarters. Who was hollering?

I found George in the tiny beam of light, on his back, his mattress partly over his legs, one hand feeling the back of his neck, him moaning he was dying. A can of Burma Shave, with its red, white, and blue stripes, was lying on the floor against the wall by George's head. I saw a big jagged hole in the can. Foamy shaving cream was everywhere. I wanted to laugh out loud but didn't, because I was greatly relieved that my old buddy wasn't going to die at all. I whispered to him, "George, the slopes blew up your Burma Shave can, and what you are feeling is hot lather from that can." He was very still for at least thirty seconds. Then he yelled, "Those sonsabitches! Sonsabitches. It took me two months to find a can of Burma Shave and now they've ruined my shaving. Oh, shit, shit, shit."

We snatched our flying suits and made a dash outside, climbing over debris, choking on smoke. What we found as we came into some light was pandemonium. I grabbed his arm and yelled in the blasts of sounds, "Let's go to the bunker, come on." I tugged his arm and pulled him with me toward a large sandbagged bunker. We had no sidearms or carbines and had no idea how we'd protect ourselves if a VC came around the corner of a building.

Daylight came and the target of the attack was clear: the main flight line. Medics and doctors were working on three people who had been pulled from the barracks. By an ambulance lay four body bags. I gulped. Not too far away, the perimeter wire around that part of the base could be seen. Air Police were working to cut four VC bodies out of the tangle of concertina wire. A lot of the shooting we'd heard was from the base perimeter guards as VC were trying to get over the wire. Some did but were killed as they ran helter-skelter in their dash to throw their satchel charges.

As I stood looking at the smoking black pile of rubble that had been our barracks, I saw a golden gleam in the ashes. I walked over and kicked at the debris. The corner of a brass plaque, nailed to a stained plywood board, came into view. One corner was charred, and the plaque was tarnished badly. I picked it up from the ashes and wiped it off on the seat of my flying suit. I strained to read the words that were embossed on the plaque: "War is an ugly thing, but not the ugliest of things. The decayed and degraded state of moral and patriotic feeling which thinks that nothing is worth war is much worse. A man who has nothing for which he is willing to fight, nothing he cares about more than his own personal safety, is a miserable creature who has no chance of being free, unless made and kept so by better men than himself." I took the plaque with me and, later, cleaned it off and hung it on the wall of where I stayed. And I defied anyone to mess with it. The words on that piece of brass said a lot to me.

CHAPTER 2

Check-out Time

Each and every pilot who'd been ordered by the Air Force to become a forward air controller, an FAC, belonged to the 504th Combat Support Group, Bien Hoa Air Base, Republic of South Vietnam. FACs were the heart throb of every major engagement that went on, as well as many more skirmishes and impromptu fights. When on the scene, an FAC was *the* commander of all operations going on in support of troops. He was the ultimate approver and disapprover of all air support efforts by *any* organization.

After a pilot checked in with the 504th and had his records reviewed, he would be temporarily assigned to Phan Rang Air Base, Phan Rang, South Vietnam, for about a week, in order to be re-qualified by instructor pilots who had already been FACs in Vietnam for six months or more and flew the type of aircraft the new FAC had been checked-out in back in the States at Eglin. While most of a pilot's "check-out" at Phan Rang—located on Route 1 Highway where Route 11 intersected it, some 30 miles south of the big base at Cam Ranh Bay and about 45 miles from Dalat—was performed in safe, permanent, air-conditioned buildings on base and in reasonably safe flying areas near base, some actual combat sorties were flown farther afield in support of American and Korean soldiers.

There were three types of aircraft at Phan Rang used for re-qualification and the "check-outs" of new pilots who were to become FACs: the Cessna O-1 and O-2 and the North American OV-10 turboprop. I'd been checked-out in the O-2 back at Hurlburt. Thus, that was the bird I'd fly, as ordered, in Southeast Asia. I would, though, also check out in the OV-10 and A-1E Skyraider because of "in-the-field needs," squadron losses, and personnel transfers.

Sometimes the world is a very strange place. My instructors were three young lieutenants whom I had taught to fly back in the States. I made every effort to be a respectful and cooperative student. They had learned well after graduation from the Undergraduate Flying Training Program, going on to become fighter pilots and then FACs in Vietnam. My instruction under them included time in the classroom as well as in the air. One time, my instructor took me out over the South China Sea to show me a battleship and to direct naval gunfire without briefing or preparation. We flew some 10 miles out with no Mae West or other life jacket. I couldn't believe this instructor—whom I had taught to fly!—had taken us so far from land without an ounce of survival gear.

I had been through Temperate Survival School at Stead AFB, Arctic Survival School in Alaska, local SAC survival schools in Texas and Ohio, Ocean Survival School in Florida, Nuclear Weapons Survival Training School, the SEA Jungle Survival School, and half a dozen other schools from jump training to parasailing—and I was not pleased with this "indoctrination" ride. I chewed my IP's ass for his stupidity and took command of the aircraft, turning it back toward shore and proceeding to do my own calls to the Navy in order to familiarize myself with naval gunfire. I told him to "pink" me, fail me, and I'd pack my bag, but on the way out, I'd be in his boss's office relating his stupidity at taking a student more than 10 miles out over the ocean with no survival gear or vests. I was sure I could get him reassigned by the 504th to a nice place in IV Corps. I told him not to schedule himself with me again; I'd do my in-country check-out with some other IP.

My week at Phan Rang went rapidly. I did my best to be humble and absorb as much of the information I could that was given by the instructors who served there at "FAC U," and except for the stupid trick pulled by my ex-student playing IP, there was no further incident. He even came to me one day and apologized for his actions and lack of brain power in taking me out to see the battleship and try to impress me. He impressed me all right, but not in the way he figured. Anyway, we had a laugh and shook hands, and I took him to the club and bought him a beer—and gave him one of my "friendly" lectures on how to bring his butt home—even though he had seven months real combat time on me there in 'Nam.

After "graduation," we were handed a set of orders from the 504th Combat Support Group. Those orders assigned us all over South Vietnam—from the 504th TASG itself at Bien Hoa, to the 19th TASS, 20th TASS, 21st TASS, and 22nd TASS. Assignments were to remote Army and joint Air Force locations to large airfields like Saigon's Tan San Nhut. And, crazy at it seemed, I was assigned TDY to the 21st TASS at APO 96205, or Nha Trang, about a 100 miles up the coast from Phan Rang. But the catch was, I was to be air liaison officer (ALO) to a Korean element of the ROK Capital (Tiger) Division at Dalat.

While the ROK Forces Vietnam Field Command had established a corps-level headquarters at Nha Trang, near the U.S. I Field Headquarters, the primary area of responsibility of its two divisions—the Capital Tiger and 9th White Horse—was the central coast of II Corps, from Phan Rang to Qui Nhon. Various ROK forces were stationed throughout their area of responsibility. The 504th's crystal ball gazers had seen fit to assign me to the 21st TASS as an ALO to the Tiger Division's ROK element of 800 men at Dalat. I was to "provide guidance" to our allied friends as they went about their chore of insuring security for their part of the world around Phan Rang and Dalat. I was to be in TDY—temporary duty status—with the 21st and the ROKs until "further advised."

Being green as spring gourds on a vine, I really didn't give a shit where I was assigned. I was told that the ROKs needed an experienced officer in aviation to better protect their area of responsibility. The ROK element at Dalat ranged far and wide in its sweeps throughout their area and my job would be not only to provide aerial strike capability for them, but to insure that ROKs and U.S. forces did not get in each other's way or engage each other.

Once in Nha Trang, the administration officer briefed me on my job and assigned me the call sign of "Cutie." I already knew I was going to take a shit pot full of fun-poking for that. There was nothing for me to do at the TASS's headquarters, and I was cleared to take myself to Dalat. I was told, however, that the ROKs there were in make-do quarters and that I'd be living with the ROK commander, a Major Kim. I was to be in command as far as FACing was concerned. My job would be to keep the ROKs out of trouble if at all possible. There would be two O-2 aircraft at Dalat, and a ground/maintenance crew would keep them operational, fueled, and ready to go around the clock. I would assist and perform FAC duties for U.S. and other allied forces as required, and I should check in with 21st TASS operations daily and as needs arose for emergencies and unusual situations. It sounded like total insanity.

CHAPTER 3

To Find a Way Out of My Job

Living in a hole in the ground while attached to the ROK Tiger Division was not my idea of fun. First of all, the Republic of Korea troops all seemed half bananas. They had but three things on their minds at all times: kill as many of the Viet Cong and North Vietnamese as they could find, make as many of the women as they could get, and buy all of the BX merchandise they could haul away in their six-bys—in that order. Mix in some booze, and you had all the makings for complete chaos. However, as the commander of the 50,000-strong ROK forces, Lt. Gen. Chae Myung Chin, said, "Where ROKs are, it is 100 percent secure." To that I can say only "Amen." The Viet Cong had learned the hard way to avoid the ROKs.

The area that the ROKs were assigned to look after extended from Qui Nhon along the II Corps coastline to Phan Rang, south of Cam Ranh Bay, then west to a bit beyond Dalat, about to Ban Me Thuot along Route 21, then wobbly on to Hau Bon, Route 19 to Anke and on down back to Qui Nhon. It was a pretty fair-sized bit of real estate to try to control. Some of the geographical area on the western edge of the area of responsibility was impossible to identify; there was no river or main highway to identify for sure where the ROK area stopped and the rest of South Vietnam began. You just did what you had to do and call the map coordinates as you saw them wherever the action was.

One day, I accompanied some ROKs to the Phan Rang BX, looking for a new Seiko watch and a 35mm camera. While there, I ran into an old student who mentioned that he saw an announcement that the 504th Group was looking for SCAR FACs. I hurried over to the base ops building, went in the double doors off the flight line, and asked an airman behind the counter where the bulletin board was. On it, I spotted an 8 x 10 sheet of pale blue paper. "Two SCAR FACs needed Out-Country Immediately. Call 504th Combat Support Group, Bien Hoa Air Base, South Vietnam, Number 4762. Ask for M/Sgt. Craig. Only experienced pilots with high flying time, rank of Captain or up need apply." It was one day old. Here was opportunity knocking on my door.

Down a long hallway, painted the standard Air Force puke green and tan colors, with a white ceiling, I spotted a telephone sitting on a shelf. I picked it up and told some operator, "Ring me number 4762 at the 504th Combat Support Group, Bien Hoa."

There was a buzz in the line, a peeping, a click, then, "Master Sergeant Craig speaking here, can I help you?"

"Uh, Master Sergeant Craig, this is Major Hathorn calling you from Phan Rang at the moment. I am looking at a note I copied off of the bulletin board here that says to call you about a SCAR FAC job needed immediately out-country. What can you tell me? I'm presently the ROK ALO in II Corps at Dalat."

He replied, "Well, major, the 23rd TASS is short two O-2 pilots after, ahhh, an event where they fly and we need to replace them. You interested?"

"Sarge, if I wasn't interested, I wouldn't be on this phone. The ROKs are great people, but they are driving me nuts. And the living is like a permanent campout."

I heard a snicker. "Just a minute, major, hang on, I want to get your folder out and take a look. Hang on, okay?"

"I ain't going no place, sarg, okay?" I answered.

I heard a low whistle. Then he asked, "Major, you still there?"

"Yep, I'm still here. What's the story?"

Sergeant Craig said slowly, "Major, you more than fill the bill of what they need over there. I see you have 4,000 hours of time now from fighters, bombers, big bombers. Five years as an Air Training Command Instructor Pilot, date of rank as a Major back to '67, yessir, you're what they are looking for. When you want to go?"

"How about today?"

"Well, Major Hathorn, I have to talk to Colonel Wisner. He's the boss, you know, and whatever he says is what I'll do. If it is a go for you, I'll get right on the orders for you. When can you call me tomorrow?"

"Well, look, I have a ten o'clock takeoff in the morning and it should be about three hours of reckie-tech for some Ranch Hand spray birds. I'll do a land and refuel job here at Phan Rang and give you a call about 1400. How's that sound?"

"Great."

"And sarge," I added, "if I can get to Bangkok while I'm waiting to be contacted when I get the reassignment, I wouldn't be surprised if Santa Claus didn't come to see you with a surprise." I was deliberately sweetening the pot for his help. I knew damn well old sergeants like him ran our Air Force and him talking to the colonel was only a square-filling exercise. He was the guy who made the decisions since he worked with all assignments on FACs in Southeast Asia.

The next day, the spray mission went well. No ground fire was taken, and no enemy forces were seen. An area along Route 14 where it nears the Cambodian border, northwest of Quang Duc, was the target. At 1110 the flight of four UC-123s checked in, UHF. Ranch Hand lead briefed me that he had a flight of four; two were carrying 1,000 gallons of "Orange" and two were carrying a 1,000 gallons of "White." Lead was the left bird with Orange, two was next on the right carrying White, three was next with Orange, and four was on the far right with White for a line abreast. Altitude would be 150 feet AGL while in spray mode, at an air speed of 125 knots. That speed, for me in the O-2 with a near-full load of fuel and two pods of Willie Pete rockets, would be pushing my engines harder than I cared to do. I asked lead if he could give me 5 knots less. He rogered that he could do that for his "little friend." He also briefed me that the flight of four would be running side by side at approximately 80 to 100 yards from each other in their spray formation. I gave the Ranch Hand leader a briefing that I had reckyed the intended line of spray for some forty minutes and had seen or heard nothing. Part of the spray area was open land with rice paddies, some scrub-covered terrain, and some thick jungle-treed areas bordering Route 14. If any heavy fire was encountered, I had fast-movers standing by for support.

I had tooled over and along the area in normal FAC fashion, jinking, turning, climbing, and diving like a drunk pilot, but never remaining in any one place long enough to draw attention to myself. At an altitude of 1,000 indicated, I had a real good look-see, and while rudder-flying the Oscar Deuce drunkenly, I could see really well through the 7x50-power Bausch & Lomb binocs. Here and there, I'd spot villagers working in a field, walking on the road, an ox cart with a buffalo attached. Nothing out of the ordinary. However, I knew that Seventh Air Force, through its Tactical Control Center (TACC), directed the Ranch Hand squadrons' missions and that, therefore, these guys would not be here unless intel to Seventh had indicated there was "activity of interest" here, so close to the Cambodian border. I did wonder, though, why two birds had Agent Orange on board and two carried Agent White.

As the Ranch Hands checked in, I watched the UC-123 Providers move into line to begin their run. I armed the rocket pods and told lead I'd give him a mark to run on, then move on down track and mark a terminating point. As FAC in control of the mission, I'd be crisscrossing their formation as their eyes and ears in case of trouble. I watched the four birds line up like cotton sprayers I'd seen so many times back in my native Louisiana. And on his count, lead triggered the spray. Simultaneously, the other three aircraft let go also. Spray, looking like white smoke, billowed behind the birds like the swirling contrails I'd seen so very many times during my 2,000 hours of flying B-47s, RB-47s, and the EBs. Their spray fanned out far and wide and drifted upon the wind, gradually sinking down onto the foliage and crops below and filtering into my aircraft. It had a wood-smoke smell.

Bidding the spray birds adios, I set a course for the Phan Rang airdrome. I punched the mike button and contacted the tower there. "Phan Rang tower, Cutie Zero Six," I said.

There was a rattle, and the tower answered, "Go, Cutie Zero Six, this is Phan Rang tower."

"Ahh, Phan Rang tower, Cutie Zero Six is inbound, an Oscar Deuce, needing refueling, say landing instructions, over."

"Roger, Cutie Zero Six, tower has you in sight, you are cleared to land runway 22 left. Winds are calm, altimeter is 30.10, over."

I rogered his instructions and knew he was putting me onto the 10,000-foot aluminum planked runway, which was no problem for me and the O-2 because our landing distance would be short. I could get a quick runway turnoff, and save the 10,000-foot concrete runway for the "big" birds, fighters, and transports.

The blue "follow me" pickup truck made a 180-degree turn in front of me to lead me to the refueling ramp. Another airman stood at the end of a curving yellow line on the tarmac and motioned me into a specific spot. I locked the brakes and chopped the power to both front and rear engines. The right passenger door opened—the only way into or out of the Deuce—and a three-striper asked, "What can I do for you today, major?"

I swung my boom mike aside and yelled, "Fill it up, clean the windshield, and gimme green stamps." He smiled and gave me a thumbs-up.

I went into base ops to call Master Sergeant Craig.

"I got a real deal for you, major," Craig told me after he clicked onto the line. "The Thailand unit lost two pilots in their ops, and they want you and the other volunteer ASAP. Can you travel in two days?"

"Sergeant Craig, I can travel in two hours. All I need to do is get my stuff."

"Well, major, it will take us the rest of today and tomorrow to get your orders cut and have the boss sign them. So here's the deal. You are being reassigned effective day after tomorrow, officially, that will be July 30. On the afternoon of the thirty-first, a C-123 will land there at Phan Rang at 1300 with your orders hand-carried by the aircraft commander. The plane and

crew is stationed here at Bien Hoa. They will make an intermediate stop at Phan Thiet to pick up some ARVN Rangers and
drop them off there at Happy Valley. The aircrew will fly you
from Phan Rang to Bangkok, Thailand, landing at Don Muang
airport. The crew will remain overnight that arrival night, have
next day off as R & R, remain overnight, then depart for back
here the next day. You will check in to the U.S. military hotel
there in Bangkok, the Chao Phya. You will remain at the Chao
Phya until you are contacted. Understand?"

"Yeah, I got it all, sarge, but it all sounds like Double-O-
Seven to me," I answered him.

Sergeant Craig continued, "Major, this program is top
secret. What you will be doing we are not doing, understand?
Every pilot and navigator in your new organization is a volunteer, like you. We have picked each one and everyone is experienced. Just today we have also selected the second SCAR FAC
needed there. He is, like you, a very experienced pilot and we
want to get him to Bangkok at the same time you are there so
that we can have the both of you transported to your new
organization together. And one more thing: there is a 5th Special Forces unit stationed where you are going. I have coordi-
nated with MACV-SOG in Saigon about you coming into, ahhh,
our program, and your flying background and experience. You
will be contacted later on when you are in position about perhaps joining the SF unit there to fly missions for their troops. I
inform you now that you are not to talk to or with anyone
about where you are going, what you will do perhaps, and mum
is the word. Understand?"

My mind was whizzing. I was in stunned silence, wondering
what in hell had I gotten myself into.

"Major, are you there?" Sergeant Craig asked.

"Yes, yes, I'm here, sergeant. I'm just in a state of bewilder-
ment and reassignment shock is all," I told him.

He laughed and added, "Congratulations, sir, welcome
aboard. Keep in touch. And, sir, good luck."

"Master Sergeant Craig, I am genuinely appreciative of
your help to me in my reassignment. Therefore, when I get an

opportunity I will be sending a Christmas present to you, for you and your wife. I assume you are married?"

"Yes, sir, I am. And by the way, sir, do you know a navigator by the name of Chandler?"

More puzzlement flashed through my mind, and I slowly answered, "Well, yeah, I had one by that name back when I was in SAC, why?"

"Just wondering, sir. We know a guy by that name in a roundabout way. Good luck again to you," he said. Then the line went dead.

Back with the ROKs at Dalat, Maj. Yo Chin Kim was not overjoyed at the news of my reassignment. He was dejected, but my having only one day left with him didn't stop him from calling a mission for six the next morning.

There had been a smattering of trouble to the northwest of Dalat, mostly from some VC who were hiding out in caves in the hills during the day and who would sneak out at night to shoot up villagers. U.S. straight-leg Army grunts had tried to rid the area of VC but hadn't gotten anywhere. So the ROKs got called in to see what they could do.

I wasn't sure what Major Kim had in mind, but I should have known. He had only one method of dealing with the enemy, which was the same thing you might do with a rattler in the road—run it over with a ten-ton truck and skid the wheels. I got a hint of Kim's intended tactics when a jeep with a recoilless rifle mounted on it showed up, followed by another jeep with a pair of ROKs with large satchel-charge canvas packs. The crowning touch was a third jeep with two more ROKs with flamethrowers. This could be interesting.

Four six-bys, a supply truck, and the three jeeps, all led by the major with his Thompson sub-machine gun plainly showing, wound its way off base and into the hinterlands toward the village. The convoy surprised four VCs who had lingered in the village too long. At the sight of Kim's team, they bolted for the brush. Big mistake. Up came the major, his Thompson roaring. An M60 mounted in the back of the first six-by blazed. All four VCs went down.

Then the ROKs drove up to the entrance of the nearby caves, where the flamethrowers unleashed the fires of hell into them. Orange flames poured in; black smoke rolled out. There was no doubt in my mind that the "problem" with the VC near this village had been solved—for a while, anyway. As the convoy rolled back to base, I turned the radios off.

What a way to earn a living.

CHAPTER 4

A New World

The morning of my reassignment, I woke early, packed, ate breakfast, and turned in my equipment. As it neared ten o'clock, I commandeered Major Kim's jeep, bribing the driver to take me to Phan Rang. Sergeant Craig had said the 123 would be landing at Phan Rang at 1300. Knowing the punctuality of the many-motor troops, I figured I damned sure best be there ahead of time. In the Phan Rang ops building, I was given a message from Craig: "Hang tight at the Chao Phaya until you are contacted by Thai person by the name of Thammarat. Second SCAR name of Barker, look up at Chao Phaya. Good luck."

The Provider came loping in, staying high on base leg and turn to final to stay away from any small-arms fire. I watched the bird touch down with twin puffs of blue-white smoke as he did a squeak job landing the bird, holding the nose up, then gently letting the front wheel down. I heard the twin recips reverse, then change pitch, and the green and tan everything-hauler turned off the active runway onto a taxiway and idled straight up for the base ops where I was standing.

The 123 rolled smoothly to a stop, the No. 1 engine was shut down, right engine was kept running. The ramp came down at the rear, and a whole gaggle of mud-spattered and dirty, fresh-from-the-field RVN troops began to hop out the back of the bird and throw their gear down.

A flight-suited figure wearing a headset connected to a long, black cord appeared on the tail ramp of the bird. He spotted me and waved. I waved back, grabbed my two bags, and headed for the rear of the bird.

"Your name Major Hathorn?" he asked, lifting an earphone.

"Yes."

"Welcome aboard, sir. Have a seat."

Don Muang Airport in Bangkok was the epitome of a bustling international airport. Aircraft from around the world were coming and going. The military parking and loading area was on the opposite side of the field, and I gawked at the people in business suits who were totally oblivious to us killing each other only a few hundred miles away across the mighty Mekong River.

The Chao Phya military hotel in downtown Bangkok was another surprise. It was a plain, well-decorated, and clean building overrun with a variety of mostly "roundeye" males who were obviously American military personnel. A few females were mixed in here and there. Inside the two front doors were two of the largest elephant tusks I had ever seen anywhere, including Africa.

I didn't know a soul in the hotel, so I hired cabs and went to all the Bangkok tourist sites, like the Temple of Dawn, Floating Market, Emerald Buddha, and Timland; rode a huge bull elephant; watched some Thai guy walk around in an enclosure with hundreds of cobras; saw some chicken fights and Thai boxers kicking the shit out of each other; gorged myself on blue cheese–stuffed steaks at the Rama Hotel; and did a lot of late-hour drinking at Lucy's Tiger Den, where I managed to get shit-faced with Air America pilots, fighter pilots, mercenaries, and—of all people—my old flight commander when I IPed at Laughlin.

One morning, after six days at the Chao Phya, there came a soft knocking on my door at the ungodly hour of ten o'clock. I had barely survived a "drunk front" at the Tiger Den the night before. I opened the door in my shorts and was staring at a neatly dressed Thai military officer in a starched khaki uniform.

"You Major Hathorn?" he asked courteously.

"Yeah, that's me."

"I am Colonel Thammarat. I have been instructed to inform you personally to be at the Don Muang military passenger terminal tomorrow at 0800. You will check in with passenger service with your baggage, be in uniform, and ride the USAF C-130 aircraft to Nakhon Phanom Royal Thai Air Base. Okay?"

I stammered, "Uh, okay, colonel. Thank you."

The next morning, the military terminal was a beehive of activity with forklifts and personnel scurrying around loading and unloading crates, boxes, and plastic-covered pallets of stuff. Four-engined C-130 transports were making regular shuttles into and out of the terminal. I went into the terminal and handed an airman behind the counter a set of written orders. He looked at them, raised his eyes at me, and told me softly, "Major, if you will go through that door immediately to your right you will find a waiting room with four other officers in it. Please take your bags with you and have a seat. You will be contacted. Thank you, sir." He handed me my orders back.

I entered a large square room that was painted in a light sky-blue color, spotted four other Air Force officers, two majors and two captains. We introduced ourselves to each other, and I asked where the C-130 was bound. NKP and Udorn, I was told. One of the majors was going to Udorn to fly F-4 Phantoms and the captains to participate in the "Steven Canyon Program," whatever the hell that was. The other major said his name was Barker.

Shaking my hand, Barker said, "Master Sergeant Craig mentioned there would be another SCAR FAC going to NKP. I guess you must be him, huh?"

"Yes, Major Barker, I am him. I also had been told there would be another SCAR FAC going where we are going. I tried to look you up at the Chao Phya but wasn't able to."

Barker laughed. "Well, after four months at Ninh Hoa, I, uh, was seeing the sights and sounds and, uh, pleasures of Bangkok, and I wasn't around that much."

"I copy," I replied. "Sights, sounds, and pleasures of Bangkok."

Nakhon Phanom was way up on the Thailand frontier, the end of the road, three hours by Herkey Bird. And stepping off the C-130 at NKP was another new experience. It took no genius to cast an eyeball around the ramp at NKP to see and

understand that this was a very unusual place. Rows and rows of
World War II–era A-26 light bombers squatted on the ramp.
Rows and rows of A-1E and A-1H Skyraiders were there, too. A
long row of C-123 Providers, painted brown and green, some
with black bellies, foretold out-of-the-ordinary missions for these
birds. Some gray T-28s sat here and there, displaying the Lao
three-headed elephant on a brilliant red shield. A glance up-
field revealed Helio Couriers with open chutes on their sides, as
if something was dispensed through them. Then way down on
the far end of the airdrome, I spotted the Jolly Green Giant
choppers, and more big CH-3E helios, which belonged to the
"Knife" squadron. And, lo and behold, I spotted two long rows
of O-2s. There were not only the usual gray-and-white-topped
wings of the normal FAC birds, but also about eight birds
painted dull black, with no windows on the right side. Nowhere
on any of the aircraft did I see a single "U.S.A." insignia. Each
aircraft had only a few numbers and "TT" on the vertical stabilizer. I wondered what the shit I had gotten myself into.

While I was standing there taking it all in, a neatly dressed
second lieutenant walked up to me and Barker and asked, "Are
you two Majors Hathorn and Barker?" I was startled. We
answered in unison that we were. He snapped a salute, which
we returned. He went on. "I am from the 23rd TASS, the FAC
Tactical Air Support Squadron to which you have been
assigned. We've been expecting you. We need you." He then
picked up our bags and led us to a blue crewcab pickup. On its
side door I spotted a painting of a cricket—Jiminy Cricket, to
be exact, from Walt Disney—hanging under an open umbrella,
pointing at something, and obviously yelling his head off at his
find. The lieutenant explained that it was the squadron's
emblem. Throwing the truck into gear, we took off down the
ramp. I leaned forward for a better look at the lieutenant's
wings, and my thoughts were confirmed—a navigator. Only
navigators could drive like that, meshing gears with a clatter
and making vehicles lurch.

Signing in at the 23rd operations shack was done in quick
time. The operations officer was there, a tall, lanky major
dressed in washed Air Force–issue fatigues with a black rank

insignia sewn on the collar, along with black wings and black name tag. A lieutenant colonel navigator was there, too, as well as two more majors and three NCOs. We shook hands all around, and I thought that this place was rank-heavy for a bunch of FACs. Then two more majors came through the doors. Big grins came across their faces, and one said, "New cannon fodder, huh? Welcome aboard the Nail ship, guys."

Any new guy in the squadron was of interest to everyone. Not many replacements were coming through, it seemed.

"Best kept secret in the world is being here," a major said to me as he walked up, sticking his hand out. "Hi, I'm John Silva. And welcome to the Nails."

I was sort of flabbergasted. This place was crawling with rank. Most of the pilots I spotted were majors, a few captains, the one second lieutenant who'd picked me and Barker up at the 130 off-loading area. I commented on the rank situation and the second looie.

"Oh, you mean Lewis?" another major laughed. "We use him for a mascot. He's a good kid. We look after him. How he got here is anyone's guess. First assignment."

Then I spotted another lieutenant colonel navigator. "Who's he?" I asked pointing at the lanky guy, also in green fatigues.

"That is Jim Regal. He's our squadron's lead navigator, the senior one here," Silva commented.

"What's with all these navigators around here?" I asked, adding, "FACs don't normally need a navigator to get from point A to point B." I was puzzled.

"Don't you know?" Silva asked me.

"Well, no, I don't. That's why I asked," I replied. "I have no idea what goes on here. And over in 'Nam, where I just came from, you are on your own to take care of yourself, buddy, and you fly alone most of the time. I was with the ROKs playing nursemaid to them, and you'd often be up on a mission two, three, even four times a day. Short ones, maybe thirty minutes, maybe two hours for a long one."

"Well, we have an entirely different operation here. We use the navigators to fly with at night where we look for trucks moving on The Trail, the famous Ho Chi Minh Trail. They hang a

Starlight Scope out the right window of the airplane and look up and down the road we are over with 180 degrees of vision. The Starlight Scope magnifies light 29,000 times, and we can see a match burning at our working altitude of about 3,000 feet, maybe up to 4,000 feet. Everything has a green glow to it looking through the scope, and I guarantee you any driver stupid enough to have driving lights on gets waxed. Our night birds are black, no windows in the right side and have all the running lights shielded so only our strike aircraft can see us from above. Our night-strike aircraft are the A-26s, call sign of Nimrod. And we also use the A-1s here with call signs of Hobo, Firefly, and Zorro. The Aussies fly for us at night with their B-57 Canberra bomber, call sign of Yellow Bird. So we have a lot of night action here. Those C-123 aircraft you saw when you came in are also used at night, under call sign of Candlestick. They have very large Starlight Scopes installed in them, and our navs fly with them also."

Silva continued, "I gotta warn you now, this is entirely a secret operation with everything we do and what all is here. So keep your mouth shut. We are, officially, not here. No media people are allowed anywhere near this place. Also, the antiaircraft fire over in Laos and on The Trail at night is heavy. Fierce. The best July 4th fireworks display you'll ever see anywhere, any time."

Another major chimed in, "We here at NKP fly in what is called Steel Tiger. There's an operating location farther south at Ubon AFB, but they fly in the Tiger Hound area. Laos is broken up into areas called Steel Tiger, Tiger Hound, the PDJ, which means the Plain of Jars, and Barrel Roll. During the day we fly normal FAC-type missions up to five, maybe six hours' duration, on the network of roads over in Laos. Everybody calls them The Trail, but it's really a network of roads, trails, ruts, through the landscape over there where the NVA and Pathet Lao transport war supplies down into Cambodia and on into South Vietnam. Our job is to interdict and to prevent as much of those supplies and materials as possible from getting through to the war in South Vietnam. We have only fighter-bomber aircraft that we can use on targets we find. There are no friendly troops in Steel Tiger or Tiger Hound. None. If you go down, or bail out, any and everyone on the ground is your enemy. Don't be caught either. The bad guys hate FACs. Nobody is taken alive if caught."

I swallowed hard at that torrent of information. Then Silva added, "Reggie, anything that moves across the bomb line is a legal target. You will learn where and what the bomb line is as you complete briefings at intelligence. Simple, huh?" He laughed at my eye-rolling gesture.

From nowhere, Lieutenant Lewis said, "And we fly, sir, with the Army's 5th Special Forces here on some of their missions. Like Operation Heavy Hook and Prairie Fire. Then up to the Lima sites for General Vang Pao. And we do special missions inserting radio transmitters and receivers under Operation Igloo White so TFA can tell what is moving in Laos."

I was overwhelmed with all of the information thrown out for me. I remarked, "Then tell me about all of these different missions, especially what we're doing with the Special Forces."

Silva spoke up, "No, Reggie. No can do. Unless you are involved in the missions and have a need to know what goes on. Like I told you, everything is secret around this place. Unless you have a need to know something, you won't be told squat." He paused. "Come on. Let's go over to the club and chow down for the evening. I think you will like the place. Ain't the Waldorf, but it sure beats a GI kitchen or dining hall and is, by the way, the only place here where you can eat. Unless you end up flying night missions and stop by the airmen's dining hall after midnight. It has great, I mean *great*, food for next to nothing. All you can eat and pack off for about a dollar."

As we headed to the O Club to eat, Silva told me about the 23rd running a satellite operation down at Ubon Air Base, in order to have FACs covering southern Laos near Cambodia in the "Tiger Hound" area. By having the satellite operation stationed at Ubon—called OL-1—it put FACs nearer the operating area. To have flown there from NKP on regular missions would have made too much going-and-coming time and less time over the target. So some twenty-five pilots and navs in a mixed force, plus the maintenance personnel, were stationed at Ubon constantly. Ubon, some 150 miles south of NKP, was also the home of an F-4 fighter-bomber wing that included the famous "Triple Nickle" squadron, the 555th—home to MiG killers and aces.

Normal 23rd FAC missions, day and night, were airstrike missions against trucks, boats, personnel, truck parks, anything that moved beyond the bomb line. The "special missions" involved the 5th Special Forces, the Cricket West Operation, the Igloo White sorties, the missions to the PDJ and the Lima sites, and anything else 7th Air Force levied onto the squadron.

Everything that went on at NKP in 1968 and 1969 was top secret. The world did not know that the U.S. had an operational base in Thailand for launching clandestine combat missions into Laos. Nor did the world—or anyone outside the personnel directly involved—even dream Air Force FACs were directing search-and-destroy missions inside Laos or directing and controlling U.S. Army Special Forces missions by inserting U.S. and indiginous long range reconnaissance patrols (LRRPs) into Laos. In plain English, the U.S. was not supposed to be conducting an armed shooting war inside Laos. But we were.

CHAPTER 5

Welcome to the War in Laos

"Watch the SAM, watch the SAM," my indoctrination pilot, a captain, was yelling at me. His orange Yosemite Sam mustache was quivering. His beady black eyes were intense. He was staring at a lump of brush-covered real estate down on my side of the aircraft. He had the O-2A Cessna Skymaster turned up on its right side to a pure vertical position. Nothing below seemed out of place to me. It was quiet on the ground. Or so I thought. A twisting, rutted, sienna-colored dirt road met the equally twisting Xe Namkok River beneath us. The river was green, whipping along with a nice flow. You could see white water where the current smashed and washed over a shoal. Emerald green banana trees lined the shores on both sides of the river. The tiny village of Ban Kengsep was a squatting cluster of seven thatch-woven, pole-and-grass huts clinging to the side of the hill beyond.

He was yelling in my ear, really excited. He was making quick movement corrections with all the controls: ailerons, rudder, elevator—all at the same time it seemed. The dove-gray aircraft responded to his every movement like a flapping swallow attempting a landing, darting this way, then that, and whipping around in flip-flop circles. I was tense. Never in my life had I seen anyone do the things with an aircraft he was doing—and I had just completed almost five years as an Air Force instructor pilot teaching young officers how to fly. *Whoosh!* I saw a flash of fire and smoke and dark metal go streaking past the window on his side.

"Damn!" he exclaimed. "They nearly got us that time!"

"They did?" I asked stupidly.

"Yeah, didn't you see that surface-to-air missile launch and come up for us?" he asked, looking at me.

"No," I said. "I did not see it."

"Well," he added, "this is your first mission. Maybe you will learn something out of it."

"I sure hope so," I replied, feeling like a beginner clod.

He pointed out the front windscreen on my side and said, "That is the Banana Karst, as we call it. We believe that there is an underground cave there that is a repair point for vehicles going down The Trail to Cambodia. It is just too heavily fortified with ZPUs, 37s, and SAMs to be anything else. We see an awful lot of trucks in this area. Mostly at night, but sometimes during the day. I was looking at that area when I saw the SAM launch. I saw the puff of dust that it kicked up and watched it wobble as it came off the launcher. They are usually heat seekers, but there isn't that much heat generated by our engines. They, the SAMs, give the jets fits."

"Whew," I replied, "I sure am glad that you were watching."

"Aww, that's okay," he mumbled. "The longer you stay out here, the more you learn, and you learn where to look. You gotta remember, I am almost ready to go back stateside. That is why they put you with me today for your first ride. I'm an old timer, a short timer."

I looked over at him. He might have been thirty-two years old. His bald head was invisible underneath his olive-drab helmet, but his black eyes twinkled and sparkled. His orange mustache gave him a Fu Man Chu look. The waxed ends had gotten limp in the heat and humidity of the Lao air, not to mention the heat in the cockpit of the aircraft. The mustache drooped down around his mouth. His heavy fiberglass flak jacket was open in the front. I felt as if I were being boiled to death by mine. The vests were bulky, cumbersome, and hot as a Turkish bath. His hands and feet moved in easy rhythm, making the Skymaster climb a little, slip sideways, dive a little, then come back up in another climbing turn in the opposite direction. He called it "jinking." "Never want to fly around out here on a straight and level course," he had said. "The Gomers down there will get you for sure. They just sit and watch to see how stupid some guy will

be. Always, always, fly like you are drunk, and you will stay alive."
I remembered that. It saved me more than once.

We had begun to work our way back up the Ho Chi Minh
Trail from where the SAM had missed us, on past point Foxtrot.
There were a lot of alphabet-coded choke points along The
Trail, places where the road crowded the river or a cliff. The sky
was clear and absolutely blue like a maiden's eyes. Below, the
pocked, moon-like surface of the ground along the road was
dusty and orange. Here and there a few scrub bushes remained
from the intense daily bombing that went on all along The Trail
whenever the FACs could find a target to drop bombs on. My
mind was wandering, observing the pure beauty of the gray-
green mountains off to the east in North Vietnam, the waterfalls spewing down the mountain's sides.

I was jarred back to reality in a hurry. "Hello," Captain Butts
said. "Would you look there—what we have going down the
road?" I peered over the nose. Just then, my pilot cranked the
O-2 around some in a sideways slip. He pointed. "See? Look
there at one o'clock. See them?" There was a long, huge trac-
tor-trailer tank truck going up the road. A gasoline truck—
beautiful. And there was a regular army-type truck following
the tanker. In front, leading the way, was a smaller vehicle, sort
of like a command car.

Butts was elated. He flipped his radio over to a strike frequency and began calling for air support. "Invert, Invert, this is
Nail 27, over," he called.

Invert Control answered immediately, "Go ahead, Nail 27.
This is Invert, over."

Butts replied, "Roger, Invert. This is Nail 27. I have three
movers at the 075 degree radial on Channel 99, approximately
eight-zero miles, request air support, over."

There was a pause, then, "Nail 27, this is Invert. You have a
flight of two, I say again, two, F-105s inbound to you. Their call
sign is Buick, over."

"Nail 27 copies, Invert," Butts said. I tingled all over. Now I
would see a real strike.

We shadowed the small convoy for a few miles. Suddenly, the lead command car whipped into some shade alongside the road and stopped. A small creek crossed the road there. The trees were fairly heavy on either side of the road. They were lush and thick, almost overlapping the road.

"Aha," Butts exclaimed. "They have seen us. No need to try and play coy now. The jig is up."

Butts kicked the machine over on its side, pulled the nose up, and pointed up and to the right, to the two o'clock position. High up I could see the pair of Thunderchiefs streaking toward us. The wingman was tucked in real nice on his leader. The slender, bullet-like shapes of the Thuds looked like arrows shot from a bow with their slim, swept-back wings. Sheer power, they were bigger than a B-24 of World War II—and carried far more bombs in tonnage and destructive power than a B-17 or B-24.

I marveled at the sleek sharks as they began a slow turn and swept across the sky over us, their white bellies turning to brown as they turned up on their sides.

The radio crackled, "What's your position, Nail 27?"

Butts banked the O-2 back the other way, letting the nose fall in a nice, easy-rolling turn. I noticed that he had both hands on his map. He was rudder-flying the bird, letting the set power and aerodynamic stability of the aircraft bring it up and down, then over and down and up as he eased in a little left rudder, then a little right.

"Roger, Buick lead. This is Nail 27. We are underneath you, sir, at this moment. Please look directly below and you will see your friendly FAC. We are grey on the bottom and white on the top. And we are pulling white smoke for you, sir. Your target is one, I say again, one gasoline tanker, one staff car, and one army personnel variety truck. Your winds are 180 degrees at 10 knots. Your bailout heading if you take a hit is 270 degrees. Channel 99 is your nearest friendly landing base if you become crippled, at 79 nautical air miles. Your target elevation is 200 feet. Highest terrain in the target area is 1,060 feet one click to the northeast. There are no friendlies in the area. Consider all personnel on the ground if you go out as hostile. You have heavy 37mm and

ZPU antiaircraft defenses in the target area. There is a known SAM site to the south about 10 miles. I suggest you make your runs from east to west, with turns to the north, over."

We were watching the pair of Thuds. As soon as Butts told leader that we were underneath him and pulling smoke, we saw the pair ease up onto their sides, then go back down.

"Roger, Nail 27. Buick Lead has you in sight. You can terminate your smoke, over."

The O-2A was equipped with a small auxiliary oil tank. By pushing a button on the instrument panel, the pilot could inject pure oil into the engine cylinders. The sudden influx of oil into the cylinders produced heavy exhaust smoke—just a bit like an old car with bad rings burning oil, like a skywriter doing tricks overhead at the circus.

"Watch close," Butts said. "We could take fire at any time now. They have seen us for sure. Pulling that smoke is just like advertising for it. So watch real close."

He banked sharply to the left, dumped the nose, and made a beeline for the trucks that were hiding in the shade of the heavy trees, at the same time telling Buick lead to hit his smoke. He held the dive for only a few seconds, long enough for him to get a stable shot with a marking rocket. I saw him squint through the gunsight up on the dash, punch the red fire button under his thumb, then twist the controls sharply to the right, standing the bird over on its side, way past the vertical point. *Whooosh!* A single rocket sped away, out of the right pod just before he made the quick turn. He whipped the bird back to the left and let the nose slide down.

"Buick Lead is in hot, 27."

Then the 105 was screaming down the slot from 16,000 feet. The brown, green, and white 105 shot across the target; a pair of 750-pound fragmentation bombs arrowed toward the trees and the three hidden vehicles. Twin explosions came from just beyond the vehicles. A large cloud of black and dusty tan smoke billowed upward approximately 100 meters to the west, and Buick Lead was calling off the target, and Number Two was saying he was in hot.

"Make it about four road widths to the east, Buick Two," Butts told him just as the second 105 began his run.

"Roger, Nail 27. Buick Two is in, hot," came the slow reply.

We watched the F-105 roll off of his perch and come barreling down the chute, dead on for the three vehicles. A pair of 750-pound fragmentation bombs left his 105 and came streaking down to where the trucks were parked. I watched the black missiles crunch into the middle of the road, then explode with a tremendous flash. This was followed immediately by a gigantic, earth-shaking explosion and ball of fire that shot skyward in a plume of orange and black. He had hit the tanker! There was an immediate secondary explosion. Then a third. More fire and smoke shot skyward in a miniature atomic-like cloud.

"You got them, Buick Two. You got all three! Oh, watch out! Watch out! You are taking 37mm fire! Jink, Two, jink!"

Suddenly, the air behind the streaking 105 was filled full of white popcorn looking puffs in the air. Buick Two was going upward like a streak of lightning. All the white puffs were well behind him. One thing for sure about an F-105, it could really carry the mail. It could really climb coming off the deck with full afterburner. The tremendous speed of the 105 was a main reason why we FACs liked to work them—that and the terrific ability of the 105 drivers. The Thud pilots were aggressive as hell, possessed real skill, and had an absolute dedication to their job. They were great, just great.

With the three vehicles destroyed, Butts called in his thanks to the Thud pilots and gave his battle damage assessment to Invert Control. Then he remarked, "Well, let's tool on up to the Buffalo Plain and sedate a buff or two. Whaddaya say?" he asked me, grinning.

I told him, "If I knew what you were talking about, I might agree with you. But you have to remember that I am the new guy on the block, okay?"

"Uh, roger on that. I just forgot for a second," he answered. He increased the power on the bird and began a climb, turning toward the north. "Up about the 50 degree radial of Channel 99, NKP, at the 36 mile point, there is a real nice flat plateau.

We call it the Buffalo Plain. There is an airstrip there also. Only it is abandoned. Been bombed a lot. We go up there every once in a while to see if we can catch a pack train of buffs bringing munitions down along Route Eight. There is some really rough country up there, and you find that the NVA and the Pathet Lao will use this kind of transportation to get the arms and ammunition to their mountain outposts. So let's go have a look."

Flying time up to the Buffalo Plain was not that long, but it was definitely a scenic route. Butts swung the Skymaster over along the North Vietnamese border. The 2,150-foot peak of Nui Bai Dinh, on the border between Laos and North Vietnam, was beautiful. So were all the other mountains in the area. They were bright green, just as if an artist had come along with a palette of fresh watercolors and splashed paint on. Bright greens, dark grays where the volcanic karst rocks showed through the vegetation, and all of it laced with geysers of blue, green, and white waterfalls. The turquoise sky illuminated and highlighted the brilliance of it all like a scenic poster for a vacation land.

As we began our westward swing toward Ban Sopma, an abandoned village on the Buffalo Plain, we noticed a large number of small abandoned villages. We commented on the fact. Why the small clusters of houses in the various villages were empty and where the former residents had gone were anyone's guess. The war? Famine? Disease? Who knew? Chances of enemy antiaircraft fire were practically zero in the area, so we loafed along like on a Sunday drive—indeed a rarity for a combat FAC.

"Buffalo Plain coming up ahead," said Butts.

There was a veldt of green expanse growing larger in the windscreen. I thought of Africa. It stretched left and right. It was basically flat. Mountains surrounded it on all sides and sloped down to the billiard table–like plateau. The Nam Theun River ran along the east side. I could see the Lao airfield of Ban Taleo. It was a pock-marked ruin, unsuitable for anything except maybe a helicopter. Route 8 ran along the western side of the plain from where we were.

"Be careful here," Butts advised. "There could be 37mms stationed along the road over there." He pointed with a gloved finger, bare forearm, sleeves rolled up on his jungle fatigues. "See those black dots down there along the edge of the river?" he asked.

"Got 'em in sight," I answered.

"Well, my new FAC friend, those dots are buffalo. Let's see you do your stuff, okay?" he told me.

I rolled the UHF radio channel selector over to Invert Control and spoke in my best FAC language, "Invert, this is Nail 27, over."

Static. Then Invert answered, "Go ahead, Nail 27. This is Invert, over."

"Roger, Invert, this is Nail 27, requesting air support for some fifty pack animals. Do you have any chicks airborne looking for a target, over," I asked him.

"Stand by, Nail 27," the controller said.

Butts was making a slow circle, descending down to about 3,000 feet, and doing some slow jinking as we went.

"Nail 27, this is Invert Control. I have two Hobos inbound to you from the PDJ. They are looking for a target to expend on. State your rendezvous position, over."

"Roger, Invert. Send your Hobos to the 050 degree radial of Channel 99 at 40 miles," I instructed him.

"Roger, 050 at 40," the voice said.

The black dots were single file and moving down the river at a slow pace. I peered through the binoculars and told my pilot, "There is a man riding the lead buffalo. And it looks to me as if there are bundles slung under the bellies of the pack animals."

"Yeah, I suspect so," Butts answered slowly, taking a square of tobacco from a pouch that he took out of a pants pocket, cutting a chunk off of it with the commando dagger he kept in his other boot, and plunking the foul-smelling stuff into his cavernous mouth.

Altitude was holding at 3,000 feet. The Hobos were checking in. He was telling them to come on down. There appeared to be no antiaircraft defenses on that side of the plateau. The

O-2 rolled up on its side, and Butts let it slip downward in a falling leaf maneuver, tilted the wings back level, and told the A-1s to hit his smoke. With that he fired a single Willie Pete rocket toward the lead buffalo. The white smoke of the rocket billowed upward. Animals began to run in all directions.

Butts called, "Follow me down, Hobos. I'll round them up for you." From one side of the herd to the other he flipped the Skymaster, shooting rockets at will. When nearly all fifty of the animals were in a group, he zoomed up and out of the way to let the A-1s do their work. I watched.

Like a pair of swooping hawks on a rabbit, the green and brown A-1Es with dirty white bellies roared down the slot, their 20mm wing cannons blazing. Both aircraft were in formation, just like a Luftwaffe fighter storm, in a short line abreast. The high-explosive incendiary shells went walking through the herd like Roman candles. Sparks and dirt were flying. From the number of shells fired into the herd on the first pass, I had expected to see the entire herd fall down, but only four animals were down. Rather than scatter, the animals all took off in a cloud of dust across the plateau. Butts rolled in behind the A-1s and walked several Willie Petes up through the buffs. Another one went down, seeming to explode as a 2.75-inch rockets centered the animal. Then we were up and climbing in a right-handed half roll.

"Come back around, Hobos," he was telling them. "It is free shooting. No one home around here."

The A-1s were back around for the second pass. I heard lead tell his wingman that they were going to drop some Daisy Cutters. A Daisy Cutter is a fuse-extended, 250-pound fragmentation bomb. The fuse extenders were two-foot metal rods that stuck out in front of the bombs, set to explode on contact. These A-1s were carrying four Daisy Cutters each.

They began the run with the 20mm cannons. The HEI shells slashed through the running animals like hail. It was a good pass. The Hobos were down on the deck, coming up fast, raking the animals from the stern. I saw four go down, then two more, then another. Just then, when the A-1s were nearly over the remaining animals, each dropped a pair of the Daisy Cutters. The four 250-pound frag bombs exploded in pairs left and right in the herd. Animals went down kicking all over the ground. There were too many to count through the dirt and dust.

"That's enough, Hobos. Take it up. Hold high and dry," Butts said around his plug of tobacco. To me, he said, "See if you can get a body count when we come around for some BDA, okay?"

I acknowledged. As the O-2 swept back along the line from where the animals had come I began counting the downed buffs—one, two, four, eight, ten, eleven, fifteen, then up to thirty-seven. "Uh, I think they did pretty well. I can count thirty-seven. I could have missed a couple," I told him.

"No sweat. That's close enough for government work," Butts replied. He thumbed the mike and talked into it nonchalantly, "Okay, Hobos, take it home." Almost in the same breath, he finished the transmission with, "Invert, Nail 27 with BDA, over." Invert answered. We gave them the bomb damage assessment.

To the uninitiated, the shooting and bombing of water buffalo may seem like a cruel and inhumane thing to do. Under normal circumstances, it would have been. However, it must be remembered that this was war and the NVA and the Pathet Lao forces used the buffalos on a regular basis as vehicles of war. Each animal was capable of carrying up to fifty pounds of munitions under its belly and considerably more in a pack on its back. It would require a sharp-eyed pilot to know the difference between an animal packing ammunition and one lolling along a trail. Every one that we took out of action meant that much less ammunition would reach the enemy troops.

After four hours of sitting in that stinking, growling, hot machine, I was ready to call it quits. So was Butts. He struck a course for home, wandering and weaving all across the sky as we went. Never in my life did a river look so good. The muddy Mekong passed under the wings after four hours and fifteen minutes in "enemy territory." The wheels screeched gently on the PSP. The Skymaster settled down on all three wheels and rolled along like a tired goose after a long flight. I unbuckled the backpack parachute, slipped out of the harness, and took the flak vest off. I was soaked. I vowed I would not wear one of those stupid things again, not that kind anyway.

"Well," I said to Butts, "thanks for the ride."

He grunted, leaned forward, and spat. "Glad to have had you along. Hope you learned a thing or two today."

Butts had jockeyed the O-2 into the parking area by the Nail maintenance building, shut down both engines, and held his hands up so the ground crew could install the wheel chocks. Then he unsnapped his helmet strap and pulled the olive-drab helmet off. His bald head shined with sweat, and he looked like Mr. Clean with an orange Fu Man Chu mustache hanging down five inches on either side of his mouth. He shook my hand and held it for a moment and said slowly, "You take care out there and always remember to jink and jink some more. And be like an owl. Keep your head rotating so you can look around and look around some more. This is my next to last flight, really, and I'll be gone back to The World in about a week. God bless you." He let my hand go.

I unlocked the right door and opened it, then asked, "Butts, this completes your second tour, does it not?"

"Sure does," he replied.

"How much combat time you logged?"

"Well, with this sortie today—I think it makes me right at a thousand hours and 359 sorties," he answered.

I looked him in the eye and said, "Butts, it is time to go home."

He looked back at me and said slowly, "I feel like you are right and I have just enough luck left to make one more. I'm tired. And The Trail is no place for tired people. They make mistakes. Mistakes will get you killed out there."

CHAPTER 6

Cricket West

I had screwed up. I had committed the worst possible sin that a pilot could make. I had allowed fighter aircraft to close on me unseen. Not only did they close on me without me seeing them first, they had me completely boxed in. One minute Lieutenant Sohn and I were sitting there minding our own business and the next we were surrounded by F-28s.

It happened in the blink of an eye. The 28s had zoomed in on us from behind, coming down out of the sun. My eyes got bigger and bigger as I saw the slate-gray fighter sliding up on the right wingtip, its red- and white-tipped black propeller a whirling blur. My head snapped to the left: There sat another one just off the left wing. I looked up through the Plexiglas in the top of the cockpit: There was another. It was so close I could see oil running along the belly in quivering streaks from the blast of the slipstream. I looked over the side: There was a fourth one. Two white-helmeted figures were staring up at me like creatures from outer space. Their oxygen masks pointed up at me and their dark green sunvisors gave them the appearance of giant bugs. The pilot of the plane to my left gave me the finger. Then, as if to rub salt into my wounded ego, he cocked his thumb back, pointed his index finger at me, and made a motion like a pistol firing.

The 28 sitting off the right wing undulated up and down; the white triple-headed elephant on a blood-red background on its side made me breathe easier. They were Lao F-28s—friendlies.

Lieutenant Sohn and I had taken off from NKP at 0800, as we had done every morning for a week. We flew low, just over the trees, and made a beeline for Tahkhet across the Mekong.

It was standard operating procedure to "buzz" the Royal Lao Army camp there to get them up. It seemed that the Lao Army slept late no matter which way the war was going, good or bad.

I cranked the O-2 around in a tight circle, jazzing the rear prop. Sohn was peeking over his side of the cockpit to see if there was any activity down in the camp. I whipped the controls over, kicked right rudder, and stood the Skymaster on its side, pulling back stoutly on the yoke. The bird groaned under the quick load of Gs. A running figure came into view on the bare, swept ground below. Some guy was busily hitching up his breeches and tightening his belt as he came out of a little shed. The headset crackled as the FM radio came to life. I heard Sohn talking excitedly to the radio operator on the ground. Then I noticed he was not writing with his black grease pencil on his side window. He laughed.

"Knock it off, Lieutenant Sohn," I told him. "Let's get on with the business of the day."

At that he said something in Lao and began to write. I could make out map coordinates as he put them down. More excited jabbering. When we received instructions, I could never tell whether they were discussing the party from the night before or a strike we were supposed to make.

"What did he say, Sohn?" I asked, releasing pressure on the yoke, leveling the gray and white wings, and making a readjustment on the throttles and mixtures.

"Bad men at Charlie One," he yelled over to me. "PL men mortar camp."

"How bad?" I yelled back over the roar of the engines and the whistle of the wind coming in the side.

"Plenty, plenty bad," he said, readjusting his mouth boom mike. "Plenty bad men drop mortar shells down on camp."

I pushed both throttles up against the firewall, with mixtures at full rich. The bird began to climb quickly. The flat, lush green valley of Muang Khammouan was falling behind. I punched the interplane mike and said to Lieutenant Sohn, "See if you can raise Charlie One. Find out what their situation is." He nodded and rechecked the Fox Mike on 47.6 freq. I thumbed the UHF.

"Hello, Smoky Control. This is Nail 31, over."

Almost immediately I got an answer. "Ah, roger, Nail 31, this is Smoky Control, over."

"Rog, Smoke, this is 31, we have troops in contact at Charlie One. Request Eagles at the six-zero degree radial of Channel 99, two-zero miles, over."

There was a pause. I pulled the throttles back to 23 inches of manifold pressure and the props back to 2,100 rpms. Then I twisted the armament control buttons to the "in" position. Ahead, the gray karst crags of interior Laos were looming huge in the windscreen.

I heard Sohn jabbering."Camp taking heavy mortar fire," he said, his black eyes as bright as diamonds.

"Nail 31, this is Smoky Control, over," stuttered the headset inside the heavy fiberglass helmet.

Sweat was running down the back of my neck. "Go ahead, Smoky, this is 31, over."

"Nail 31, you have a flight of four Eagles, call sign Eagle One, bearing 345 degrees, Angels five, from your position. Ordinance is two, I say again, two 250-pound Daisy Cutters each, with mini pods, over."

"Copy, Smoky, Nail 31," I acknowledged. I knew Eagles were F-28s, sold by the U.S. to Laos, fighter-bombers with props. Mini pods were 7.62 Vulcan gattling machine guns.

I began calling, "Eagle One, Eagle One, this is Nail 31, over." No answer. I rolled the O-2 over to the left and scanned the rough ground below. The karst was like rock needles. Over to the right was flat plain. I had the camp in sight. There was a puff of dingy gray smoke even as I watched. Then another. 60mm mortar fire. The squiggly line of trenches that was the outside perimeter of the camp's defense looked like a stream of chocolate syrup on the dusty orange ground. I circled the camp, scanning the area all around it. I saw no one. A water buffalo was lying on its side on the ground, its head at a crazy angle. Puff! Another dirty gray cloud erupted right alongside a hooch. A flicker of organge crept up the side of the thatch building. A column of white smoke was rising.

"Where in the hell are the Eagles?" I asked Sohn. He grabbed my right shoulder and pointed. The slate-gray fighter was in on us before we knew it. They had come down out of the sun—a favorite trick of a fighter pilot. The four fighters had bracketed us in a flash.

My astonishment was short. "Stack up, stack up," I said in the mike. "Hit my smoke."

As quickly as they had come, they were gone. Up and away from us the four F-28s zoomed. Going high, off to the right. I pulled the nose of the O-2 up and watched the airspeed fall away: 100 knots, 90, 80, 70. The bird shook a bit. Left aileron, forward pressure, and left rudder—all at the same time—and the bird came over in a nice dropping turn. I pulled back on the yoke and watched the yellow rings in the gunsight center a cave on the side of a karst hill overlooking the camp. The yellow pipper dot in the center of the sight hung on the cave's mouth. Airspeed was building fast. At 140 knots I punched my finger onto the red fire button. A 2.75-inch white phosphorous rocket went streaking away, corkscrewing its way down. I saw its impact flash, just above the cave. Back on the yoke, hard. I didn't want to hang around to give anybody a shot at us. We went streaking off to the side in a slipping fall, airspeed building rapidly.

I craned my neck back to look out the top of the bird. Eagle One Leader was rolling in. He leveled his wings momentarily. Two black dots left his underside. Then he was up and away. Both bombs exploded just above the cave. Dirt and gravel slid down. Two was in, hot. Both of his Daisy Cutters flashed to the right of the cave. More dirt began sliding. Three was in, then four. Three's and Four's bombs exploded above the cave slightly. Then there was no cave. I saw little figures running down the stream bed.

"Follow me down, Leader," I told the flight. "Hit my smoke."

Sohn's eyes were huge in his small face. He was transfixed in his canvas seat. The yellow rings in the gunsight picked up four running figures. They had broken from the brush on the side where the cave was, where the steep hillside met the dry creek bed. I was already in on the firing pass, intending only to mark the bushy area from which the figures had bolted. I had felt that it was a good likelihood some ground troops would be hiding there, waiting to make an assault on the camp perimeter wire. Experience told me that it was not likely that only one mortar crew was in the area—that the mortar crew was most probably backup support for another and larger force. The Pathet Lao liked to overrun the small Royal Lao camps any time they could.

It was a simple matter in the dive to skew the nose around and line up on the running figures. They were really making it up the wash, shirts flapping out behind, looking over their shoulders at me coming down on them. Just as I centered the yellow pipper among them, one decided to be a hero. He stopped, jerked his AK-47 up, and hosed me. At that same instant I punched the fire button. I saw my pair of Willie Petes go streaking down at him, his tracers coming back up at me. I kicked right rudder, twisted the yoke, and let the bird slide down in a slip. The rockets exploded left and right of him. He went down in a heap. But his green tracers flashed like streaks of sparks over the cockpit. Then I was up and away, letting our 200 knots carry us high and to the right in a half roll.

I heard Eagle Leader. For the first time, an unmistakably crisp Yankee voice rattled in the headset. "Eagle One Leader is in hot, 31," he said.

I banked back the other way to jink—get away from anyone tracking my flight path. Never flying on the same track more than a few moments. More green sparks whizzed by the window. Figures were running all through the brush below. I saw Eagle Leader flatten out on his pass, his 7.62 mini gun was blazing orange under his bird, like the breath of a dragon flicking out. His tracers were white-hot, lacing the brush in a dust-spattering crescendo. Some figures sprawled in the dirt.

"Two's in, FAC," I heard in broken English. More white-hot streaks. More dust in the air. The four figures had turned into about thirty. We had flushed the whole force. Three and Four went in. They were taking it head on. Small-arms automatic weapons fire right in their faces. I saw Two take hits.

There was some jabbering in the headset. "FAC's in, hot," I spoke firmly, yanking the old bird over in a sideways dive, coming in 90 degrees from where the F-28s had begun their run. The little figures on the ground were so intent on the line of 28s they were not expecting the gray FAC bird to come swooping back like a hawk. I needed to give the 28s cover fire if I could. Two was up, climbing, trailing a whisp of dirty white smoke from the engine cowl flaps. I doubled two pairs of Willie Petes into the fracas below, pulling hard to stay above the withering machine-gun fire of Three and Four. I pulled back on the yoke, hard. It was heavy with the high diving speed. The four rockets flashed and exploded among the running and crouching troops. Their surprise was immense. They were distracted enough for Three and Four to get in and out on their pass with an immediate slackening of fire on them.

"High and dry," I yelled to Eagle Lead. "High and dry." I watched the four 28s form up. Two was still smoking some. "Eagle Two," I said, "take up a heading of 270 degrees. Maintain your present power. Your nearest safe landing is 22 miles. Proceed to that point. I will alert Jolly Green, over."

I did not want the pilots to have to bail out. I didn't know if they were Thai, Lao, or American. It didn't matter. The Pathet Lao did not take prisoners. I had seen what had happened to two Thai pilots who took ground fire and crash-landed their F-28 on the flat plain outside the village of Ban Kabout. They had been machine-gunned in the cockpit before they could get out, and their heads had been hacked off. Whoever these pilots were, I didn't want them to meet that fate.

Eagle Lead herded his flock together. They went droning away. Lieutenant Sohn and I were left alone as we always were. We surveyed the situation. A few people began to emerge in the camp. We could see men coming from the bunkers carrying weapons. They were still undecided about whether or not it was safe to venture very far away from their holes. Sohn and I had pretty well used up our rockets and mission time. I told him to see if he could raise the camp on the Fox Mike. While he fiddled with the radio, I set up a pass on what was left of the troops below. A good many figures were sprawled in the dirt. I counted seventeen through our binoculars, but I was not sure if there were any remaining in the brush or not. I thought it would be a good idea to salvo the remaining Willie Petes into the brush and see if I could catch it on fire. A good brush fire might flush any remaining troops into the open.

The gray and black nose of the O-2 rose to meet the rising sun as it climbed higher into the blue sky. The bird shook a little and quivered, as the airspeed sank. Then around came the nose. The yellow-tipped prop was a solid circle as we slid down into a final run on the brush below. I started on the front edge of the brush and marched the remaining Willie Pete rockets up through it. I thumbed the rockets out in singles, stitching a line through the thick foliage. We climbed and circled to watch. The men from Charlie One had gotten their courage up. A few were crouched on the downwind side—bent on catching any stragglers hiding in the bushes. God! There were some. We could see them fall as they ran headlong into the waiting guns of the men from Charlie One. Five. Then six. One was kicking on the ground. Somebody walked up to him, pointed an M-16 at him. Then he was still.

The guy waved his rifle back and forth to us. We wagged the gray and white wings back at him. I felt a little bit sick. But I knew, in rationalizing, that had we not of done what we did, another free Lao camp would have been overrun. Each and every person in that camp would have been murdered.

While we were Americans, the strike had been sanctioned by the Royal Lao Army. Lieutenant Sohn, a Royal Lao, had assisted me in the direction of the strike—on his soil, to save his country. Things were like that in Cricket West. We were U.S. pilots flying unmarked U.S. aircraft with a serial number on the tail of the birds. Each day, some few of us flew from camp to camp to camp to camp, looking and checking, in an effort to be certain that these camps—mountain village strongholds, valley village watch points, Mekong River watch points—did not fall into enemy hands. We always had a Royal Lao Army observer on board. While we were flying in "free" Cricket West Laos, he would be alert and intent. However, fly in an area outside of his "free" Laos, and he would go to sleep on you, leaning back in his seat and taking a nap.

Around and around we went, up one valley, down another, along roads, along the rivers, looking and hunting for targets— boats, vehicles, motorcycles, troops, columns of buffalo. We looked and searched for targets of opportunity—anything that was related to the enemy. It was our job to seek out and deter the enemy as much as we could. A lot of the free Lao people in the camps and villages were, in reality, free guerrilla fighters. Therefore, they were equally as aggressive and hostile to the Pathet Lao and NVA troops as these troops were to them. There was no taking of prisoners on either side. Whichever force over-ran the other meant total annihilation to the loser. A downed pilot was a thing for celebration among the captors, and a pilot could never be absolutely certain that any village he walked into, even in "free Laos," would be friendly toward him. Some of the hill people were absolutely hostile. A horde of angry vil-lagers could kill you just as quick as a platoon of NVA or Pathet Lao. While the NVA would generally, that far west, machine-gun you in your tracks, the villagers would stone you to death with rocks, poke you with pitch forks, or hack you with machetes. The Pathet Lao, on the other hand, had more quaint practices: tying you to a tree and skinning you alive; cutting you apart one piece at a time; sticking your head on a pole; cutting your liver out and cooking it on a stick—symbols, I guess, of their total vic-tory over an enemy.

Consequently, those of us who flew the missions in Cricket West wore jungle fatigues, tiger-striped camo to try to blend in with the foliage if we went down or had to bail out. We all car-ried weapons, lots of them. We FAC pilots knew the likelihood of return if captured was zero. Therefore, we took precautions. The "fast-mover" pilots who came to us to drop their ordinance were not indoctrinated into the hostilities and atrocities that waited for them on the ground if forced to bailout. The fast-movers, the jet pilots, had little hesitation to bail out if their craft was hit, whereas we FAC pilots had learned to stay with the bird as long as it would fly, as long as we had altitude and airspeed and were not burning or coming apart. We did. Our losses were low, ten in a year. The jet pilots from the F-105s and the F-4s had a high casualty rate among those who punched out into Laos—sometimes, as many as six or eight a day. An unfortunate pair of F-4 pilots bailed out in Cricket West. They walked into a village they assumed was friendly. It wasn't. The GIB (guy in back) from the F-4 hid in the brush and watched his aircraft commander walk into the village with his hands in the air. For his surrender attempt he got a belly full of AK slugs—a whole clip, thirty rounds. Then they chopped his head off. The GIB hid and made his way up the valley. It required two days of intense search-and-rescue efforts to get him out, at a loss of two A-1E aircraft and two other pilots.

I carried enough personal armament to start my own personal war in Cricket West if I went down. I was determined that I would not ever be taken alive. Consequently, I carried a 9mm Browning pistol; a 9mm Swedish K submachine gun; ten clips of 9mm ammunition for the machine gun with thirty-two rounds per clip; two extra clips of thirteen rounds each for the pistol; 300 extra rounds for both weapons; four plastic B compound hand grenades; two survival radios; a blood chit package; medicine; maps; compass; a commando dagger; and a large hunting knife.

I was a "prize" to the Pathet Lao. They knew me and the other five FAC pilots who flew Cricket West. They knew us by call sign. We had a $10,000 price tag on our heads if we could be caught.

As pilots in the 23rd Tactical Air Support Squadron, we were not concerned with the politics of Laos, really. They changed daily. Laos was a pawn in the chess game for Southeast Asia. Long before any war was being fought in South Vietnam, American airmen and equipment were in combat throughout Laos in the late fifties and early sixties. The main support to the

Lao forces was in the form of supplies, equipment, and advisors. Then came American pilots. By the early sixties, United States Air Force personnel were flying sortie after sortie into and over Laos. Aircraft losses began to mount in 1966–67. Nakhon Phanom Royal Thai Air Base became a staging and logistical support base for operations into Laos.

U.S. Navy T-28B aircraft were sold to Laos in numbers. These aircraft were modified from the trainer, or T configuration, to that of a fighter, or F, aircraft, adding guns and ordinance stations on the wings and underbelly. They were painted green and black. On the sides of the fuselage, where country markings would normally go, a U-shaped channel of metal was riveted, leaving the top open. Into that U-shaped slot an emblem of a country could be slid at any time, an emblem of whatever country was appropriate for the situation or mission. Most of the F-28 aircraft that we put in on targets in Cricket West carried no emblem whatsoever. Sometimes they sported the triple-headed Lao elephants. Sometimes they sported the roundel of Thailand. Some of the aircraft were dove gray in color. Some were green and black. Along with the F-28, which we FACed in on targets in Laos, Cricket West, there was the durable old U.S. Navy A-1E Skyraider. They belonged to the U.S. Air Force and were stationed at NKP (Nakon Phanom). They never carried national markings. Their green and brown paint blended well into the Lao countryside, a mixture of karst mountains, jungle, tall teak forests, and rice plains. The A-1Es were used constantly in Cricket West. The A-1s carried a big load of ordinance: hard bombs, napalm, CBUs, mines, rockets, and a good amount of ammunition in the wings for the 20mm cannons. We FACs loved the old A-1s. They were slow, but they packed a punch and were excellent for the low and close-in work we were doing—close-in work on guns, vehicles, boats, water buffalo, villages, troops in contact.

The war in Cricket West was a daylight operation. Not much went on at night. There, even the PLO and the NVA slept at night. We flew no night activities in CW, except on a very special basis. The two special exceptions that I was on were an attempt to capture American POWs in a camp and an effort to take a PLO hospital. Both episodes were routs.

Despite our most valiant efforts, Cricket West was slowly being eaten up by the PLO and the NVA. You could see the area shrinking daily—and becoming more and more like the face of the moon, cratered and bare. It was bombed and burned into oblivion.

CHAPTER 7

A Hotbed of War

During the period of 1968 and 1969, the war in Laos was at its zenith. Most of the world was unaware of this. The war in Southeast Asia, so the majority of people thought, was being waged in South Vietnam with some bombing raids by the U.S. in North Vietnam. This was true. But it was only a part of the big picture. The intensity of the bombing in North Vietnam was not known to the general public. It was fierce. Day after day after day, the F-105s and F-4s of the Air Force pounded it "up north." The losses to aircraft and pilots were equally fierce. The North Vietnamese were claiming something like 2,000 aircraft shot down. Our government was saying it was a lie.

What the world did not know was that, in actuality, the difference between the numbers of aircraft North Vietnam claimed to have shot down and the numbers the U.S. admitted was in Laos. Over half of the aircraft that the North Vietnamese were claiming to have downed were shot down in Laos. U.S. air activity there was heavy. The Air Force was flying in Laos, and so were the Navy, Marines, Army, and CIA. So was the International Control Commission. So was North Vietnam.

The air was full of aircraft. The Air Force had F-4s, F-105s, F-102s, F-101s, B-52s, O-1s, O-2s, OV-10s, A-1s, A-26s, C-130s, C-123s, C-47s, and F-111s. The Navy and Marines were flying F-4s, A-4s, and A-6s. The Army came and went in helicopters of the Loach type, Hueys, and Mohawks. The CIA used Pilotus Porters, C-123s, German Dorniers, and all types of helicopters. The Australians flew their own B-57 Canberras. Then the Lao pilots used F-28s, although you could never tell who was flying them because on some days Thai pilots flew them and on others Americans.

There was not too much NVA or Russian activity in Laos in aircraft. Once in a great while we would spot a MiG 19 or 21 over the area, but not often. A few old prop-type aircraft were seen up on the PDJ, Plains des Jars, once in awhile. One industrious FAC even shot one down with a handheld machine gun stuck out the window. Air supremacy was generally ours.

It was a standing joke in the squadron and on NKP when the International Control Commission came around. Word would filter down from the higher headquarters that the commission was going to have a look in Laos to determine if there actually was a war going on there. On such days none of us would fly. It was as simple as that. We just did not fly. We took the day off. The International Control Commission must have been a planeload of idiots not to have seen what the place looked like, and realized what was happening. Up and down the Ho Chi Minh Trail, the ground looked like the face of the moon, crater on top of crater. Trees were burned to blackness all along The Trail. Whole villages were burned down into charred ruins. Sections of the jungle were burned into oblivion by napalm. Some whole sections of ground were as bare as a plowed field in spring.

The CBUs, the cluster bomb units, made little evidence of damage to the ground, but they were dumped into Laos by the equivalent of a ship full a day. Roads were mined with anti-personnel mines. They were called Gravel and Dragon's Teeth. These little mines had a two-fold purpose. One, they were very effective against enemy troops walking and vehicles that were unlucky enough to roll over them. Two, Nakhon Phanom Royal Thai Air Base was wired up like NASA and the moon shot. Stationed there at NKP was an outfit called Task Force Alpha (TFA). We called it Disneyland. TFA was an intelligence gathering organization. It had four absolutely huge thirty-foot dish-type antennas set up on base. Laos was wired for sound.

One of the prime missions of the 1st Air Commando Squadron at NKP was the dropping of these devilish little mines all over the country. The Dragon's Teeth mines looked like a pie-shaped bean bag. The Gravel Mines looked like small bean bags that were round. And they looked like rocks—thus, the nick-name. Both types of mines were carried to the target in large cylinder canisters under the wings of the A-1s, usually one or two under each wing. The usual procedure was for the A-1s to proceed to their target coordinates in Laos in a flight of four aircraft. Prior to the A-1s arriving at the target, a 23rd TASS forward air controller would be orbiting that target. As the A-1s came on the scene, the FAC would dive and mark with a 2.75-inch rocket the beginning of a line where the mines were to be started and an ending rocket where the mines were to cease being dropped. Thus, with two columns of white smoke in the air, all the A-1 pilots had to do was dive and swoop so that the mines were dispensed between the beginning and ending columns of smoke. The pilots absolutely hated this kind of a mission. The old Skyraider was a fine airplane. It dove like a lead brick and 400 knots in the dive was the norm. However, once the pilot pulled out of that dive and rotated to begin his climb out away from the target, his airspeed fell off immediately, back into the 140 to 160 knots category. The A-1s were sitting ducks for the antiaircraft gunners with their 37mms, the 23mms, and the 57mms, not to mention the 85s and 105s, the surface-to-air missiles, and the deadly .60-caliber quad-barreled heavy ZPU machine guns.

The A-1 drivers had to face all of this on their mine-dropping missions. The FACs did not like to run the A-1s on these missions. The chances of the gunners getting one or two of the A-1s were great. I flew in South Vietnam some, but the missions in South Vietnam in no way compared to those over Laos and North Vietnam. In South Vietnam an FAC might be up and down on three to five missions in a day. He might have to face small arms and some heavy machine guns, but not like it was in Laos. The normal mission for a daytime FAC in Laos was two to five hours—usually about four. During those long day missions, the FAC encountered all types of antiaircraft defenses. Antiaircraft fire, once the guns got going at striking aircraft, was absolutely fierce. It was not unusual to see thirty or forty strings of antiaircraft shells in the air at the same time. Expose a slow-on-

the-getaway A-1 to such fire and he was meat in the pot. Therefore, we FACs took very careful precautions to avoid areas where
we might get our A-1 pilots shot down.

The whole purpose of the mines that the A-1s dropped was
for TFA to monitor the "popping" sounds that they made as
troops on foot and vehicles stepped on them or ran over them.
The intensity and frequency of the popping sounds coming out
of Laos told TFA a particular area of the country had increased
traffic in it. Quite often, while we FACs were airborne, we
would be diverted from one area to another to "check out"
those popping sounds that TFA was hearing.

In addition to the mines that the A-1s dropped on a daily
basis, the F-4s dropped strings of radio transmitters all over
Laos. The procedure was the same on the F-4s as with the A-1s.
We FACs marked the beginning and the ending of a sensor
string run—two columns for the fast-moving twin-engine heavy
jet fighter-bombers to run on—at 600 knots. The sensors that
they spewed out were about seven to fourteen in number and
resembled tree limbs. The sensors came out of the F-4 pods
like spikes and stuck in the ground, leaving the radio transmit-
ter portion above ground. In this operation, TFA now had real
audible sounds to track on—like voices, truck engines, wheels
rolling, and the clank and bang of troops.

However, TFA and their listening operators, who sat at
large console tables back at NKP, were not infallible. One night
I was on the Ho Chi Minh Trail. My navigator and I were busy
striking trucks going and coming up the main Trail. It was a
good night. We had some "movers," which is what we called
the trucks. Right in the middle of running a pair of Aussie Yel-
lowbirds onto a trio of trucks, the nav and I got a call from
Invert Control. A set of coordinates was given to us, along with
instructions to hustle on up there, take a look, and make a
strike on *tracked* vehicles. That really got our attention. We felt
sure we would find tanks rumbling up the main dirt road. We
had two World War II–vintage A-26 Nimrod light bombers on
their way to us. I broke the Aussies off, had them salvo their

stuff out in the weeds, and chugged on up to the coordinates that TFA wanted us to check out.

Night operations on the Ho Chi Minh Trail were an entirely different world from our daylight activities. First of all, it was blacker than being inside a whale with his mouth shut. Second, the night-version O-2A aircraft were entirely black and had no windows. And third, armament was different. While the pilot made right-handed circles along a road, the navigator peered out the window with a Starlight scope, which magnified lights by 29,000 times. A vehicle with its parking lights on was quickly spotted from 3,000 feet. A man walking with a flashlight could be spotted. Campfires were like torches to the scope. When looking through the scope, everything in the field of vision had an eerie green and yellow cast to it.

When my navigator and I arrived at the coordinates that were passed on to us, we received a shock. The nav commented, "You ain't gonna believe this! You ain't!" I was expecting antiaircraft fire, which came in ever-present strings and could come from any direction. If seen in time, we could easily get away from the strings of 37mms. The 23s took some fancy footwork, but the cluster of red balls, usually about thirty in number, could be side-slipped easily—again, if seen in time. The 23s moved much faster than the slower 37mms. The 37mms always came up in thirty-foot strings of five or seven shells that looked like orange beer cans coming up about two feet apart. If the shells were moving on the window, you were in good shape; they would miss you. However, if they became round orange balls on the window and were not moving on a line across the window, you best move *fast*; they were coming head on.

The 23mms came up fast in a cluster, like someone shooting a huge shotgun at you. The 57mms, the 85mms, and the 105s gave you no warning. If you were watching, you could spot the muzzle blast on the ground. Otherwise, you had no warning you were being fired on by the big stuff until you received a big bright flash near you. In the daytime, you got a big black

greasy puff in the air. We did not like the big stuff. You usually
did not know you were getting it until you got it. The Zepes—
or ZPUs, as we called them—were the .60-caliber twin- and
quad-barreled anti-aircraft heavy machine guns. Each barrel
fired 600 rounds per minute—that is, a four-barreled gun could
put about 2,400 rounds of .60-caliber slugs all around you in
just a minute or two.

So I was expecting the worst when the nav told me I
wouldn't believe it. "Whatcha got over there?" I asked him.

He laughed. "Five elephants pulling guns up the road."

"What?"

"Yeah, five big tuskers."

"Well, targets are targets. Let's go get them."

There were a few napalm fires burning along the road. So
we set the A-26s up on an ambush run. Out of NKP, the Nimrods flew on The Trail only at night, usually packing eight .50-
caliber forward-firing machine guns in the nose, four "funny
bombs" in the bomb bay, and eight fixed-wing stations carrying
750-pound napalm bombs. Sometimes, they varied their load
and carried half napalm and half frag bombs.

The nav and I set our trap. We continued our right-handed
circles along the road. We did not want to drop a parachute
flare. That would alert the drivers with the elephants and they
would all take to the brush. So we had the Nims concentrate on
a particularly bright little fire along the road. I asked the Nim
leader if he had the particular fire in sight. He acknowledged
that he did. Meanwhile, as I was briefing my 26s, the nav was
keeping a watch on the five tuskers plodding along up the road
pulling their big guns. I told the Nimrod leader to use one
funny bomb on this outfit below. I felt a funny would do the
trick. Funny bombs were thermite bombs, phosphorous. They
looked exactly like 52-gallon hot water tanks. Once the bomb
left the bomb bay and cleared the aircraft, the casing on the
bomb would split in half and spill the contents out into the air.
The phosphorous ignited upon contact with the air, and the
whole mess would spew over everything under it. If dropped
from the right altitude and airspeed, one funny would cover

the area about the size of a football field. It was deadly and could burn right through an engine block or truck body. The ones the 26s were carrying were leftovers from World War II.

As the five elephants neared the fire on the ground, I talked the lead A-26 onto his downwind leg of the run, i.e., the far side of his rectangular pattern. Then, as the elephants came closer to the fire, I had the A-26 turn on his "crosswind" leg, the short side of the far end of the rectangle. Just as the elephants came abreast of the fire, I had the Nimrod turn on his "final" approach, or the other long side of the rectangle. He came in on a long diving run. Just before he came abreast of the fire, he dropped his ordinance load—in this case, a single funny bomb. He was perfect on altitude, airspeed, and line of flight. I saw the funny pop open, the load of gleaming silver phosphorous ignite and cover the whole scene—elephants, drivers, and guns. The whole scene was an instant fire. He got them all in one big pool of silver, burning phosphorous.

We had him climb back to altitude, then called Invert. "Invert, this is Nail 31," I said into the boom mike.

"Go ahead, Nail 31. This is Invert, over."

"Standby to copy BDA, Invert," I answered. "Uh, Invert, this is Nail 31. You ain't gonna believe this."

"Say again, 31. This is Invert, over."

"Yeah, rog, Invert. This is Nail 31. Tell TFA that the tracked vehicles they had us check out at those coordinates were, uh, five elephants pulling big guns, and that is our bomb damage assessment. All are crispy critters now, over."

"Roger, 31. Understand. Invert, out."

In addition to the funny bombs, the dragon's teeth, the gravel mines, and the radio sensors, we used millions of tons of conventional bombs on Laos, from the 250-pounders through the 500- and 750-pounders, on up to the 1,000-, 2,000-, and 3,000-pounders. Frag bombs were mostly 500- or 750-pounders, as were napalm bombs, which were standard armament on

fighter-bombers. Although dropping napalm bombs was standard at night, you couldn't do it in the day unless you had
troops in contact or had a special purpose, like rescuing a
downed pilot. To clear LZs, we had 10,000-pound "block-
busters," which were dropped out the ass end of a C-130 Hercules cargo plane and created an instant LZ.

One of my favorite weapons to use on trucks was the CBU,
which came in CBU-14s, CBU-19s, CBU-22s, CBU-24s, and CBU-
25s. All were deadly when dropped from the correct altitude
and airspeed. A single canister of CBUs could cover the area of
a football field like a shotgun blast. Every square foot of the area
would be saturated with red-hot ball bearings. Some CBUs were
filled with nausea gas, used exclusively on SAR missions to rescue downed pilots and crew members. The gas would make anybody who came in contact with it deathly sick, instantly.

Laos was a proving ground for weapons. "Fat Albert," as we
nicknamed the great propane bomb that came to NKP, was a
test bomb. It was gigantic. Hanging under the wing of an A-1, it
looked like half of a railroad tank car. The theory of Fat Albert
was that it was to be used on troops in bunkers and trenches.
The bomb, upon hitting the ground, burst in half, spewing
eight little igniter capsules all around. The propane inside was
designed to flow over the contours of the ground like fog,
creep into crevices and bunkers, holes and ditches, then burst
into flames when the igniters set the gas off. The blast was like
a miniature atomic bomb. A great orange and black mushroom
cloud ensued, rising 6,000 feet into the air.

Perhaps one of the more sophisticated, and complicated,
bombs that came into our employ was the "smart bomb" that
we used on The Trail at night. It was too complicated and faded
from the scene, even though it had devastating effects in the
short time in which we used it. Those of us FACs at NKP that
were old timers had the opportunity to check out some pilots
who joined the squadron from Da Nang. These pilots brought
with them their North American OV-10 Broncos—a twin-
engine, turbo-prop, twin-boomed aircraft, with a large Plexiglas
canopy. It was a fine airplane that cruised at 200 knots indicated
and dove at 400 indicated. We employed this aircraft a lot on

The Trail at night, with the smart bomb. The way this bomb worked was sort of on the flashlight principle. A pilot, or a navigator, in the back seat of an OV-10 would hold a device like a laser onto a target. A pilot in another airplane would drop his smart bomb at the target. A sensing device in the nose of the bomb, much like an eye, would home in on the beam that the other airplane was directing onto the target. The result was usually pinpoint accuracy. However, the bomb was far too costly to be used on single trucks.

Night work on the trucks on The Trail was exciting—and dangerous. FACs and fighter-bombers, diving on trucks in the night, amidst the towering karst mountain krags aged fast—if they survived. The night pilots who worked The Trail were a special breed of cat unto themselves. Many pilots dreaded the night dive-bombing runs down into the murk, and the wild pull-offs into the swinging, swaying shadows cast by the parachute flares coming down around the target—not to mention the climb outs amid laces and crisscross strings of antiaircraft shells.

Frankly, I liked the night flying. I always felt it gave me the "edge" in case I took a hit and had to bail out. You could jump out, if you had to, and likely wouldn't be caught. Plus, at night, you could see everything that was being shot at you except the really big antiaircraft stuff or the SAMs. During the day you often had a tough time seeing a stream of antiaircraft shells coming up at you. I liked the night so much that I had myself taken off the daytime sorties and flew only night missions for four months. During that time we killed seventy-five trucks, a great many guns, many stores of munitions, one helicopter—and five elephants.

There was always plenty of enemy activity at night, especially in the Steel Tiger and Tiger Hound areas of Laos. The NVA and Pathet Lao moved mostly during nighttime hours down the Ho Chi Minh Trail. We waited for them along Lao Routes 911 and 912, constantly circling up and down the network of roads and directing strikes against the traffic below.

While it was our mission to interdict the flow of men, arms, and supplies in Laos before it got to South Vietnam, it was also our mission to prevent or delay the whole capture of Laos by

the NVA and the PL. Both missions proved fruitless. No
amount of interdiction could stop the flow of personnel and
supplies going south into South Vietnam and Cambodia. It simply was not possible with the tactics we used and the amount of
pilots and aircraft we had available to us, though we had many.
Laos was bombed and bombed, but still the enemy came. We
pilots knew it was a lost cause, but McNamara and the Pentagon apparently did not.

CHAPTER 8

Scratch One Gun

The mission started out like a milk run. I had done the same thing so many times before that I wasn't particularly concerned about the outcome. Our short missions were about two hours long, usually flying out to a set of map coordinates to mark for a pair of F-4 Phantoms to put in radio sensors that monitored troop and vehicle traffic along The Trail. That's what I was scheduled to do this day.

Just like every day for the past week, I crawled into the little O-2, strapped myself to it, and climbed east. The Mekong was a wide, muddy snake sliding beneath the rocket-laden wings of the gray-on-bottom, white-on-top observation aircraft as it soared into the blue Thai and Lao skies. A bus of some sort careened along the single hard-surface road beside the Mekong. I wondered what sort of urgency necessitated that sort of speed at 0800 in the morning? But who really cared? Life and death played out all around us each day, and each scene was like a page flipping in a drama of high suspense. My page for the day lay somewhere ahead, and to deviate from the plan would foul up a whole string of events that had been put into motion the day before. My fighters would be on time. I knew that. They depended upon me to be on time, too, no matter how seemingly stupid it was to risk the lives of five aviators and hundreds of gallons of av gas and jet fuel just to drop eight radio-receiver transmitters, looking like tree limbs, into the jungle along a dirt track somewhere in the middle of nowhere.

It was still the wet season on The Trail. No motor vehicles moved. They couldn't. The mud of Laos would bog a snipe, but you could not tell that to the people down at Blue Chip. They always said to get on with the plan at all costs. The blue sky was deceiving. By the time the sun was up for a few hours, there would be thunderstorms towering to 50,000 feet, and it would rain again, rain like you have never seen before, turning the jungle into a sea of mud and slop and green steam.

Once I crossed the Mekong, I was in Laos. It was a bad place to be, and the farther east, north, and south one progressed, the worse it got. I had developed the habit early in my career as an FAC to climb in a wide spiral after takeoff to gain altitude before I crossed the river. An O-2 is no great shakes as a speed machine, and when it's laden with fuel and two pods of Willie Petes, there's not much margin of error, especially at low altitude.

As I reached 4,000 feet, I pulled the throttles back to 22 inches of manifold pressure, adjusted the props to 2,150 rpms, and reset the mixtures for optimum fuel saving, but still rich enough to allow the engines to run cool and smooth. Then I leaned back to enjoy a smoke. I had a thirty-minute run to my target. I let the old bird climb slowly as she lightened ever so slightly with consumed fuel en route. My head itched. I stuck the grease pencil up under the edge of the bulletproof olive-drab shell and scratched. The jungle fatigues still felt clammy from all the sweat, even at so early an hour, but they were drying some as the wind tunneled through the cockpit.

At 7,000 feet I leveled off and reset the trim, opened the little triangle window by my left hand, and threw the Camel out. The butt sparked with new life as the slipstream breathed on it and splashed it down the side of the fuselage in a spatter of minute shell bursts. I prayed silently that they would, indeed, be the only actual fire on the thin gray skin all day. Less than an eighth of an inch of aluminum does not provide much sanctuary and haven from the wrench and tear of heavy shells. The Trail was infested with big guns where I was headed.

An FAC—alone in his cocoon of thin aluminum, Plexiglas, canvas, and tubes and knobs and life-giving fluids to his steed, shielded by a layer of paint on crackerbox-thick aircraft skin— is truly alone. Unlike the fighter pilots who almost always flew in four-ship formations, or the A-1 jocks growling along in a

pair with big R-4350 engines and 14-foot props howling, the
FAC had nobody to talk to except through his radios, the FM,
HF, VHF, UHF, SSB, or Prick 25. More often than not, there
was not anyone in the cockpit of the little gray birds except one
single steely-eyed, mustached, sun-burnt aviator, usually loaded
for bear with a big knife on his chest, a big pistol on his hips,
spit-shined jungle boots, and a sack full of maps and charts.

The FAC was truly a man alone in his gallant bit of a tiny
machine, a frail craft that whirred and hummed like a huge
chainsaw as it flitted and flirted this way and that, up and down
and around, never making the same flight path twice. A loop
here, a roll there, a climb, a dive, then straight and level for the
breadth of a second. That was the way and manner in which
the FAC flew. He appeared to be as a great drunk all of the
time with his airplane flopping through the halls of hallowed
space. And just when you knew that the man was insane, bent
upon killing himself, the machine would miraculously hesitate
for a blink of an eye, and a rocket would *whoosh* away with a
bright flash from the wings and go streaking down with a thin
trail of vapor to smash into a target with the deadly accuracy of
a gunfighter long accustomed to getting the first shot before
the victim even knew he had been selected.

FACs drove the NVA and Pathet Lao antiaircraft gunners
nuts because the FAC, the true FAC, the steely-eyed tiger in the
little bitty airplane, never did as he was supposed to do. The
FAC did not fly by the rule book. He couldn't—if he wanted to
live to be a ripe old age. He laughed in the face of death each
day, tweaked the nose of fate, and switched the sleeping dragon.
Then he went scampering merrily away, gleeful, props running
completely out of sync, flying sideways like a bird caught in an
awful crosswind—nose pointing in one direction but in reality
going another, looking for a second dragon to kick while the
first was still roaring and thrashing and belching fire into the
heavens.

Unless I was forced to take an observer along, I didn't. I
even had my crew chief take out the right seat today for this
mission. I figured that the weight of the second right seat might

make the difference in whether I returned to NKP if the chips were really in the fire. The O-2 flew quite well on both of its 225-horsepower engines; however, take away one of those six-cylinder horizontally opposed powerplants, and the machine floundered in the air like a goose with oil-soaked feathers. But it could fly if odds were in its favor—if it wasn't too heavy with fuel and stores, if there weren't too many people on board, if you could feather the prop on a failed engine. There were always a lot of ifs. That's why I liked to cut the odds down before I flew. I figured that the extra pounds of the observer, his gear, and the seat decreased my chances of getting home by 50 percent. Furthermore, bailing out of an O-2 is not an easy task. Unlike a fighter, it didn't have a hot ejection seat. The only way into and out of it was through a single door on the right side. The pilot got in first and out last.

The subtle green on the land below looked so utterly peaceful. But I knew it wasn't. The land was a sleeping alligator, docile in the hot sun until a morsel fell from heaven. At that moment toothy jaws would open wide and make every effort to consume you, turn your mortal body back to dust. The roving bands of the Pathet Lao and swarming hordes of NVA Regulars were the same as the alligator, always lurking and waiting for the unwary, the unfortunate, the stupid, the cripple, to gobble you down, savoring each mutilating chew before swallowing and excreting your parts across the land that reeked with the stench of communism and enslavement.

The deeper I flew into Laos, the taller the teak trees became—200-foot giants, as thick as hair on a dog's back, 6 feet through at the base, towered toward the sun and the moon and the stars. I smiled to myself as I peered straight down and thought of Jack and his beanstalk. I marveled at the stalks of the trees here, shooting upwards more than 100 feet above the forest floor before the first sign of a limb appeared. Then, the canopies of the upper limbs formed double and even triple layers of green, through which a downed pilot would have one hell of a time getting through should he have to come down into it in a parachute. We had found the remains of one Navy lieutenant commander who had been shot down long ago and hung there until just a few rags and bones remained, high above the ground, still buckled into his chute, unable to get down, swinging in the wind for all eternity. Bright flowers dotted the foliage at the tops of the trees. I thought of the bee landing lightly onto the nectar of the Venus Flytrap, duped by an illusion.

The main Ho Chi Minh Trail was only 62 miles from the Mekong at the point where I was going. Takeoff had been at 0800. At 0900 I had a pair of F-4 Phantom fighter-bombers coming to me for a sensor drop. At 1015 I had another pair of the same due for a similar drop on another target not too far away, the second pair of F-4s having been diverted to me in a last-minute change of tactics.

The Phantoms were to be carrying their radio sensors in belly-slung canisters. I had been briefed by the intelligence officer to mark their start-of-run point at a specific set of coordinates on a map and their end-of-run point at another set. This would provide a line on which the pilots could lay the eight transmitter-receivers. All they had to do was line up the two columns of smoke provided by the pair of Willie Pete rockets, run in at full power, pickle at the split-second time, and zoom off into the blue—and another pea patch in Laos would be bugged. The whole country was already so wired-for-sound that I really couldn't see how a mouse could defecate without it being recorded forever back at NKP at Task Force Alpha—Disneyland East, we called it.

At 40 miles out of Nakhon Phamon, I could begin to see the Nam Phanang River. There The Trail ran on its west side. I dug out my maps, the ones so nicely provided by the intel boys, the maps made up into bound volumes with acetate coverings that you could write upon with a grease pencil. Then I laid my aerial photos out onto the floor of the cockpit where the right seat would have been. Though I knew the area intimately, when you are searching for one particular hair on the dog's

back, one specific hairpin curve on a dim road, you need all
the help you can get and the aerial photos were it. The mark
for the Phantoms had to be precise. Fifty meters right or left of
the drop line and we may as well not have even come out. The
sensors had to be just off the road, but far enough back in the
brush to not be readily seen by walking troops. Even though
the sensors were designed to look like tree limbs sticking in the
ground, foot soldiers often found them. They knew what they
were after finding a few and it got to be sort of funny. The soldiers would shout into the receiver and make unprintable comments about Nixon and the "imperialist dogs" and tell jokes.

The sensors were to be dropped on a fairly straight stretch
of road on the main Trail near Ban Thapachon. It was normally
a heavily traveled section. Apparently, an air strike had taken
out the string that was there. The location had been without a
monitor string for a few days. It was my job to see that the place
got re-bugged. The river valley at that point was a deep gully set
between a 4,500-foot mountain on the east and a 1,666-foot
karst ridge on the west. The only successful-looking approach
for the fighters would be north to south, or vice versa. It was a
bad run-in heading either direction. Big guns were all around.

With about twenty minutes to go before the F-4s were to
check in, I reached up and armed the rockets and turned up
the pipper in the gun sight, then began a long descending glide
down to 3,500 feet. Twenty minutes would provide me with a
good VR of the area to see if any hostiles were about and in
sight. I didn't want to spend too much time circling the area. It
would alert the gunners that something was going to happen.
So I made a wide turn, got the sun to my back, and cruised up
the road like on a Sunday ride, trolling like a green, stupid FAC.
I didn't really want to get anybody riled up down there, but if I
had any trigger-happy gunners in the near area, I wanted to
know it before I went down into the bushes. You never could
tell for sure about those Gomers on the guns. Some days they
would shoot at you at any distance and on other days you could
fly right over them while they squatted in a circle and ate their

lunch. We always said it depended upon if they had shot up their monthly ammunition allotment.

Anyway, nothing happened by my acting dumb so I motored on over the ridge and recky-tecked a little. Route 911 ran straight for a 1,000-meter stretch at Ban Thapachon. I was to mark just north of a fork in the road. At that point a towering piece of karst we called the East-West Karst was immediately off the fork in the road. This was bad, very bad. The karst was pocked with caves. Guns were dug in up on top of it. From quite a distance away, I drunkenly rudder-flew the bird with my feet while I surveyed the situation with 40-power gyro-stabilized binoculars. I wanted to know what was happening back there, but I did not want any gunners that could be awake and watching to think I was supremely interested in that particular piece of real estate. The night FAC had reported both 37mm and ZPU fire from the EW Karst. There was one gun that I could see, but it was halfway up on the front side and I could not tell for sure whether it was an old burned-out gun or a live one.

The hands on my Seiko watch showed 0850 when the headset rattled for the first time as the initial pair of F-4s checked in with me.

"Nail 31, this is Bigot, over."

"Bigot, this is Nail 31, how do you read me?"

"Loud and clear, 31. What's your position?"

"Bigot, I am 76 miles on the 095 radial of channel 89, at 3,500. Come to me."

"What's your position and angles, Bigot?" I asked.

"Angles 16, heading 050 degrees, crossing the Mekong off of channel 99, Nail."

At his speed I knew the F-4 and his wingman would be on me in six or seven minutes. I was ready. I had a couple of minutes yet to look some more. Right close at hand was a place called Papa 2881. There, at coordinates WE 755, 340, the Nam Ngo River flowed past a karst cliff. A main road ran under the cliff next to the river—a perfect interdiction point. Too, the road was a direct route to North Vietnam through the Deo Mu

Ghia Pass only a few miles away. The karst cliff above the road
was infested with various caves. And the caves housed countless
NVA troops and their road repair machines—plus stores of
munitions and supplies. A B-52 raid, Arc Light, had gone in on
the place during the previous night. The raid of the big bombers had been useless. The 750-pound frag bombs that had been
dropped had only made a gigantic gravel pile for the road
crews to get hard-surfacing material from. The trucks and their
supplies were so deep inside the maze of caves that only an
atom bomb might get them out. Besides, with it being a semi-
wet season, not too many of the trucks were moving at all. It
was true that things were beginning to look better as the moons
changed and the rains got fewer and fewer. But it was really not
the time for the trucks to run. During most days at any time of
the year, and during the monsoons, the trucks and accompany-
ing supplies were simply stored. But one never knew; you could
and may just catch a few out and about if the roads were dry
enough to move locally. There were no paved roads or tracks
along The Trail, and it took some time for the whole landscape
to dry out enough for the long and regular run from Hanoi to
Cambodia. So while the ground dried sufficiently, activity of
supply movement was slow.

Time after time, we Nail FACs had informed Saigon that
their techniques of Arc Light B-52 bombing on Laos during
the wet season was a waste of gas and bombs. All the bombing
did was to make gravel for the road crews to use when it finally
got dry out there. Saigon wouldn't listen. But when we really
needed the tremendous fire power of the B-52s during the dry
season and the heavens over The Trail at night were laced and
crisscrossed with streams of antiaircraft, we could not beg nor
buy a single B-52 raid.

The only way, we suggested, to make the labyrinth of caves
completely unlivable at any time for the enemy and force them
into the open was to use mustard gas on them. Saigon and
Washington would not hear of that. So we continued to watch
as troop strength built and had no way to stop it. It was frus-
trating. About all we could do was pick off a truck here, a few

trucks there, a few troops now and then and hope we did the GI some good down where he was catching hell—in the South.

Squinting up through the roof window as I circled, I soon spotted the fighters. They were dark and sinister looking. Their wings turned up on the ends and dirty plumes of brown smoke trailed them.

"Gotcha in sight, Bigot. Start a left turn, Bigot Leader, I'm at your ten o'clock position. I'm low, Leader. I am in a slow right turn and got my smoke on. Roll out, Bigot. I am now at your twelve o'clock position. Am white on top. I'm west of the north-south river over the ridge line."

Bigot Two cut in. "Tally, Leader. FAC's just off the right and straight down."

The two F-4s set up a circle over me as I briefed them on their target. It was short and to the point—as the fighter crews had been briefed by intelligence before takeoff.

"Your target winds are 150 at 10 knots, Bigot. There are hostiles on both sides of the river for 10 klicks. Your run should be north to south. If you take a hit, bail out heading is 270 degrees. If you can't get west, go to the high ground to the northeast. Your FAC will be holding east at 3,000."

"Okay, Nail. Give me smoke in two minutes."

"Roger, Bigot," I answered.

All the while I had been talking to him, I had been rudder-flying the O-2 over the target and searching with my binoculars for guns. I remembered the ZPU the nighttime Nail had said was active on Delta 18.

"Hey, Bigot, there was a Zepe on the karst just south of your target last night. I don't know whether he's home or not."

"Roger, Nail, we'll keep an eye peeled."

"One minute and counting, Bigot," I advised, while continuing to fly like a drunk at an air circus—up and down, sideways, and running the props out of sync to try to confuse anyone who might be watching. I had dropped to 2,000, and I continued to rudder the O-2 around this way and that, never doing the same thing twice. I intended to flip off and over on one of those crazy climbs and dives I was doing for a running dive just long enough to get a pair of rockets off. I'd need about thirty seconds to do it, and I figured I'd have about one straight free pass before the gunners realized what I was doing.

My watch showed thirty seconds to go. I wanted time to shoot, then a few seconds for the rockets to hit and the cloud of white smoke to rise so that the streaking F-4s could spot it and alter course a few degrees as needed to make the run true.

"FAC's in," I stated. "Mark's away."

I had been hanging on the prop at 65 knots. The O-2 was grumbling and shaking its head at the low airspeed. Full left rudder and she swapped ends in her own length. I was looking at the blend of red dirt and green jungle in about a 45-degree dive. I pushed on the yoke, stuck her nose down, and aimed the pipper at the road. Airspeed came up fast, 100 knots, 120, steady, 140. I punched the thumb button for fire—*whoosh*. A 2.75-inch Willie Pete rocket streaked out of the right wing pod and went whizzing away in a corkscrew pattern. The road was running through the yellow rings on the sight. I was a sitting duck then. The sight pipper settled again on the spot to hit that would terminate the sensor drop line point. Airspeed was 150 and building fast. Punch the firing button—*whoosh*, left rocket away. I pulled hard on the yoke and banked away in a flat right turn. I saw the rocket writhe toward target, then straighten out and streak straight home. A flash of yellow and white smoke began to erupt.

"Mark's good, Bigot, I'm off to the east," I told him.

I twisted in the seat and saw a satisfying column of smoke billowing from two nice bullseyes up through the trees and scrub brush by the road. I also spotted the F-4s. They were streaking in over the smoke at 500 knots plus, their war paint making them look like great green and brown bats scared from the jungle by my rockets. They were difficult to spot against the mottled blotches on the earth. Vapor trails poured off the tips of their wings as they rotated and pulled straight up in a beautiful climb, afterburners bellowing and winking at me like the eyes of a pair of wakened monsters. Their white bellies reminded me of great manta rays leaping skyward, as if hurled from the bowels of the ocean.

"Okay, 31, got any targets for us today?" asked Bigot Leader. "Whatcha carrying, ol' buddy?"

"Oh, we have the usual soft stuff, Nail."

That meant CBU's and rockets. I knew that was okay for troops and guns.

"I have a gun, I think," I told Leader. "There was one in the saddle on the karst south of your target. He fired last night. Want to try for him?"

"May as well."

I briefed him on the target. When I had the fighters in a high orbit, I got set. The sky was so blue, without a cloud. The emerald green of the jungle stood out vividly. It seemed as if you could get out and walk on the thick carpet of the tree tops. If it had not been where I was and the job I was doing, I would have considered it a Sunday flight. Laos, despite all the enemy traffic and air activity of war, was a beautiful little country.

I swooped the Skymaster in on the gun position in a head-on firing run. The karst loomed big and rapidly got bigger in the yellow circles of the gunsight. I had the hole the gun was in wired. The bright yellow dot of the pipper was dead center on it. I waited, waited, waited, and pressed the pass. I wanted to get the Willie Pete down in the damn hole if I could—2,000 feet, steady, 1,000 feet. My finger quivered on the button, the tiny red button on the yoke the size of a pencil eraser. 500 feet—punch, punch on the button. Two rockets whizzed out of the left pod. Just as I fired, I saw a pair of gun muzzles come winking to life in the hole. I could see the slugs coming—fast—green and yellow tracers. I gutted the old bird out with full power instinctively and pushed forward hard on the yoke. My lap belt strained and cut into my belly as I floated in the seat from the negative Gs. My shined jungle boots pushed hard on the rudder pedals, polished from countless scrubbing by nervous feet. I went straight for the trees. The gun was a ZPU, a .60-caliber heavy machine gun. Usually, they came in two- or four-barreled versions for use as an antiaircraft gun. This one was a two-barreler. The rate of fire for each barrel is about 600 rounds per minute. Every fifth round was a tracer. You could never be sure about the tracers. Some were red. Some were green. Most seemed to be yellow.

I saw five or six long, bright yellow streaks pass over the top of the craft. The smell of cordite was strong coming in the open window, pungent in my nostrils.

Bigot had started yelling as soon as the gun fired. "He's home, Nail! He's home! Jink, Nail, jink!"

I will never forget the pilot's voice. He was warning me, and he was really worried. To him, little brother was in trouble. We had a comradeship, FACs and the fighters. We never knew, usually, who was flying the fast-movers. They did not know who was putting around down below in the Reynolds Wrap bombers either, but the fighters knew that the FACs were the guys that would come looking for them first if they had to bail out or went down. He'd be first on scene, and he'd be the guy that would bring in the Sandys, the Jolly Greens, and monitor the whole show. Even Sandys and the Jollys didn't do anything unless the FAC was on scene. The FAC would be the eyes and ears for rescue if he needed it. Fighters were shot down everyday over Laos and North Vietnam. Nothing could move or be done without a FAC.

My mark was good on the gun. I told Bigot to hit my smoke. Both birds made passes and dropped CBUs. The softball-sized bomblets exploded all over the karst, making bright little glittering flashes in spasmatic groups. I could imagine the steel ball bearings cutting and slashing through anything in their path within a 50-meter radius of each tiny flash down below. The gun was dug in well. It kept right on shooting just as soon as the CBUs quit going off. The F-4s made another pass, this time with 2.75-inch HEI rockets. The dirty brown trails of the rockets converged upon the area in a pulverizing wither of blasting steel fragments. Then the smoke became so dense—smoke and dirt and flying debris—that I could not see the target. I told the fighters to hold it high and dry for a few minutes. We'd let the wind blow some of the crud away. They wanted another mark.

I reached up with my right hand and tipped a right and left arming pod button to give me a pair of rockets on one shoot. The manta rays were circling overhead, watching, dragging brown plumes of exhaust trails.

"FAC's in hot," I said.

"Jink, 31, jink, little buddy," he screamed.

I knew what he was telling me—the gun was after me. I had rolled the O-2 in on her nose with a wingover from a shuddering seventy knots, kicked right rudder, and was looking straight down at the gun hole. The airspeed hung there for just a moment, really not doing anything. I bicycled the rudders back and forth and wallowed the nose up to circle the hole with the yellow sight rings. Airspeed began to build rapidly as gravity took over. The rocks on the karst began to blossom and come into focus more sharply. I figured the gun couldn't get me shooting straight up. It had turned into a duel. I was gonna kill that sonofabitch if I could. The fighters had been taking fire on each pass. The guy on the Zepe was as intent as we were. I watched the gun muzzles winking inside the gun sight and watched as the pair of rockets went like streaks of death toward the hole. A Willie Pete is a devastating piece of little machinery within a small circle despite the bull put out that they are only "smoke rockets." The gunner got a rocket on each side of his hole. It made him duck—just long enough for me to get away. I sucked the yoke back into my gut. The bird groaned and creaked.

"FAC's off south," I told Bigot.

"We're in, Nail," I heard him say.

Never being one to stay on one heading for more than a few seconds out over the trail, particularly over a raging-mad stung antiaircraft gunner, I kicked left rudder, twisted into a fake left slip, then flipped over to the right in a wingtip stand. Long yellow and green streaks flashed by the tail, where I just had been. I saw both Bigot Lead and Wing take fire—long bursts, maybe 1.000 rounds each. Leader turned his rockets loose in an apparent salvo, followed immediately by Wing. Part of the wingman's rockets went straight into the gun hole. There was a terrible flash, explosion, and a column of black smoke came up like a miniature atom bomb.

"You got him, Bigot. You got him. Musta put one smack into his ammo box!"

The karst shook with another explosion—evidently stored ammo. Rocks and stuff went skyward and a rolling cloud of orange fire snorted from a small cave by the gun's position. The hole the gun had been in was now bigger.

"Nice work, boys," I said.

"Thanks, 31. We'll see you tomorrow, same time, same stand. Got a BDA for us?"

The bomb damage assessment was given to them in cold, flat terms. They knew and I knew that it would be passed on to intelligence back at debriefing and stored for inclusion into the package of facts and figures that would be passed on to PACAF for briefing of the brass the next day. To the weeneys, sitting somewhere in Hawaii, in an air-conditioned "war room," it would scarcely be noticed, if at all. To the FAC pilots at NKP and the F-4 pilots at Ubon and Udorn, a small red circle would be put on a map, to advise others that a gun had been there. The wise pilots would know that the hole would be silent for a few days, but sooner or later another gun would take its place.

I had another pair of fighters to put in on another target. And while my comrades in the F-4s headed home to a cool shower and a cold beer, I wiped the sweat from my brow, moved around in the seat some to get the circulation going again, and headed on up the road. Quite likely, we'd do the same thing all over again within a few minutes. I hoped not. If luck was on my side, we'd get the string of sensors in, dump on a suspected truck park, and call it quits for the day. Daylight activity on the trail, at high noon, was practically non-existent. You had to stir it up, troll for guns. I was hungry. I didn't feel like trolling anymore—not with me as bait.

CHAPTER 9

The Mission That Never Was

Captain Whittaker stabbed at the big wall map behind him with a vengeance. His standard-issue Air Force pointer bent under the strain. Its black rubber tip squashed on a fly speck of a hamlet. His beady, grape-like eyes glistened at me. His non-regulation walrus-type mustache twitched back and forth as he savored my puzzled look. I strained forward in the cold, gray metal folding chair for a better look at the wall map. Really, I did not relish or care for what I saw. But since I did not know what the orders for the day were and where my mission would take me, I didn't say a word. I just sat back, crossed my legs, and waited—and stared the impudent son of a bitch right in the eye.

He always was a pain for a few of us squadron pilots, seemingly taking delight at handing out the really weird missions. He knew the "funny ones" were always bad and even took bets on whether or not we would come back. FACs were considered illiterate in his book, and anybody who charged 37mm AAA guns for an O.K. Corral–type shoot out in an unarmed observation aircraft had to be some sort of a mental nut case—to him, at least.

My silence was killing him.

"That, major, is your target for today. Ban Phontan."

"Okay," I answered him. "Ban Phontan. . . . Now what is so damned important about that hole in the wall?"

"Aha!" he chortled, pointing the bent stick of a pointer squarely at my face like a spear. "You are going to land there and complete a mission of real value."

I cut him off. "Now just a minute there, hot shot. Every mission we fly is of real value, and as far as this one is concerned,

81

you are just as aware as I am that we do not land operationally fit aircraft inside Laos on any sort of a normal strike mission."

"This ain't no normal strike sortie," he growled at me.

I snarled back, "Well, whether it is or it isn't, I am not putting my machine down over there, other than at Long Tieng or Vientiane, without written and verbal orders from someone who has more horsepower than you do."

"Will I do, major?" a voice spoke up from behind me.

I turned in my chair. An Army colonel I had never seen before had just slipped into the back door of the intelligence briefing room in time to overhear my comments to Whittaker. He glared at me from within a set of new-looking starched-and-pressed fatigues. Everything about him yelled "strap hanger" at me. That's what most of us old FACs called staff weenies who got no closer to armed conflict than a local bar and ran their part of the war by what was read from intel reports.

"Well, colonel, I don't know whether you will or not," I retorted. "In all due respect, sir, the rules of engagement prevent USAF aircraft from landing inside of Laos without a higher headquarter's approval and nobody's only verbal say will convince me to not abide by that rule."

He softened his stance and even smiled. "Would you accept a TWX confirmation from Blue Chip?"

"Yes, sir, I would that," I replied.

"Read this then."

With that he thrust a communications-type, perforated-edged, line-o-type sheet of paper at me. I took the piece of paper from his left hand, which had a big West Point ring on the third finger. My stomach did a flip-flop at what I saw. I felt that strange tingling sensation I get around my ankles when things are really turning to shit and are beyond my control. Words on the TWX read: "Have small, unarmed, observation aircraft proceed to prime target of Ban Phontan with a Royal Lao army observer on board. STOP. Land. STOP. Have Royal Lao observer take possession of one NVA captured Lt. prisoner held by Hmong road-watch team. STOP. Pilot is not to put foot on Lao soil. STOP. Depart pickup point with subject. STOP.

Land Muang Nakhon Phanom. STOP. Hand prisoner over to Special Forces officer at MNKP. STOP. This mission never happened. STOP." I did not, indeed, care for this one. My stomach churned at the idea of landing in Laos.

I looked up at Whittaker and remarked, "You gonna take bets on this this time, Whit?"

"Sure, why not?" he grinned back at me.

"You sadistic bastard," I said back. I looked over at the grunt colonel and asked him, "Can I pick my own Lao observer?"

"If you wish," he replied. He then turned on his spit-shined heels, and went out the door. The armed guard saluted him smartly. He returned it. The guard silently closed the thick metal door.

I said to Captain Whittaker, "I'd feel a whole lot more comfortable about all of this if I knew who the colonel was, where he came from, and what sort of a blessing he has from our own people."

Whittaker looked at me in a moment of normalcy and replied, "He works with the Company is all you need be aware of, and your only concern is to complete what you are expected to do." Then he handed me a thick, black, heavy, plastic mission packette, adding, "Is there anything else you need before you make yourself familiar with the package here?"

I answered him as I slid the heavy chrome-plated zipper back, reaching in to pull the pad of maps and papers out so I could read everything. "Yes, it would be a big help if you would call down to the Nail hooch where our five Lao Army lieutenants live and see if you can contact Lieutenant Seri. He may be still asleep because he had a night go with Nail 10, but it is just coming on 0500 and he's had enough sleep for this. I want him because he knows that area of Laos real well from his flying in the Cricket West Program."

"Very well," he remarked as he stepped up onto the briefing stage, pulled the dark blue velvet drapes closed to hide the maps behind them, and vanished through a door curtain into the bowels of the intelligence building. Then he was back with coffee in hand for himself.

Contents of the mission pouch were fairly standard: maps, radio and navigation frequencies, call signs of different organizations, descriptions of fighter-bomber ordinance. This pouch was different in its inclusion of a blood chit pouch and an incineration device to destroy the top-secret mission pouch when activated. The instructions read: "In the event of hostilities where the contents of this packette cannot be safe-guarded, it is recommended all pouch contents be shredded and tossed into the slipstream if in an airborne aircraft. Should there be inadequate time to shred contents of this pouch, and tossing same into slipstream, therefore be advised to activate destruction device. To do so, simply depress and turn red button located on top of the 1-inch x 3-inch x 6-inch gray metal bar secured within this packette. CAUTION: Activation of the destruction device permits only a 5 minute time delay before detonation. Vacate aircraft if airborne, remove self from aircraft vicinity if on ground. (C-4 and magnesium detonation likely to be violent at expiration of time lapse.)"

My eyes got big and round when I read that. I knew that no pilot in the world would be able to shred the pouch contents if he had a shot-up airplane. Plus, three ounces of C-4 with magnesium powder was likely to cause a violent explosion. In no shape, form, or fashion was I going to detonate the pouch.

The pouch also had a small American flag in it and printed on it were words in Thai, Lao, Vietnamese, Chinese, French, Hmong, and Cambodian. I couldn't read any of it, but I knew what they said: if I were to go down and be captured and the captors treated me well and turned me over to friendly forces, those captors would receive $10,000. A year's wages for a Lao villager was about $50. I felt honored to be worth so much.

Whittaker dialed the Nail hooch on the black wall phone, then thrust the handset back at me, and said, "You talk to the little slope."

My eyes flashed fire at him, and I showed him my boot knife, telling him simultaneously, "He ain't no slope, Whit. He is an honorable Lao officer on our side. Say it."

"Okay, okay," he stammered. "He isn't a slope. Don't get so riled up. I take it back, okay?"

"Okay," I answered, sliding my pants leg back over the sheath. "That Lieutenant is fighting for his country and homeland, and he has saved my buns more than once out in never-never land, so don't you ever let me hear you bad-mouthing him again. Or his four buddies."

The phone rang three times, four, five, then six, and a sleepy voice with an accent of Asian sing-song pitch said, sort of like Elmer Fudd, "Hello, this Lieutenant Seri, sir. Who you wanna speak?"

"Seri," I said, "this is Nail 31. I am at TUOC being briefed for a mission in your Cricket West area and I need a Lao Army observer to fly with me. I'd be honored if you'd fly with me today on this one because the mission is number ten and there are lots of bad guys going to be around. We go bring back one bad guy."

There was total silence on the other end. Then, the sleepy voice was gone and in its place came, in a sharp and distinct Laotion rattle, "I come, I come, we go, we go."

I bent over and picked up the black naugahide pouch, looking through it a lot more carefully, and its contents, rather than just studying about the damn destruct device. There was the standard folder of acetate-covered maps on the area we'd be flying in, over, and around. But on one page of a single-sheet map there was a lone red circle, around the tiny village of Ban Phontan with data written in about the village—elevation, population, ethnic variety of the population, and a caution note that said it was believed the population was anti–Pathet Lao and NVA. Or so the Intel weenies believed. Upon my return, if I made it, I'd confirm it.

There were never any sure-fire things in the "secret war" in Laos. Everything changed all the time, often hour to hour. So all I could do was follow my orders, and my instincts, and try to pull this charade off. The instructions on the TWX that the colonel had handed me were specific in nature. In cryptic boldness they'd told me to fly to the prime target, at very specific coordinates, and land, and have a trusted Lao Army observer on board with me. I was to land at my target, but not set a foot on Lao soil. I would have my Lao Army observer get out, obtain the captured NVA officer, put him in my airplane, and we would fly him to Muang Nakon Phanom. I would deliver the prisoner alive if possible, and turn him over to a 5th Special Forces "Snake Eater" officer at MNKP. I groaned and wondered what was so special about this dink officer? The 5th Special Forces troops all so often hung out with "those people" who liked to wear the loud Hawaiian flowered shirts and flew around in French Pilotus Porter airplanes like were used in the Swiss Alps.

I felt that tingle around my ankles turn into a stinging itch. This trip was going to be the kind of mission that turned pilots' hair gray before its time. And, if anything went wrong, anything at all, none of it, or its nature and purpose, would be admitted to. Even if it went perfectly, only the fewest of essential people would ever know it happened at all. That's the way things were done. Only those personnel directly involved with an operation knew what was going down. Nobody talked. NKP was so secret, and what went on there was, too, even roommates never knew exactly what the other guy did specifically. Loose talk meant dead people.

My Lao observer walked into the Tactical Units Operational Control (TUOC) briefing room quietly. The armed guard at the door knew him, knew him by sight, and knew he often flew with me, and had let him in to complete the mission's briefing with me. I simply handed Seri the TWX the grunt O-6 had given me. He looked at me, then began to read the very official TWX. Seri's almond-shaped eyes actually got round as he viewed the content, and got meaning, of what was there on paper. I heard a little gurgle as he sucked in his breath and he stared up at me. His look was that of pure astonishment—fear, too. There was no denying that because the probability of an unforeseen fuck-up was always present.

"Yeah, I know what you're thinking, Seri," I told him in consoling frankness. "It will come off fine. Everything is in good shape and I will rub Budda's butt fourteen times, okay?"

He smiled. "Okay, sir."

He knew I believed in Budda, Saint Christopher, rabbits' feet, God, Santa Claus, guardian angels, and anybody else who I thought might be able to help get us home and not get too many holes in the gray and white "Reynolds Wrap Bombers" we flew, which the U.S. Air Force called O-2s.

I dialed the wall phone again, this time to Nail operations. It was still very early morning.

A sleepy voice came on the line and said, "23rd TASS Ops, Sergeant Denvers speaking, sir."

"Sergeant Denvers, good morning to you," I said. "This is Nail 31. Take a look at the flying schedule board and tell me the tail number of the bird I am supposed to fly this morning on my mission, please."

"Just a moment, sir." There was a pause, a hissing in the line, and then he said, "Major, it says here that you have number 455."

"Well, damn!" I exclaimed.

"Sir?"

"Forget it, sarge, but look on the spare-bird board and tell me if the *Pink Panther* is operational, No. 212."

"Just a moment, sir. . . . Yes, sir, it is."

"Great. 455 has too much fuel in it for what I need to do today, so switch me from 455 to 212, then call maintenance about the switch-a-roo and have Master Sergeant Dill put only a half-load of fuel in 212. Got it?"

I well knew that 455 was a hangar queen of a bird and often developed gremlins of one sort or another, and this day was sure as hell not a time or place for gremlins to be queering the show. I wanted the best machine I could get my hands on without tipping off the world as to why. My friend, the *Pink Panther*, was an old friend. It had new engines and flew very well, was quick and easy on the go, and we had been shot at together before. To be perfectly honest, I was superstitious about the bird. She had luck built in it seemed. The 37mms, 23s, ZPU 60s, and .51s had all tried us before, whizzed all around the *Panther* on five missions in it that I knew of. Either its luck or my guardian angel, or both, had brought us home each time. Three of those missions had been to Tchepone. It was about the baddest of bad places to go to or fly by. The fourth mission had been to Mu Ghia Pass, the fifth to Ban LaBoy Ford. There the *Panther* and I took out ten 37mm AAA guns, and I got my first DFC.

I picked up the phone again and punched up the 23rd TASS's armament shop and told the crew chief for No. 212 about the tail number switch and that I needed only a half-load of fuel for my mission rather than a full one. I also thought that high-explosive incendiary rockets would be preferred over Willie Pete smoke rockets today. The crew chief was an old, savvy sarge.

"Good morning, major. This is Master Sergeant Dill. Figured you'd be calling. We saw Lieutenant Seri go by on the hustle toward TUOC, and we know he goes where you go a lot, and Denvers gave us a call on the horn, too. What can we do for you?"

I told him my preferences.

"We'll have the bird ready to go as you wish, sir, and warmed up for you. . . . Sir, we wish you both godspeed."

He hung up. But the thought stuck with me. We tried to look after each other, and it was a cold, hard fact that none of us pilots could do our job without the superb dedication and skills of our maintenance crews. The sergeant's concern and professional competence were deeply appreciated. While I had a moment, I looked skyward, closed my eyes, and did a soft whisper to my guardian angel. "I'm going to need your help this day, Lady. Amen."

The Army colonel walked back into the briefing room and asked, quizzically, eyeing Seri up and down, "Set, major?"

"As set as can be, sir," I replied. "Colonel, let me introduce Lao Lieutenant Seri to you, please. He is, indeed, a highly qualified and experienced observer. Especially for the job at hand today. He's very familiar with the territory where we have to land. He is a native-born Lao, knows the language and customs of the ethnic groups, in not only the farm-type people where we will go in, but also the mountain area Hmong tribes people all around that area. Too, he is an experienced army combat soldier with eight years of fighting behind him. I trust him, colonel, with my life."

The colonel only grunted. Seri sort of hung his head. I ignored the colonel, got Seri by the arm, and said, "Come on, soldier. It's show time. Let's hit the road." Then I whispered, "And we have more important things to do than get upset at Colonel Prickhead's manners at international relations."

The personal equipment room had the peculiar smell about it that it always did—old canvas and sweaty leather, gun oil and desecant, nylon parachutes, well-worn gray-green oxygen masks with their expandable-stretch hoses looped so very carefully over supposedly bullet-proof olive-drab helmets. The oxygen masks were for the A-1 Skyraider guys, the Fireflies, the Hobos, and Sandys. We Nail FACs were never high enough to need a mask.

To me the expandable oxygen hoses always looked like the guzzle torn out of some space-age creature from another planet. Looking around, it was clear to see that this room was a room used by serious and professional warriors. Every single piece of the equipment was arranged and hung so meticulously and carefully. Handmade Randall knives glistened in greased leather sheaths to protect the leather from the mold and rot of the tropical climate. Custom-fitted survival vests hung on named pegs. Each aircrew member could adapt his own equipment to his own personal needs, whims, beliefs and imagination. All of it meant the difference between life and death.

I went to a peg that held my gear. The backpack parachute felt unusually heavy this day. I checked it carefully, inspecting the dates on its own status booklet, then every buckle and strap, pin, zipper, steel D-ring on the right shoulder, and my second large K-BAR taped securely on the left strap. Then I looked at the two types of body armor hanging there. I dragged down the old World War II B-17 and B-24 waist-gunner type with overlapping steel plates and canvas-and-leather-covered chest and back panels. It was heavy but gave great protection from shrapnel or small-arms bullets from below the waist to neck level. The two panels snapped together, and also had straps, and looked much like a baseball catcher's chest protection padding. I'd also arranged a special section to hang down over my groin area. Mr. Cessna's Skymaster was a real fine airplane, but its $3/32$-inch-thick aluminum skin was really shitty armorplate, fit only to deflect the 3-inch long Thai and Lao rice bugs but not much else.

The survival vest was checked out thoroughly. Both survival radios were in their pockets. I had the personal equipment sarge check them out and install fresh batteries. He gave me fresh batteries for the two spares I carried.

"You going on a little hunt across the river today, major?" the sarge asked.

"Yep, lotsa skunks across the river, sarge, and we going on a skunk hunt. Ya wanna come along?"

He knew perfectly well that of the 108 crewmembers in our squadron and nearly sixty pilots, only six ever flew with one of the Lao observers, whose presence in the personal equipment shop meant one thing—a trip into really bad Indian Country.

"No, sir, not when you guys take one of them along," he answered, pointing to Lieutenant Seri.

"He won't bite, sarge," I laughed.

He looked real serious and screwed up his face into a grimace. "Sir, I ain't worried about him. It's his PL countrymen and buddies from around Hanoi that cause me concern. Man, I hear they are downright hostile to aircrew members."

"Aww, sarge, somebody has been jerking your leg."

"Well, then, if that is so, sir, how come you're packing all that iron? Like grenades, a 9mm pistol and submachine gun, three knives, and enough ammo to start your own war plus all the other stuff you do? Huh? Man, if you ever go into the water you'll sink from the weight of all that stuff you wear and carry."

"Sarge, there isn't any water in Laos, just a lot of pissed-off skunks running around the neighborhood." I gathered up my gear and headed for the door.

"Good luck to you, sir."

I held the Swedish K sub high in the air and said, "Thanks, we'll be back in about four hours."

"It's them hours that you ain't back that worries me, sir."

Seri was dancing around like he had ants in his pants. He was very, very nervous, and I noticed he was packing a Car-15 and a canvas pouch with ten clips of twenty cartridges each in it, plus a grenade pouch with six frags in it. He saw my look and my smile.

"May need! May need!" he yammered. I just nodded.

The *Pink Panther* was warmed up and ready when we pulled up beside her in the blue TUOC crew bus. She sat like a ragged old goose on the pierced steel matting of the maintenance parking area. Streaks of black smoke smudges lined her pale gray belly from the augmentor tube exhausts all the way back to the end of the fuselage. I could smell the hot oil from her runup. The door was propped open on the right side of the cabin, the only way into, or out of, an Oscar Two.

"She fit to fly?" I asked the old crew chief.

He smiled, wiping a drop of oil off the cowling from the quantity and color check, and answered, "Fit as a fiddle, sir."

I inspected the Form One. It looked good. I handed it back to him, its clear plastic cover smelling just like the airplane—of oil, grease, fresh fuel, sweaty canvas, nervous hands, and war.

I smiled to myself as I inspected the cabin's interior. All of the usually white plastic knobs inside an O-2 were vividly pink in this bird. All turned that bright color because of a cleaning fluid some Thai guy had used in his not-in-accordance-with-the-regulations method of cleaning the cabin when the bird was down in Bangkok for an "IRAN" overhaul, and both engines changed out. Some enterprising soul had taken the liberty to paint the usually black front prop spinner pink. And in pure jest he painted on the engine cowling *Pink Panther*. Both the name and color stuck because the bird was a really good one, and its "mishap" in overhaul gave it character. The *Panther* was a goer. I became firmly convinced it had luck built in.

I motioned to the chief. "Help me on with this stuff, please."

The backpack chute rested upon a chock by the right wheel. I held the front plate of my body armor against my chest. He held the back plate for me and snapped and buckled the two together on me. Then came my loaded survival vest, then my parachute. I crawled in and got settled in my left seat, wiggling to get all of the lumps just right, then secured the shoulder harness and lap belt. The sarge handed me the Swedish K, which I laid by my seat on the right side, in quick and easy reach.

Seri slid in beside me, getting settled himself, muttering, "We go, we go."

The sarge stuck his head in the open door and yelled, "How long you going to be gone, sir?"

I flipped the battery switch on and answered, "About four hours, I think."

"We'll be watching for you. Good luck, sir," he yelled and slammed the door.

Seri locked it. I looked left, right, yelled, "Clear!" and hit the start switch for the rear engine. It caught with a growl. Then the front engine caught. Both purred.

I adjusted all the knobs and dials and my seat, checked both engines again, gave the chocks-out sign. The chief was out in front motioning me straight ahead. I added power on both engines and the *Panther* rocked forward on her journey of clandestine intent—or oblivion.

I mashed the mike button and said, "NKP tower, Nail 31, taxi runway 27."

A rattle came over the radio. "Clear to taxi runway 27, Nail 31. Winds are 280 at 10 knots, altimeter is 30.02. You going on a scenic ride today, 31?"

"Yep. Ya wanna come along? I'll pick you up in front of the tower."

"Nawww, I think I best stay on this side of the river and take care of needs here. Thanks anyhow."

As I nursed the *Panther* out of the parking area and turned onto the taxiway, I noticed a few heads sticking out of the maintenance shed, watching me and Seri rock by. My rapport with the crew chiefs and maintenance support personnel was outstanding. They all gave me 110 percent effort. They were keenly aware that we had to work as a team, that lives were at stake. As a squadron we could not do what we really needed to do unless we looked after each other.

Just as I turned out onto the main taxiway, parallel to the main runway, an A-26 light bomber, modified for needs in Southeast Asia under a call sign of Nimrod, was crossing the airfield's perimeter fence to land. Idly, I watched the black and green camo-colored bomber land. He flared, chopped the two big radial engines, and settled in, coming back from a night mission on The Trail bombing and burning trucks. Day was barely breaking. I figured he'd had a good night. There was no ordnance remaining on his wings, and he should have landed long before daylight. Minding my own business and fiddling with knobs in my own cockpit, I put my head down for a moment, my gaze fixed upon the engine augmentor temp gauges. I heard the A-26's radials do a scream job as he put the props into reverse to slow down. Slightly ahead of me, no more than 150 yards off on the main runway, the bomber suddenly made an abrupt 90-degree turn in my direction and went into the ditch between us. One engine's prop had reversed and the other had not. I stomped my brakes, fearing the runaway bomber would make it to me. But the nosegear collapsed, the aircraft stood on its nose and great chunks of red mud were being sliced up, thrown into the air. Seri pointed excitedly. I goosed the Panther so hard we almost got liftoff speed while I tried to put distance between me and the A-26.

I thumbed the mike button on the yoke and said, "NKP tower, the landing A-26 just went into the ditch, call crash." I fully expected a ball of fire out of the 26, as I saw the gullwing lids of the cockpit flash open and both pilots came out like jack-in-the-boxes, hitting the ground in a run that would have won the world's record.

The *Panther* came around in a slow curve upon the end of the runway. I held the brakes and checked the rocket pods again to be sure the ordinance men had not left a red-flagged safety pin in my left and right wing pods. The pins kept the pods from firing and I would be unable to launch any of the 2.75-inch HEI rockets if a pin was left in place. Now, while seven rockets in each wing's pod is not one great amount of destructive power, I knew they could, in a pinch, prove extremely fatal to whoever was on the receiving end of one. And some "sting" out of the Reynolds Wrap Bomber was better than none.

With the *Panther* headed straight down the centerline of the runway, I pushed the two pink-knobbed throttles forward to their stop, props at full increase and mixtures at full rich. The *Panther* growled, then roared in earnest as if she knew her best efforts and behavior were being called upon. A quick eyeball check of all of the instruments said everything was in order. I eased the yoke back some, the yellow tip of the front prop cut a large yellow circle against the brightening morning sky.

The main gear lifted off. I let the bird climb, getting her speed up, saw a rise on the VVI needle, altimeter, then lifted the gear handle. There was a whine from somewhere in the bowels of the machine, the wide gullwing gear doors opened behind us, and there was an audible clunk, clunk as the left and right mains came up. All three of the gear lights and barber pole hatches went out, and away. Airspeed read 100 knots at 100 feet. The bird felt good. Throttles came back to 25 inches of manifold pressure, props to 2,500 rpms. The runway's end came up and I began a sharp right turn, circling over the airfield as I climbed to 4,000 feet to keep away from any Gomer who might be lurking in the bushes off the end of the runway. I wanted altitude before I took up a heading out over the Mekong. It was my habit to climb above basic small-arms fire range before I got to "bad guy country," in a spiral, because we had had several A-1s shot down right off the end of the approach runway and one O-2. I was not anxious to have my day ruined by AK slugs so early in the morning—nor my mission either.

It was really smoky today. It was the dry season now, and the burning of the rice straw on both sides of the Mekong made visibility from air to ground and air to air a terrible problem—two miles vis at best. A combination of the smoke in the air, hanging heavy in the muggy humidity, and the thick, wet, early-morning air gave everything an eerie cast. The sun was blood red through the murk of total gray. Once it got up and burned off some of the haze, visibility would improve a bit.

I peeked over the high side of the cockpit as we started our turn and spotted the junkpile that was the village off the end of the runway—a brown jumble of teak boards, cardboard, tin, and whatever else the natives could steal and haul in to make their shacks. Every structure was built flat on the ground, no airspace underneath. We were all sure the inhabitants were strong sympathizers of the NVA cause. There really was little doubt of that among us pilots as the Jolly Greens had complained about automatic-weapons fire coming from there often. The Knives, our other helicopter squadron of CH-3Es, in their patroling of the perimeter of the base at night, had gotten sprayed with smallarms fire more than once from near that village, and I had taken a clip of 7.62 AK rounds myself one night.

I'd learned it was much safer to climb to altitude over the airfield in a spiral climb before heading out over the countryside. I usually went up to 3,000 or 4,000 feet to level off, then headed out on course to where I was going. We'd lost one A-1 Skyraider just off the approach end of the runway two days prior; the pilot was killed in the crash. The bird had not burned and the pilot had been stripped naked of his clothes and gear before the crash trucks could get on scene, though only some twenty minutes had elapsed between the bird's crash and the firetrucks getting on scene.

The engines growled nicely. Years of flying experience had tuned my ears and body to sense any irregular rhythm the engines might make during performance or unusual creaks, groans, or vibrations an aircraft might give off if everything wasn't just right. Number one engine was out of sync a few revs from two, but that was not unusual. The black and white sync meter was ticking over slowly. A tap on the number one engine throttle and the sync meter was steady with its black and white bands perfectly still. The "McCullough chainsaw," as we called the Cessna O-2, purred smoothly once again. It felt good today. The old bird was smooth and steady, as I recalled our rides; everything even smelled right—the stink of the smoke in the air outside, the musty smell of canvas in the cockpit.

I settled back in my seat, wiggling again to get a missed lump out of the pad behind me.

"NKP tower, Nail 31 switching to Invert Control, over," I spoke into the boom mike attached to my helmet.

"Roger, 31, you are cleared to Invert."

We made our turn and started the climb back across the field, well out of the way of any birds who may be taking off, and certainly out of range of snipers who may be lurking in the bushes.

A little back-pressure on the yoke, a spin of the elevator trim, and the airplane settled down rock solid in a smooth, steady climb with its half-load of fuel. Seri weighed barely a hundred pounds even with his gear on. That is exactly what I wanted. I'd figured if we had to go into a mountain village and bring somebody out, I didn't want to go in with a near full load of fuel barely an hour after takeoff, thread the needle through 1,000-foot karst peaks, and then try to make a get-away climbing over 800- and 1,500-foot high hills. That was a quick way to the grave, and I wasn't going to give Whittaker the satisfaction of collecting any bet on me.

"Invert Control, Nail 31, airborne from NKP, passing 3,000, heading 360 degrees."

"Nail 31, good morning, sir. Invert has contact. You have bogeys at your now two o'clock position, 3 miles, angels five, a pair of A-1s."

"Roger, Invert. And a happy one to you, too. 31 has no contact on the bogeys."

Seri pointed. I let Invert know I had them, a pair of Hobos coming back from the Plains des Jars—returning from a night strike no doubt. The leader waggled his wings at me. The wingman duplicated the act. I returned the salute.

"Got a tally-ho, Invert, on the Nail," I heard through the radio. "Whaddaya say, 31. You're out and about early today, huh?"

"That's a rog, Hobo. Got a little business that needs taking care of," I answered. "You guys been up on the PDJ?"

"Roger, 31, one of the Lima sites, 36, had some bit of trouble early this morning. Gomers on the wire."

"Understand. Have a nice day. See ya."

"Same to you, 31. . . . Drinks are on me tonight, come by the Hobo's Lair."

Gomers on the wire meant only one thing—Pathet Lao troops, or NVA regulars, attempting to take Nha Khang, real close to Route 6 in some sort of an offensive. In northern Laos the Lima sites, like 36, 85, and 20A were always under fire in efforts by the PL and NVA to control the vital positions. Some Lima sites were nothing more than clearings on top of Karst hills with a short dirt landing strip where some helicopters stood alert in efforts to do SARs on the fighters coming back from Hanoi and the Red River Valley. The choppers waiting to catch the cripples from the raids in Route Pack Six. The big F-105 Thunderchiefs were really catching hell from raids in and around Hanoi. Not a day went by that two or three 105s didn't go down over there, victims of the withering AAA fire and SAMs. A standard joke with the fighter jocks was that if the triple-A fire or a SAM didn't get you, then the MiGs would. So it was imperative that the Lima sites be kept in friendly hands.

"Invert, Nail 31, over."

"Go ahead, 31."

"Uh, Invert, 31 will be low for awhile. If you do not hear from me in one hour, from now, mark, launch a SAR effort for the position of 52 miles of the NKP TACAN's 003 degree radial, over."

"Understand, 31."

The troops that manned the radar site knew by my call sign that I was one of the handful of FACs who flew Laos regularly and worked with the Lao Army, often using the Lao call sign of Eagle Red as we operated in the area called Cricket West along the Mekong. Therefore, it was not unusual for those of us flying the Cricket West and Heavy Hook missions to be out of radio contact for short periods of time.

Of course, I was not about to tip my hand and let Invert know that I would be on the ground in Laos that short period of time. Nor was I worried about the NVA or PL being able to tell specifically where I was in Laos by the information I had given to Invert. They did not have the data to be able to pick up the TACAN radial and distance I'd relayed. Had the info been a set of map coordinates, then I'd be in big trouble. The Gomers could read a map as well as we could.

The terrain below was rough as we crossed the Mekong. I did not worry about anyone seeing us at the moment. Enemy troops in the mountain karst valleys would require a long period of time to walk just a few miles, which was a prime reason that someone wanted this NVA officer brought out by air pronto. Apparently, the NVA lieutenant had been caught several nights before by one of the 5th Special Forces' Hmong roadwatch teams. The team had laid in ambush somewhere along the Lao roadway that went through Ban Nape, thence through the river pass 10 miles farther on, into North Vietnam. The road eventually made its way into Vinh, North Vietnam, barely 40 miles from the Lao and NVA border. The road was a prime and decent passageway for materials to be brought into Laos.

The NVA lieutenant had been caught as he rode, dead asleep, in an NVA 6 x 6 canvas-covered truck in a convoy passing out of Laos. It seems the NVA officer had been riding shotgun in the last truck with a PL driver. The team had set up their ambush site well in a sharp curve of the road, and when the other trucks in the convoy made the turn, old tail-end Charlie was out of sight of his buddies for a couple of minutes. Movement of the trucks had been slow on the mountain valley road and it was an easy matter for two members of the team to hop on the left and right side running boards of the Soviet truck, stick a pistol in the PL driver's ear, and get him to stop. At the same time the NVA lieutenant got the cold snout of a Browning 9mm stuck in his right ear, the driver tried some heroics on his Hmong capturer and was eliminated.

The road watch team had turned the NVA lieutenant over to Meo soldiers friendly to Lao General Vang Pao, who, in turn, established radio contact with a Raven FAC patrolling the area. The Raven reported back to his headquarters at Long Tieng about the capture of the truck and the NVA lieutenant. The CIA operators at Spook City became really excited at the capture of the lieutenant. It seems he was some sort of intelligence officer. Nobody seemed to care about the truck, so it was pushed hard to get out of the area and driven to the Mekong, then ferried across, complete with one Soviet 14.5mm Type 75-1 heavy machine gun up in the bed, with ten cases of ammo. This type of heavy machine gun, along with the four-barreled versions of the 12.7mm machine guns, was among the weapons FACs feared the most.

I had to give this situation some thought regarding the best way to get into and out of the place, with a minimum of advertizing my presence until the last few minutes. That was both good and bad. It meant I would have to be nearly on top of the village before I spotted it, and it also meant that my gray airplane, in the gray haze, would be equally tough and difficult for enemy eyes on the ground to see until I was virtually on top of them.

I let the *Panther* accelerate on level-off, up to 115 knots, then slipped the power back and adjusted the props and mixtures. I was deliberately running them heavily on the rich side to keep them cooler and on the higher power side to avoid backfiring if I needed power fast. Seri got out the maps and we took a long in-flight look at the situation of where we were headed and to see if the maps and ground agreed. Sometimes they didn't. Ban Phontan was one of three tiny villages close together on a mountain road that was barely 40 miles from the NVA/Lao border, passed through Ban Nape, had 3,000-foot mountain peaks on each side at the border, then went to the NVA city of Vinh, a major sea unloading port.

All three villages were within a mile or so of each other on the Nam Theun River. And all three were down in a hole in the karst mountains, around some sort of a flat river plain. The whole sink-hole looked to be about 3 miles wide. That looked good, but the place was ringed with hills varying in height from 1,500 feet up to some 3,000 feet, with several peaks showing 4,239 and 4,731 feet south and west. To the north and east were higher hills, over 5,000 feet.

The altimeter was reading 5,000 feet indicated. Compass said 360 degrees. At our speed it would only take a few minutes to reach the 52 mile TACAN arc. I wanted to play it coy. A heading of 360 took us right by the sink-hole. We could see it just under the right wing. Looking straight down through the smoke was not too bad. But I realized that once I moved too far away it would be some trick to find the place again at a lower altitude. The peak by Ban Nahin Nak was 4,239 feet. We could see that as a good landmark. We'd use it as an IP to start the run to the village.

I throttled back both engines and pushed the mixture levers to the full rich position, then both props to full increase pitch, and told Seri, "Get over in the back and get the window open and load the C-15. I'll make one pass down the valley, over the village, then pull up in a right-hand turn. If we get no fire, I'll come around and stay in close, getting the gear and flaps down, and land. If you see anyone shooting, return fire and I'll get the hell out. Okay?"

He nodded and crawled over the seat on his side.

"Then," I continued as we began a zig-zag let-down, keeping the peak in sight, "I'm going to taxi right up to the edge of the village on the road. Once I stop, you jump out and go see if you can find someone. I'm sure we will be met. Seri, when you are on the ground, I will give you five minutes to get the job done. You understand? And if we do not make contact with a friendly village person, you get back quick."

I held up five gloved fingers. He nodded that he understood. The Lao lieutenant was so nervous he had the shakes. I was not far behind him in that department either. Sweat ran out from under my helmet. I had handed Seri my Browning 9mm pistol as he got ready.

There were two ways of flying in Laos to avoid fire—either way high up or right on the deck, low enough to scare the birds out of the grass or trees. In this case, I chose the low method. I wanted to get in and out fast. Seri was rustling behind me in the large cockpit open space behind the front seats and in front of the bank of six radios. I could hear him mumbling to himself in Lao. I pushed everything up to clear the engines, then back on the twin throttles, and let the bird down in a high-speed, on the red-line, left wingover turning dive. Seri was pointing and holding on for dear life, down on his knees behind his seat. I was busy and couldn't pay him any attention. Airspeed was over maximum. Then I understood my observer's gestures. Shit: There were some thirty people coming down a footpath out of the mountains. We were over them and gone in a flash. They looked like Gomers in green uniforms. The *Panther* shuddered a bit as I jinked her around right, then left, brought both throttles up smoothly, and zeroed in on the village of Ban Phontan. The *Panther* was humming. I pushed her on down to the grasstops along the river. The bird was stiff on the controls with the high speed, knocking 200.

I called to Seri over my shoulder, "Put the grenade pouch up front and take this."

I unsnapped my shoulder holster and handed him an extra clip for the pistol. He obliged on both counts. Dead in the middle of the windscreen I saw the village. I turned the big gunsight up to full bright. The yellow rings and pipper glowed against the deep green of the scrub brush coming up. We were in the grass. The road I followed had a thick layer of dust. The river was clear, and both river and road ran straight toward the village. I was so low the *Panther* was trailing a plume of dust like a race-boat. As careful as I'd been, I was drawing attention to our stealthy sneaking-in mission.

I pushed the rocket switches to arm and fire. The pods were hot. All I had to do was punch the red fire button under my thumb. I prayed I wouldn't have to shoot, that we could get in, get our passenger, and get out. I was in, on, and over about ten people near the village before I saw them. Some skinny little kid was leading a water buffalo by the nose with a rope. A man was cutting rice straw with a sickle. They scattered like a covey of bob-white quail.

"Ahhh, hell," I told Seri. "The jig is up. They know we are here." I could now see people running left and right. I pulled back on the yoke and the *Panther* pitched up like a wild thing in a tight, right, climbing turn. We shook the tin roofs of the thatch and pole shacks. In that instant, when we started the pitch-up, and were slowing in a tight right turn, I surveyed the situation. If we were going to take ground fire, it would be coming just as I rolled out level briefly, dropping the gear and flaps almost simultaneously, and immediately making a 180-degree base to final turn. There was none. I let my breath out in a gush. Gear and flaps were down, three green lights on the gear. The *Panther* slowed, throttles at idle, 90 knots, 80, 70, 65. I felt the low speed buffet and eased up on the back pressure on the yoke, then added just a tad of power to lighten the touchdown. I was close to the village, within 100 yards of the biggest building by the road.

The *Panther* settled in on the dirt road with a clunk, clunk, two mains and nosewheel. I slapped the flaps to the up position, held the throttles at idle, and got on the brakes. I did not want to risk going into reverse on the props because one may not come out. On the ground inside Laos was not a real good place to be with a propeller stuck in the reverse position. The bird slowed quickly in the dust. It was two inches deep. We couldn't see. The wind and our own passage had enveloped us in a red cloud of dirt. I goosed the throttles and held a right brake, as we spun in place. The dust was gone, and I spotted the biggest building, which I took to be the meeting place for the inhabitants of the place. I wheeled the bird around to line up on the structure, my thumb poised to launch twin HEI rockets at the place if we took fire. We were sitting ducks. Nothing happened. Then a brown hand waved up and down from a barely opened door, holding a man's blue shirt of some kind. My tenseness eased up a little.

A figure appeared in the doorway and waved. I let up on the brakes and let the *Panther* creep forward.

"Get ready," I yelled at Seri.

The figure waved once more and made a motion to come inside.

"Out," I told Seri. "Go get him."

The little lieutenant opened the door and unsnapped his chute leg straps in one motion, then the chest strap, and he was gone. For an instant he hesitated, looked back at me, then ran toward the doorway. His tiny figure—less than 100 pounds dripping wet, thin, and jet black hair glistening in the bright sunshine—disappeared inside the building.

I let the engines run, props at full increase, mixtures full rich, in case we needed a quick getaway, and set the flaps to 25 percent down. I was nervous. I was anxious. Sweat was running out from under my helmet again, into my eyes, and it was not all because of the tropical heat of at least 100 degrees inside and outside the bird. I wiped it dry with a gloved hand. Heads began to pop up here and there in windows, and figures darted across doorways.

What was keeping Seri? Everything was supposed to be ready to go. I couldn't see behind the bird and was afraid some-one might just slip up behind me and toss a grenade in through the open right door. I locked one brake, goosed the *Panther,* and spun around in place. All was clear. I felt better but kept craning my neck around to watch where Seri had disappeared to. I reached over and got my 9mm submachine gun and laid it across my lap, bolt back, a hot round ready to go.

Back in the direction of where we had started our run on the village, and had seen the "people" coming down the trail, I spotted figures running across the open ground. They had weapons. They were a long way off yet, maybe 700 or 800 yards. At that distance I could not make out if they might be friendly Meo soldiers or enemy, but I was not going to sit there and let them come on and me take a chance. They didn't strike me as friendly, and I shifted the *Panther's* position a little bit to line up on the figures, inched up the power some, lined up the pipper in the gunsight at the figures, and hit the fire button for a single release. A 2.75-inch rocket went streaking away. I watched it corkscrew itself through the air, leaving a trail of gray smoke behind. Far away, just beyond the figures, it hit with a bang. The figures fell flat. They got my message. But then they were up and popping off their rifles of whatever kind. I could see the muzzle flashes.

Seri was running back toward me, pushing a small man before him with the pistol in his back. The man was in a greenish uniform, had his hands tied behind his back, and wore a rag of a blindfold. I could see some sort of insignia on his olive-green shirt. He was terrified. I flipped the righthand seat back down and made a motion for Seri to throw the guy in behind it. He did.

The running figures were some 400 yards distant now and coming fast. I punched the fire button once, twice, three times, four times, and fired high-explosive incendiary rockets. Seri jumped in and slammed the door.

"We go! We go!" He wasn't even in his chute's harness. He pounded the dash with a fist, yelling, "We go!"

I took a hint and firewalled the *Panther*, wheeling to line up on the road, downwind. Taking off downwind was not the best way to get the machine in the air, but doing it into the wind would have taken us back toward the Gomers shooting at us. The *Panther* wobbled and bumped along, gathering speed. The airspeed hung at 60 knots seemingly forever. I began to talk to the bird.

"Come on, baby. You can do it. You know you can. Come on!"

The trees ahead were looming larger with every second that passed. The *Panther* lurched and broke ground. I held her steady for half a minute, saw a rise on the Vertical Velocity Indicator to be sure we'd stay in the air, then sucked the gear up. Airspeed increased some as the gear clunked home, I pulled the flaps up. We gathered speed. Like a wounded turkey, the bird gallantly gathered her composure and started to hum. But the hills ahead were marching down to the road we were following. The Nam Theum River was just before us if we could make it. If we could, we could swing left and head downhill over the ridge

on the getaway, then climb out. If we couldn't, we'd be a ball of
fire on the hillside at the 950-foot level. I was counting on popping through the ridgeline gap at Ban Nahin Nok, leaving the
1,500-foot and 2,000-foot hills on either side left and right of us.

About the time that the gear went up and the airspeed
began to build a little, a group of scrawny trees came full into
view in the windscreen. I could see right through them. They
were full of monkeys eating some sort of fruit. I suppose my eyes
were as big as theirs. I eased back on the yoke, had the flaps up
in time, and roared by the monkeys in a perilously close pass
over the trees, just missing the tops by inches. I roared with
laughter. The situation was ridiculous. Death was only inches
away in those trees, and I was laughing like an idiot as monkeys
were jumping and falling out of the trees, and hitting the dust
below in puffs of red dust.

I saw a gleam of water in front of us. The river! We had
made it. The dirty brown of the hillsides changed instantly to
bright green with banana trees. Hard over with left aileron,
tough left rudder, heavy back yoke, and the bird shuddered
around, and we were running well, heading for the river. A
herd of water buffalo scattered in all directions from a mud bar
as we roared over them. Clear blue sky beckoned ahead.

There was a rustle on the floor behind me. I swiveled part-
way around to see the North Vietnamese lieutenant trying to
get up on his knees. Seri looked at me.

I said to him, "Can this guy understand you?"

"Yes."

"Then tell him to lie still or we will throw him out. If he
causes trouble, we will shoot him."

Seri yelled at him in a mixture of Lao and Vietnamese. It
got real quiet behind me. The clock on the instrument panel
told me we had been out of contact with Invert Control long
enough and I needed to make myself known to them, that we
were okay—or else Invert would, indeed, launch a search and
rescue mission just as I had instructed them to do. I did not
wish for that to happen now.

The *Pink Panther* was climbing like a homesick angel with military power on and half of our fuel burned already.

"Invert Control, Nail 31, how do you read?"

"Nail 31, this is Invert Control, go ahead."

"Roger, Invert. Nail 31 is passing 3,000, heading 210 degrees at 42 miles of NKP TACAN."

"We were getting nervous, 31, thought we might have to come look for you."

"Well, I was getting nervous, too, Invert, but everything is okay now, no sweat, but I surely would appreciate a vector to Homeplate." Then, I remembered where I was supposed to deliver my "package." "Uh, Invert, corrections for Nail 31. 31 requests a vector to Nakhon Phanom East and, again, we will be off freq and your scope for a while."

There was a long silence for about forty-five seconds. "Roger, Nail 31, your vector to NKP East is 190 degrees, your winds are 200 degrees at 12 knots, your altimeter is 30.10, distance of 31 miles."

"Invert, get on the horn and call up Walt Disney and tell him that Santa Claus is coming down the chimney with the package and will be on the ground in twenty-five mins."

"It is being taken care of, Nail 31. You are cleared from Invert's control at this time."

"Invert, this is Nail 31. I want to thank you for your assistance today. Your guidance has been of great service to this mission, and I look forward to your help on another day."

Straight-in was the best and quickest approach to the field, the civilian airfield for the village of NKP, beside the Mekong. The *Panther* wobbled some as we crossed the water of the mighty Mekong River in our let-down, then turned back toward the land. I got the gear and flaps down, adding a bit of power as we picked up a slight crosswind passing over land. *Screech, screech*—the left and right mains touched down. *Thunk*—the nose went down. I got on the brakes, stopped on the runway's far end, made a 180 turn on the runway, and headed back to the approach end where a black Ford van was waiting. As we taxied up toward the van, two figures got out. One wore tiger stripes and a boonie hat—a 5th Special LC I did not know. The other person had on a Hawaiian flowered shirt, baggy britches, and Ho Chi sandals. I kept the machine running and pulled my Browning. The guy in the loud Hawaiian shirt tried to open the door. I shook my head at him and told Seri to open his side window.

When he did, the person yelled, "Open the door, major. I want your package."

I put the Browning in his face and said, "Then show me some ID, buttface."

He looked startled. The Green Beanie Light colonel was grinning from ear to ear. Then a third person exited the black van—a major in tiger stripes that I did know, the commander of an A Team stationed back at the Marble Mountain Air Base. He gave me the finger in salute. I gave it back and told Lieutenant Seri, "It's okay, Seri. Unlock, get out, and let these pricks have our cargo."

Seri backed out the door, complete in his backpack parachute, guided the NVA person out, and turned him over to Mr. Hawaiian Shirt.

"Thanks for a job well done, major. But remember that this mission never happened."

I smiled. Seri got back in, slammed the door, and locked it, and I eased the Panther back to the takeoff position. She growled mightily and away we went, low level, just needing five minutes to make the main NKP Air Base itself.

When we taxied into the Nail parking area, the *Panther's* crewchief was there to park us, waving us in. I shut the bird down and took my helmet off. The little clock on the instrument panel showed four hours and ten minutes had passed. I was one tired troop and it wasn't even noon yet.

The chief asked, "How'd it go, major?"

I held up a thumb and answered, "Piece of cake, sarge."

He was all smiles and handed me the Form One to fill out. For a few seconds he was out of sight installing the gear pins. Then when he stood up from fiddling around under the nose, he made a face at me.

"Trouble, chief?" I asked.

He was back around by the open door, and replied, "No, not really, but it looks like you ran into some."

"What do you mean?" I asked.

"Well, you got two round little holes under the spinner, major, one going in a panel and a bigger one where a bullet came out. No big problem."

I looked dumbfounded. I thought about the matter and realized that one or more of those people we had crossed over as they were going down the mountain trail before we landed at the village had obviously shot at us. And somebody had gotten lucky and dinged the *Panther.* We had no idea we had been hit or shot at then. In short, we could have lost the entire mission had that bullet hit about six inches farther back and taken out the front engine. Oscar Twos don't fly well on just one engine in the mountains.

"You okay, major?"

"I'm fine. I'm just thanking my angel for her help. Again."

"Sir?"

"Oh, it's just a personal thing, chief. I just talk to myself at times over here. . . . You sure do have a really good airplane here." There was no doubt in my mind that the Panther's luck was still holding. I was sure, too, that my guardian angel helped.

I walked into operations and picked up the phone.

"Captain Whittaker speaking."

"Hey, Whit. You lose. 31 is back. You buy the drinks tonight, okay?"

There was silence.

"Welcome back, 31. Glad you made it."

"Yeah, I'll just bet you are. How you want me to log it in?"

"Just put the mission down as a regular combat one across the fence. This mission never was."

I was tired. I felt like having a cold shower, a cold beer, and a nap. I patted Seri on the back and said, "Thanks, buddy, for a job well done." He smiled. The blue TUOC bus pulled up outside ops and another FAC and a combat photographer got out as Seri and I were getting on board for personal equipment, Intel, then the Nail hooch area.

"Hi, 31," the pilot said. "How'd it go?"

"Slow," I answered. Only those pilots and other personnel who needed to know what was going on were told about certain missions. There were so many different missions going on out of NKP—into Laos and North Vietnam with the CIA, 5th Special Forces of MACV-SOG, the Nail and Raven FACs—that it sometimes felt like something right out of James Bond. I sprawled onto the bench seat, checking the Swedish K for the fifth time to be sure there was not a round in the chamber, then slumping into an eyes-closed rest for the bumby ride.

Next day, Seri was with me on another mission. This one was into the Cricket West areas of Laos where we Nail FACs flew and directed strikes on NVA and Pathet Lao personnel. Then we had a Royal Loation Army observer on board with us, who told us where to go and what to do. As we taxied out, parallel to the main runway, we could not help noticing a small cluster of 5th Special Forces personnel gathered around a single small figure seated upon the ground entirely encased in a bright orange suit that was attached to a long rope tha was attached to a bright orange balloon 1,000 feet up. Our "friend" whom Seri and I had picked up the day before was about to go for a Gee-Whiz ride.

"Nail 31, this is NKP tower," the earphones rattled.

"NKP Tower, 31, go," I replied.

"Nail 31, taxi into the Candlestick parking area for five minutes, we have a Herky Bird inbound now for a snatch on the package the Snake Eaters are with, over."

"Roger, Tower, Nail 31 copies. Will hold."

I turned our O-2 so we were looking straight-on at the scene unfolding in front of us. A glance back to the left showed the C-130 Hercules fast inbound like a hungry shark. Its pickup probes were wide open to catch the rope hanging beneath the balloon. The small NVA lieutenant had been sitting flat on the ground in the bright orange "diving suit." Like an umbilical cord, the rope tethered him to the balloon. Suddenly, he was an orange streak before our eyes, whizzing up, up, and away like Captain Marvel. The Herky bird made a slow climbing turn, with the NVA lieutenant being trolled behind as if bait for some big fish. He was but a dot sailing along in the 130s wake as he was cranked into the bowels of the plane.

I didn't know who wanted this guy so bad, but such was life at NKP.

When it designed its Super Skymaster, Cessna had no idea the Air Force would use hundreds of them as O-2s to find bad guys day and night. Though never designed for combat, the O-2 was reliable under all conditions. PHOTO BY THE AUTHOR

The author (right) and a combat photographer. PHOTO BY DET 12, 601ST PHOTO FLIGHT

After one of his first combat sorties over Laos, the author fills out information in his maintenance logbook. PHOTO BY THE AUTHOR

The author's O-2, painted black for night missions. After two months and forty-two missions, it had bagged seventy-five trucks, five elephants, one helicopter, ten 37mm antiaircraft guns, two wide-beamed boats, and a motorcycle. PHOTO BY THE AUTHOR

This 23rd TASS FAC inspects his O-2 in a walk-around visual inspection before flight. PHOTO BY THE AUTHOR

Strangely, temples, pagodas, and shrines could be found in the middle of nowhere in both Laos and Thailand. This complex is on the Mekong River, with no other signs of life in any direction. PHOTO BY THE AUTHOR

The Chao Phya military contract hotel in Bangkok, Thailand, was well known by members of all services as a comfortable and inexpensive hotel when one had to be in Bangkok for business or pleasure. PHOTO BY THE AUTHOR

This is a rare sight: a Lao F-28 fighter-bomber with a USAF slide-in insignia panel. PHOTO BY THE AUTHOR

The Douglas A-1E Skyraider, nicknamed "Super Spad" by the pilots of the 1st Air Commando Squadron and the 23rd TASS. PHOTO BY THE AUTHOR

Sometimes, it was necessary for an FAC to get down low and slow in order to see what was going on in a village. An empty village like this was suspicious to an FAC. PHOTO BY THE AUTHOR

This A-1H Skyraider is fitted with the large propane bomb called "Fat Albert." It was designed for use against bunkers and underground tunnels.
PHOTO BY THE AUTHOR

In late 1968 a number of OV-10 aircraft were transferred from Da Nang, South Vietnam, to Nakhon Phanom Royal Thai Air Base, Thailand, to join the 23rd TASS. They operated under the call sign of Snort. PHOTO BY THE AUTHOR

The A-26 night bombers were the guys you called whether you wanted a single truck or a whole convoy destroyed. Their slogan was "Get it done."

C-123 Providers operated up and down the Ho Chi Minh Trail at night, directing fighter-bombers onto targets. They also directed C-130 gunships.

Known as Jolly Green Giants, HH-43 helicopters like this one were used for search-and-rescue (SAR) missions to recover downed pilots and crews. PHOTO BY THE AUTHOR

The Sikorsky S-61 medium-lift variant of the CH-3E helicopter. The author often guided choppers on missions in Laos and North Vietnam to insert mines and radio transponders. PHOTO BY THE AUTHOR

Ground crew personnel of the 23rd TASS refuels an O-2 before a mission. Our crews were top notch. PHOTO BY THE AUTHOR

We had a talented aircraft maintenance crew, but even they would have acknowledged that the maintenance flight line was not like TWA's. PHOTO BY THE AUTHOR

This 23rd TASS O-2 aircraft was downed by small-arms fire in Laos and crash-landed near NKP. PHOTO BY DET 12, 601ST PHOTO FLIGHT

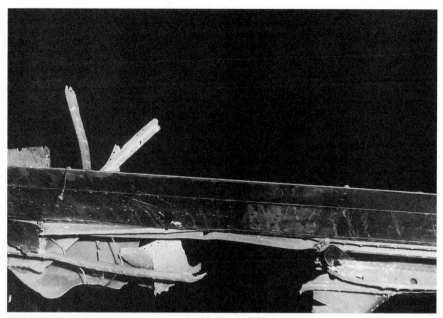

A 37mm antiaircraft shell almost cut the horizontal stabilizer in half on this night O-2, though it did sever the elevator cable. PHOTO BY DET 12, 601ST PHOTO FLIGHT

Periodically, USAF medical personnel would journey into Laos to provide the Lao people with medical treatment. PHOTO BY THE AUTHOR

Villages in Laos were primitive and simple. PHOTO BY THE AUTHOR

This "head man's house" in the village of Khahammouan is opulent by Lao standards, with a metal roof, cut tumbers, and sawed teak lumber.

PHOTO BY THE AUTHOR

These kids gathered to have their picture taken by the author. They were allowed to miss school for the day because of the medical team's visit.
PHOTO BY THE AUTHOR

On the last flight of their tour in Southeast Asia, the author and his navigator were greeted by the squadron after their return at three in the morning. The tire is from the nose wheel, which was found to be flat upon landing. PHOTO BY DET 12, 601ST PHOTO FLIGHT

The author's last flight in June 1969 was a cause for celebration for him and the squadron. PHOTO BY DET 12, 601ST PHOTO FLIGHT

The commander of the 23rd TASS awards medals to three members of the squadron. Capt. E. K. Loving shakes hands with Lt. Col. Thomas Alexander, who rotated out of the organization shortly after this event. PHOTO BY DET 12, 601ST PHOTO FLIGHT

CHAPTER 10

Merry Christmas

All of the pilots' spirits were low. Everyone moped around their hooches like zombies. They came and went on the missions like robots. Their minds were elsewhere, 10,000 miles away in the States, with wives, families, and girlfriends. It was Christmas Eve, a time for loved ones to gather at home, to have parties, to deck the tree with silver and gold and glitter, to relax and give thanks for all the blessings they enjoyed together, to look at the shine of a child's eyes, to carve a turkey at a big table overloaded with good things to eat. That is what we had on our minds. We were low, very low.

Even the ground crews moved around the dirty, oil-stained birds as if they were in slow motion. The ops officer had been good to us. He gave us a "present"—a skeleton schedule for some of us to fly. Christmas or not, the war in Laos had to go on. Someone had to fly. The squadron was fragged to cover a few fighter sorties in Laos for the day, no matter what. Under the rules of warfare, the 23rd TASS was obligated to cover those strike sorties. Therefore, six of us had to make a "go."

Besides the normal bomb-and-strafe sorties, there were always those damn "special good deals," and I was one of the handful of the squadron's pilots qualified to fly them, especially the Prairie Fire missions. The two primary pilots for these missions at the time were Capt. Bob Hobs and I—and I was the only one temporarily available for this "special." Bob had been killed on a mission in early December. He and his 5th Special Forces observer, Sgt. Jim Rush, had been leading a flight of two CH-3E helicopters into the river valley where it emptied out of Laos into the western DMZ near Ban Kapay. While leading the pair of CH-3s, call sign Knife, Bob and Jim had taken severe ground fire at low altitude. Their O-2 had done a complete wingover and half roll and struck the side of a hill in an angled crash position. The rear engine came out of its mounts and slammed through the cockpit area, killing Bob and Jim.

My mission on Christmas Eve was a middle-of-the-afternoon takeoff for a Prairie Fire insert. Winter in Laos was not a whole lot different than at any other time of the year. The sun set a little earlier. The air was a bit cooler. And a summer flight jacket felt good at altitude out over the mountains.

I did not have a whole lot of heart in this mission. I led my pair of CH-3Es with a call sign of Knife into the river valley just west of the DMZ, saw my team put on the ground near Ban Co Bai, climbed back up to altitude, and orbited for several hours to provide airborne cover for them in case they ran into trouble. Everything had gone smoothly, just like clockwork. The team was out and digging in. It was getting late. Because my fuel was beginning to run low, I could not stay with the team any longer.

The Houang Namxe river was in sight to the south of us, about two klicks distant. Ban Lalou was under the wings. I could have spit out the window and hit North Vietnam. President Johnson had decreed we were to give the North Vietnamese border a 10-mile skirting—in other words, stay away from it. We tried, but country borders in that mountain terrain were ill-defined. There was no red line on the ground like on a map. It was really easy to creep across a national border. Today was no exception. In our orbit, listening to the ground team we had just put out, listening to the fighter chatter on the radio, and intent on our own mission, our circles carried us over the North Vietnam border. While we were there, we took a look, a long look with the 60-power gyro-stabilized aircraft binoculars. The passes and trails in that part of North Vietnam were loaded with troops and munitions stacked alongside them in plain view.

Under the guise of truce, the North Vietnamese were stockpiling ammunitions and munitions all along the border from the DMZ on up north. Every pass and valley were full of stuff. Yet we could not strike it. We were not supposed to destroy the munitions. We were not supposed to be in Laos, after all. Yet I had just seen to it that a team was put out. They were on the ground. They were out to catch prisoners. They were out to blow bridges. They were out to send back intelligence. They were out to kill if they could. Still we pilots could not strike and blow up the munitions we could see stacked.

My Green Beret observer was new to me. I had never seen this guy before. He was in the briefing earlier. He said he had come from "Monkey Mountain" over in South Vietnam. I guess he had. I did not question him too closely. I didn't really care to, to be honest. All I wanted to do was get my team in, do my job, and get the hell out and back to Nakhon Phanom. Despite being half a world away from home, I knew there was a scrawny little Christmas tree back in the Nail hooch. Our wives had sent us cookies, cakes, ornaments for the tree, and candy canes, and the Nails would have a big party before the night was over.

I headed the gray bird back west, adding power and climbing a little higher up to 7,000 feet. It was a long run back to NKP from the edge of the DMZ, more than 100 miles. At our thundering, blazing, speed of 110 knots indicated, I knew it would require us about an hour to get home. So I swung the nose around and pointed it into what was left of the sun, an orange ball sitting on the blue-gray horizon. Shadows had lengthened down below. The valleys in the 900- and 1,200-foot karst mountains were purple and orange, gray and dull green. Wisps of smoke rose here and there. It was all really sort of peaceful.

The pair of 225-horsepower Lycomings were growling in the O-2, fore and aft, giving off their old familiar chainsaw hum—always just a little bit out of rev with each other. The new sergeant I had with me in the right seat was leaning forward, peering out the side window, watching the gray and purple shadows slide under the wings. I leaned back, idly puffing on my Camel, letting the smoke get jerked away out the small triangular-shaped window on my side of the cockpit. The sky was bright silver around the setting sun, blending into deeper and deeper shades of lavender the farther away from the sun you looked. It was beautiful.

Idly, I flipped over to the air strike frequency and snuggled down deeper into my lightweight flying jacket. Some chatter was coming through. I listened as I pulled the zipper up tight under my throat. It was chilly at 7,000 feet. A fellow Nail FAC was putting in a strike up at Ban LaBoy ford. Ban LaBoy was a shallow, gravel river crossing for trucks on the Nam Ta Le river, on Route 912. Barely 10 miles from the North Vietnamese border, a part of the Ban Karai Pass, a very bad area. The 37mm antiaircraft guns around that place were absolutely fierce. Lao 912 turned into North Vietnam's Route 137 there at the border, and 137 into Route 101 farther inland. All main supply routes for munitions, troops, and materials coming out of North Vietnam bound for South Vietnam via Laos and Cambodia. In the dry season of the year, like near Christmas, the routes were constantly covered with troops and supplies. Ban LaBoy was the first real choke-point in Laos along the routes. We hit it everyday with air strikes. This day was no different. I could hear the FAC directing his fighter-bombers onto the ford. They were a last flight of the day—a flight of four F-105 Republic Thunderchiefs running under the call sign of Detroit.

From what I could hear, they were catching pure hell on the strike. A line of 37mm guns was on the ridge just south of the ford. They were having a field day on the 105s. The Phou Lennik karst ridge ran there, basically northwest and southeast in direction, and the guns were on top of it—a bad situation for the fighter-bombers coming off their dive bomb passes on the ford.

Nail 37 was working the F-105s. I could hear Detroit leader saying that he was off, going high and dry, telling two and three to form on him. Number Four said he had a pair of 750-pound frag bombs left. He wanted to make one more run, the last run. Nail 37 was telling him to forget it.

"Detroit Four, just salvo your ordinance on the place. Two more frags aren't going to make any difference. Go home, buddy. It's Christmas Eve. Go home and have one on me."

Four replied, "Naww, Nail, I'll make a last pass and drop this stuff right down there where it will do the most good."

"Your funeral, friend, have at it. Nail 37 is off to the north. Hit my smoke."

There was a pause. Then Detroit Four said he was in hot.

I could see Detroit Lead and his two other chicks streaking past us overhead, and climbing, fast. Even as we watched, I saw their burners light. The three F-105s seemed to just catapult up and up. Their butt ends winking bright yellow under the terrible thrust of their huge single engines. They were going home, and they were in a hurry. Lead was calling for everyone to RTB—return to base. Detroit Four said he was taking fire, that he'd be off to the southwest. I watched. I knew his line of flight—pulling off the target—would bring him past us since we were locked in on the 105 degree radial of Channel 99, NKP, and were passing the 80 nautical mile fix. Ban LaBoy was to our left rear, nearly in sight.

I heard Detroit Four call, "Four's off dry, Nail 37. Climbing to angels two zero."

Nail 37 answered, "Rog, Detroit Four. Merry Christmas."

Then, suddenly, everything went sour. Detroit Four was excited and yelling, "Four's hit! Detroit Four took a hit!"

Nail 37 came back with a sharp and business-like query: "What's your position, Detroit Four? What's your situation?"

Four replied, "Detroit Four is on the 98 degree radial of Channel 99 at 85 miles, 37. . . . Nail 37, I think I'm going to have to get out. Hydraulic pressure is fluctuating badly and I have smoke in the cockpit."

I was alert, all eyes. My observer was looking at me. He knew something was up. He had been listening. But he was an Army troop. He did not quite grasp the immediate urgency of the situation. Light was failing. The sun had set. All we had left was the bright silver glow to the west. Purple night started to blend into the last of the gold of the day.

"Look sharp out the window," I told the sarge. "We have an F-105 coming off a bomb run and he was hit with antiaircraft fire. He is hurting real bad."

Detroit Four told Nail 37, "I'm in the climb, 37, she's still running, but I don't know how long I can stay with her, over."

Nail 37 was trying to tell him the best heading to take him away from the bad guys on the ground and brief him on the ground situation. The Thud driver wasn't really listening; he was talking all the time. I can't really say I blame him.

My observer cut in and pointed, "There he is."

I leaned forward and peered under the leading edge of the right wing. He was trailing fire and smoke. I punched my mike and told 37, "Nail 37, this is Nail 31. I have Detroit Four in sight. He is passing over me at this time. I will assist you if you desire, over."

"Roger, 31, roger. He is yours. I'm too far away to help him if he goes out, over."

I replied, "Detroit Four, this is Nail 31. Do you read, over?"

"Affirmative, Nail 31, affirmative."

"Okay, Detroit Four, Nail 31 has you in sight. You are at my one o'clock position and climbing. You appear to be about 12,000 feet. You are trailing heavy smoke, and you have a fire in the aft section of your machine, over."

"Roger, Nail 31. Detroit Four is going to have to get out, over."

My heart sank. "Can you stay with it a little while longer, ol' buddy? This is not a good area to punch out in, over."

"Uh, that is a negative, 31. I've got to go."

Then silence.

"You copy all that, Nail 37?" I asked.

"Roger, roger, roger, 31. I'm heading your way as fast as I can peddle, over."

I told the observer, "Watch the 105. See if you can spot the chute. He's coming out."

He nodded. I whirled the UHF and alerted Invert Control. "Invert, this is Nail 31, I have a crippled F-105, Detroit number four, at the 96 degree radial of Channel 99, eight-zero miles. He is in the process of bailing out. Request you inform Ops and send the Jolly Greens, over."

"There he is!" the sergeant exclaimed excitedly.

Neither of us had seen the pilot eject. Suddenly, there he was in his chute, floating down like a little toy man suspended under a white and orange mushroom.

"I have the pilot in sight, 37. He is on a nylon letdown."

We began to circle widely around the pilot as he came down slowly. Light was failing fast. I pulled the power back on the bird and began a slow, wide spiral to stay with him, to follow him down. He waved. We waggled our wings back at him. Nail 37 was telling me he was coming up onto our position and wanted to know where we were.

"Stand by, 37, and I will make smoke for you. I am down to 2,500, in a wide spiral, following the pilot down into the trees, over."

I pushed the smoke-generator button on the instrument panel. Like a skywriter, I knew I would be pulling a long trail of intense white smoke. I was not keen on doing it here, but I also wanted 37's help. I did not have the fuel to linger in this area for more than just a few minutes, but I wanted to pinpoint the downed pilot's position so 37 could take control of the SAR mission.

"Gotcha, gotcha, 31," said Nail 37. "I have a tally on you at my ten o'clock position, low."

"That's a roger, 37," I replied. "I also have a tally-ho on you, up and to my right, over. . . . Invert, this is Nail 31. What's the story on the Jolly Greens?"

Static in the headset.

"Nail 31, this is Invert, over."

"Go ahead, Invert," I answered.

"Roger, Nail 31. Command post says it is too late to make a try for the Thud driver tonight, over."

"Aww, crap, Invert," I said. "This guy ought not have to spend the night out here. We have him in sight. He is going into the trees now. This is not a good area. We can get him out. He's about the 96 degree radial of 99 at 76 miles. Coordinates are Whiskey Delta nine-nine, nine-eight, one-two, zero-zero."

"Sorry, 31, first light is the best we can do, over."

"Damn!" I yelled and smashed my fist down onto the cowl. This was bad for the downed jock.

Nail 37 was circling overhead, over me. I did not like being that low. I knew there were troops in the area. It was a very bad area. The main Ho Chi Minh Trail was past us to the east about

2 miles. It had a constant flow of vehicles and foot troops at night. And the village of Ban Mouk was immediately at hand in the plain along the river there. Fortunately, the Thud pilot had gone into the teak trees up on top of one of the ridges. I felt he would be reasonably safe during the night if no one had seen him come down and if we did not linger in the area too long.

The teak trees at the point where the pilot went in were tall, 150 to 200 feet. Underbrush was not too bad. Seeing him plough into the trees made me recoil. He hit a few limbs, bounced, then his chute began to collapse and let him fall. I could see a white streamer as he fell down through the foliage. Then the streamer stopped falling. He was hung up. I cranked the bird around in a tight circle. It shuddered on the edge of a stall. I peered over my side of the cockpit, flipped the bird over on the other side and came back around, looking all the time.

"He's hung up, Nail 37," I spoke into the mouth boom mike. "Looks like he is there for the night."

Suddenly, there came a new voice on the air. "Thanks, Nail 31, for following me down. This is Detroit Four. I'm hung in the trees. The ground is about 50 feet below me."

I was startled. Then I remembered that he must be talking to us on his survival radio. "Okay, Detroit Four," I said. "Here's the big picture. You are about 2 to 3 klicks west of The Trail. On about the 96 degree radial of the Channel 99 TACAN at about 76 miles. We have called in your coordinates. Jolly Green says it is too late to make a try for you tonight. But at first light Santa Claus is coming for you, old buddy. You hang tight. Stay in the chute if you can. Would be a good idea to loosen things up and try to get comfortable. It looks like it is going to be a long night, okay?"

"I understand, Nail 31. And, thanks, buddy. I know you did all you could do. You and 37, over."

"Roger, Detroit Four. We wish you the best, can't hang around any longer, buddy. We are low on fuel, and we don't want to attract any more attention to you than we have to. See you at first light, okay?"

With that, I pushed the mixtures up to full rich, the throttles up to the stop, full increase on the props, and began the climb out, straight back to NKP. Nail 37 was off to the left and climbing also. There was nothing else we could do for the pilot. We sure as hell did not want to leave him hanging there in the trees, but we couldn't get to him.

On the climb I marked everything well on the charts. Light was just about gone by that time. I turned on the cockpit lights, twisted them down to dim, and made my report to the command post back at NKP. They assured me that a SAR was being set up for the next morning at the crack of dawn. I was to lead the force. I slept fitfully that night, tossing and turning. I imagined the pilot hanging there in the trees in that damned parachute harness. It had to be very uncomfortable. When the alarm clock went off, I sat bolt upright. My feet hit the floor with a thud.

Four in the morning is not my time to get up on Christmas morning. But this one was special. I showered and shaved in a hurry, threw on the tiger stripes, laced up the shiny jungle boots where my Poo Ying had set them by the door, grabbed the Swedish K from its drawer, and dashed out the door. It was black outside. The dew was heavy on the short grass between the main hooch and the party hooch. It had been a terrible party the night before, a real Christmas Eve blast. Ron Himmer was lying where someone had left him, stretched out on the ground beneath the porch and propped up on a wooden platform of some kind. All he had on was his skivvy shorts and a necktie and his slouch Nail hat. It was tilted down over his eyes. He had a flower stuck in his hands. Some industrious soul had at least taken pity on him and covered his eyes. I laughed out loud as I jumped down the four wooden steps in one bound on the end of the building and ran out into the dirt street and flagged the blue TUOC crew bus. The driver was half asleep at the wheel. He traveled half a block before he realized I was trying to hitch a ride, and jammed on the brakes, standing the dumpy bus on its nose in a rocking fashion. I jumped on.

The briefing for the SAR was routine. I would lead the show. Nail 37 would be the backup pilot in case I aborted for any reason. I would take off and precede him by one hour. The Jolly Green rescue crew was there. They would be in an HH-3E chopper, under the call sign of Jolly Green 20. A second HH-3E would be standing by if 20 had to abort. There were four A-1 pilots there, using the call sign of Sandy 10 Flight. A second flight of A-1 pilots there also was backups—using the call sign of Firefly. It felt good to see all of those Super Spad pilots there. If the going got tough, we would need these guys—all of them. Their A-1 Skyraiders—Super Spads, as we called the old birds—would be loaded with CBUs, 2.75-inch explosive rockets, nausea gas canisters, and a few hard bombs. The ordinance was variable, all light stuff for use on troops in the open. That is usually what we had to contend with when trying to rescue a downed pilot. In the event that we ran into any real resistance and antiaircraft fire of any magnitude, we could call in some fast-movers, F-105s and F-4s, for fire suppression. We knew the F-105 drivers would be like mad dogs after meat if we needed them. Everyone at Udorn and Takhli knew that one of their kind was down on the ground. They would come like hornets if we put out the call.

I had no passenger on this trip. The flight shack was quiet at five in the morning. Only the night sergeant sat there by the radio. I exchanged a nod with him as I went in, picked up some maps, and left again.

"Take care, maj," he said.

"Thanks," I said and slammed the door on the run. The *Queen Bee* was hot when I arrived. The ground crew helped me on with my gear—my heavy metal-plated flack vest, my bulging survival vest, then my backpack parachute. I grabbed up the mission packette, the Swedish K, and jumped into the left seat. The sergeant shoved the right seat back, locked it, and slammed the door. I had both engines turning over in seconds. I scanned the gauges on the instrument panel for a quick check to be sure everything was running okay, had the cocks pulled, and I was taxiing out in mere minutes.

The *Queen* pitched and rolled on the PSP ramp. The blue lights that lined the taxiway seemed extremely bright this morning. Then I remembered it was Christmas morning.

I thumbed the mike and said to the tower, "Good morning, NKP tower. This is Nail 31, taxiing for a SAR, over."

"Merry Christmas, 31. You are cleared to taxi to runway 27, over," the tower said.

I jockied the *Queen* along at a fast idle. The ops officer would have had cat fits and conniptions if he had seen me. But who cared? He was probably sleeping his drunk off anyway.

"Roger, NKP tower. Has Jolly Green 20 and Sandy 10 flight checked in, over?" I asked.

"That is a roger, Nail 31. Jolly Green 20 is standing by at the arming ramp and Sandy Lead is ready to taxi now."

I wheeled into position on the arming ramp and saw a sergeant running in under the wings, jerking the rocket pod pins. I saw the HH-3E sitting off to one side, its big rotor whirling around, making bright red flashes on the ground as his anti-collision beacon rotated. The arming sergeant was out front, holding the pins up for me to see. I flashed the lights for him in acknowledgment. He was gone, running off to his alert truck.

I thumbed the mike button. "Nail 31 is number one for takeoff, NKP tower."

"Nail 31, you are cleared for immediate takeoff. The winds are 280 degrees at 5 knots. Your altimeter is 29.98, over."

"31 is rolling," I replied and ran in the power. The Queen was light and peppy in the cool morning air. There was a grayness to the east. Daylight was coming. So was Santa Claus for the downed pilot.

Jolly 20 was on his climb off to my right. I could see his black shape like a whale in the air against the lightening sky, his red beacon, going around and around. He would shut that off soon, when we crossed the Mekong. Even though the large village of Thakhek, just across the river, was friendly, we received small-arms fire from the outskirts quite frequently in the darkness. Both Jolly 20 and I made a wide circle to gain some altitude before we set out to cross the river.

I had a bit of an edge on Jolly 20 in speed. So I climbed on above him, got in front so he could see me well, and began a generally straight flight to get to where the pilot was. But with a little extra speed on the Jolly, I weaved back and forth, left and right of our course, to maintain my position with him. The Super Spads, A-1s, however, had plenty of speed and power on both the Jolly and me. They climbed on higher still, getting above the two of us.

The takeoff and climb out calls had been routine. NKP tower handed us all off to Invert radar control. Everyone went over from the 255.6 UHF tower frequency to 265.5 as they were cleared, then from the departure 265.5 UHF freq to Invert's primary working frequency of 292.3. I had been talking to Jolly Green 20 on the level off, telling him to get his PJ set up—the paramedic. Sandy flight checked in and said they had a tally-ho on us, and closed, weaving back and forth across our own line of flight like great brown pelicans in the coming light. Firefly flight was standing by on the parking ramp, ready to launch if we all needed further assistance. I knew Nail 37 would be cranking up pretty soon. He was coming on out in any case and would remain in the general area until I called him in.

The little bevy of rescue aircraft wheeled and turned as we made our way out on the 96 radial. There was no need to try any coy stuff today. The daylight was getting stronger and we wanted to be on station just as soon as it was bright enough to see down under the murk of the teak trees and undergrowth. The 60-mile arc of NKP TACAN came up. I watched it click off on the distance mileage indicator.

I thumbed the mike button and spoke clearly, "Detroit Four SAR flight, go primary rescue freq, over."

Jolly Green 20 came back quickly. "Roger Nail 31, Jolly Green 20 is going primary rescue frequency."

Sandy 10 flight acknowledged and went over. After I had all of my birds on the rescue frequency, I checked in with Ethan Control on 254.8. Ethan Control would be monitoring the whole show.

The 70-mile arc of Channel 99 was coming up fast. We were in the area. I told the Sandys to hold overhead on the 76-mile fix, begin a right-handed orbit at 8,000 feet, then spoke to Jolly Green 20.

"Jolly 20, Nail 31 will make a pass over the area before you come on down so I can see what the situation is, over."

"Roger, 31, understand," replied the Jolly.

My altitude had been 5,000 feet—way too high for any sort of a good visual check of the situation. Plus I could never spot the pilot's chute from that altitude. I eased the throttles back and began a long glide, making a spiraling turn in the let down. I felt that as long as I held the four A-1s back to the west and at altitude, they would be safe from the antiaircraft fire I knew would come from the Ho Chi Minh Trail just off to the east about 2 miles. The A-1s could get away from most of the bursting shells, but I had severe reservations about the HH-3E. So I had him hold farther southwest in a slow orbit.

I let the *Queen* on down to 2,500 feet in a graceful long arc, scanning the villages below. Something was not quite right. The little voice in the back of my head was telling me to be careful. The hair was standing up on the nape of my neck. Not only didn't I like this situation, I didn't like the bird I was in because of her bad habit of being in the hangar for repairs all the time. She flew like she had a bag of rocks dragging most of the time. She was performing quite well today, but I was superstitious about her. Once, out over The Trail, she had quit cold on me in the electrical department, leaving me above an overcast with nothing to fly by but the static pressure instruments, the altimeter, airspeed, VVI, and turn and slip. Then somebody had gotten the bright idea to paint her with a fresh coat of paint. "She's too dirty," they had said. Our standard dove-gray for the day O-2s was modified for the *Queen* to a dark gray, with bright white on top of the wings. The painting went well— except that someone forgot the clouds of red dust kicked up by the helicopters. All the dust settled onto the *Queen Bee's* fresh paint, which made the wings so rough that she couldn't generate any lift. She eventually got repainted and flew fine, but I still had an inner distrust of the old gal.

With the power set at a nice cruise setting, I whizzed over the area where I had seen the pilot go into the trees the afternoon before. Ban Mouk was in sight. So was Ban Kang One and Two. Ban Kang Two was immediately on Lao Route 911. I turned the *Queen* up on her side and scanned the road below: nothing. There should have been some people moving. As I came on around to pick up the 593-foot karst by Ban Nongkoung, I heard the stutter of a heavy machine gun out the window.

I thumbed the mike. "Nail 31 is taking groundfire. Taking gunfire at the karst just northwest of Ban Nongkoung, over."

"Roger, Nail 31. This is Sandy Lead, what is your desire?"

"Hold on a sec, Sandy Lead. Let me find the chute, over," I answered.

"Roger," said Sandy Lead. I heard him tell his chickens, "Set 'em up, gang. The store is about to open for business."

My altitude of 2,500 feet was not doing me any good. I let the *Queen* on down to 1,500. Then I saw the parachute. I whipped the *Queen* back around in a tight circle and got on the horn.

"Okay, Jolly Green 20. This is Nail 31. I have a tally on the chute. Come on down, over."

"Roger, 31. We are on our way," Jolly replied.

"Sandy flight, Nail 31 is in for a mark. Hit my smoke, over," I spoke into the boom mike. I punched the fire button and sent two Willie Pete rockets down to about where I thought the machine-gun fire had come from, close to the village of Ban Kang. Sandy flight called in hot. I caught a glimpse of them rolling in, one after the other.

"Be careful, Jolly," I said. "Something is wrong here. Last evening the parachute was a streamer and was hung in the trees. Now it is a round circle nearer ground. I don't like this at all, over."

"Rog, we copy, 31. Just don't be so jittery," he laughed.

I had a lot of reasons to be jittery. At no time during the inbound flight or while I was working the area could I raise Detroit Four on the radio. Last evening I had been talking to him. I did not like it. The little voice was yelling bloody murder in the back of my head again.

"Detroit Four, Detroit Four, this is Nail 31. Come in, over," I said.

No response. Over and over I called. Nothing from Detroit Four.

I cranked the *Queen* around in another tight circle, crossing Route 911, at 400 feet. Some figures were running across the road.

"Hit my smoke, Sandy," I called, "Hit my smoke. I have troops 1 klick to the North of the LZ, over."

The troops were too quick for me. They got across the road before I could get a good shot, but I flipped a pair of rockets down into the brush anyway.

"Get out of the way, 31, Sandy flight is in with CBUs," Lead yelled.

Jolly Green 20 was calling that he had the chute in sight and was going into his hover. I glanced out through the Plexiglas in the roof of the *Queen* and spotted him. He was just above the trees.

"PJ is going out," he remarked.

"Roger, 20," I said, "but take it easy. I cannot raise Detroit Four."

The paramedic went down on the line sitting on the jungle penetrator, like an acrobat at a circus. I marveled at those guys who were lowered into the mouth of a dragon on a string. Sandy flight was in and out. I could see their CBUs bursting all over the area and brush where I had seen the running troops.

With the PJ down on the penetrator, I felt that my job of locating the pilot was done and began a climb back to altitude. *Puff! Puff!* Shell bursts off to the right, 37mms.

I yelled, "Sandy, you are taking fire. You are taking fire. Approximately from your four o'clock position. Hold on, I will mark."

At that, I whipped the old bird over in a half roll and pulled her around in a creaking turn. In a half wingover I flipped a single rocket into the edge of the village of Ban Mouk, then scooted out of the way, straining the guts out of the *Queen* to get to altitude. The small white cotton balls were popping up all around us.

"Well," I boomed, "the little bastards are not asleep after all, Sandy. Hit my smoke."

I heard Sandy Two call, "I've got the gun. It is in a building on the edge of town. I'm in hot."

I saw him and Lead streaking in flat, just over the thatch rooftops. Their CBUs began to sprinkle the ground like hail. Their tiny flashes and spurts of dirt foretold blazing redhot ball bearings tearing through the area like a gigantic shotgun burst of fire.

Suddenly, I heard the PJ yelling, "I have the pilot. He is inert. He is inert. Take us up. Take us up."

The Jolly pilot was yelling, too. "They are under the chute! They are under the chute! We are hit! We are hit!"

"Gas the area, Sandy, gas the area." I yelled. "I have some ten NVA troops that were under the parachute. They shot the pilot."

I caught a glimpse of the Jolly. He was struggling for altitude. The PJ was out on the cable like a fish on a line, being trolled through the tree tops. I gasped in disbelief. Through the 7 x 50 Bausch & Lomb artillery binoculars, I could see the PJ as plain as day sitting on the penetrator. He had the pilot lashed to himself. He was limp. Even as the PJ was being trolled through the trees, he was talking.

"The dirty sonofabitches machine-gunned him in the harness last night. They killed him where he hung!"

My throat grew tight and dry. "Sandy Lead is in hot, Nail 31," he said. "Sandy Two is in, 31" he called. "Sandy Three's in. Four's in."

I saw the PJ snag in the fork of a big tree. The line running up to the HH-3E grew tight as a bow string, then snapped. The cluster that was the PJ and the dead pilot plummeted down like two rag dolls, bouncing from limb to limb. I could not believe my eyes.

"Take it up, Jolly 20," I called. "You just lost your PJ, over."

"Roger, 31, roger. We can't hang around. We are full of holes. We must have twenty or twenty-five up through the floor. There were about ten troops under the parachute and they hosed us with automatic weapons right up through the bottom, over."

"Rog, 20. I understand. What is your status?" I asked.

"We are RTB, 31. I say again, RTB, over." he replied.

"Hold it high and dry, Sandy flight. Let me see if I can raise the PJ, over." I said.

I called and called. No answer. I was sick inside. Not only had we lost the pilot, we had lost the paramedic as well. And the Jolly was shot up real bad. The total mission was a complete failure. I was thinking of two sets of families somewhere back in the States sitting down to a turkey dinner.

I was sitting there listening to the off-key growl of the engines, straight and level. Sandy flight was calling me for instructions. I had already pointed the black and gray nose of the *Queen* west, back into the direction of the Mekong and home.

"What do you desire, 31?"

I just sat there, then thumbed the button and remarked, "Just burn the goddamn place down, Sandy. Just burn it all down. And Merry Christmas."

I looked out behind me through the left rear window. Pillows of dense black smoke were climbing skyward in the rising sun's rays. The smoke rolled and billowed and flashed. I could hear rumbles like faint thunder. I smiled. The village was a storage area for munitions.

Two days later, one of our FACs on The Trail spotted—in an open area near where the would-have-been rescue and shootout had taken place—what looked like several bodies lying in the open. He circled the area carefully. Through his 60-power gyro-stabilized binoculars, he saw that it was two dead men in what appeared to be green flying suits. The incident was reported to Intel during mission debriefing. In those two days, we had heard nothing from the Jolly Green PJ. Suspecting that the bodies just might be the missing paramedic and pilot, a team was sent in under cover of four A-1E Skyraiders and an FAC for coordination. The team found the two missing men. Both had been killed in an unnecessary bit of atrocity. The pilot had been machine-gunned as he hung in his parachute, and the already badly injured PJ had been killed. Both could have been taken prisoner–not murdered. For the next two weeks the pilots raised hell all up and down The Trail. Anything that moved was gone with a vengeance. No one brought any ordinance home. Suspicious columns of white smoke were rising daily all up and down The Trail. Pilots went in low to draw groundfire. The nasty habit the PL and the NVA had of stashing 37mm antiaircraft guns in buildings was brought to a halt—for a while.

There is little doubt that the NVA deliberately left the PJ and pilot in an open area to be sure that both were found. The NVA and PL knew perfectly well that those of us who flew the little gray airplanes had eyes of an eagle and were constantly looking, looking, and looking at anything that could be suspicious, unusual, or a target of opportunity. The enemy was also a master at camouflage and anything they did not want seen often never was. Therefore, the cruel treatment of the paramedic and the barbaric murder of both of these American airmen were deliberate signs of the contempt these enemy troops held for us.

What I had witnessed, what I had seen, and what I learned about the treatment of the PJ and the dead pilot only reinforced my contempt of them and the absolute ruthlessness of the Pathet Lao and North Vietnamese forces. My goal as I flew in Laos was to make life as miserable as I could for the enemy and to eliminate as many as I could. It became a game between me and them. They would call me up on captured survival radios and say, "We get you today, Nail 31." To which my usual response was, "Ho Chi Minh is Number 10 and eats fish heads." That brought curses and ugly words for sure. Our exchanges of compliments to each other just reinforced each other's desire to kill each other.

I had become as cold and as hard as the LRRP CCN troopers I flew for. Our job was to kill, killing was our business, and business was good.

CHAPTER 11

Mission Failure

When I walked into the pre-takeoff intelligence briefing on the morning of December 30, 1968, I knew instantly that this was not a run-of-the-mill mission.

For a fleeting instant, the thought flashed through my mind that I had entered the wrong room. The doorknob was in one hand as I backed out enough to look up and confirm the room number overhead. Satisfied that I was, indeed, where I was supposed to be, I walked in and sat down near the rear. I felt a bit apprehensive as I looked around. The briefing room was not big, maybe 35 square feet. The stark whiteness of the walls and ceiling spoke more of a hospital room than that of a war briefing room. A young Air Force captain stood prim and proper on a small platform in front of a wall-sized map of Laos and the DMZ area of northern South Vietnam. The map was stuck full of multicolored pins and was written all over with red, blue, and black grease pencil. TACAN radials spread from the center like spokes on a wheel across the face of the mottled green, yellow, blue, and brown chart, cut with curves of mile-distance arcs.

The captain seemed to be waiting for something—or someone. He shifted his pointer stick from one hand to the other and glanced at the big clock on the wall several times. I watched the red second hand sweep over the numbers: one minute to 0800 and counting as it began another rotation. Immediately ahead of me on the next row of chairs sat a whole line of U.S. Army personnel. Next to the wall was a very strange-looking person. It seemed that he was a member of the Army group, but I couldn't be sure. He had no rank nor markings on his mottled green jungle fatigues. His legs, from the

143

knees down, and over his jungle boots, were wrapped with black plastic electrical tape. Unlike the Army lieutenant colonel who sat beside him in starched and pressed tiger-stripe fatigues, he appeared a bit rumpled around the edges. A short-barreled 40mm grenade launcher lying on the floor beside his chair, with a pistol-style buttstock, made me even more suspicious about what was about to happen. He kept writing something in a little pad. An Army major was whispering to a couple of sergeants. I recognized the five or six 5th Special Forces personnel in the room and the pilots and co-pilots of three helicopter crews. The two A-1 Skyraider pilots sat up in the first row. My own squadron operations officer was there, too. Several backup intelligence sergeants sat close to the front. It was quite a room full of people for a regular mission—if that's what it was to be.

I moved my 9mm Swedish K submachine gun from my lap and laid it on the floor beside my chair. The door clicked behind me.

"Atten—hut!" said the captain.

Everyone jumped to their feet. An Army colonel entered, trailed by two lieutenant colonels. They moved briskly to the front row and took seats. The Air Force captain pointed his stick at a spot just west of the DMZ and cleared his throat.

"Today's mission will take us to the extreme western DMZ," he began. "The purpose of this mission is to insert friendly forces into hostile territory for the purpose of intelligence gathering."

Somebody coughed.

"Nail 31 will precede the insert team and VR the area around the LZ, intended landing zone. LZ is the high ground on the side of the Banghaing River just west of the village of Ban Chay. Takeoff for Nail 31 will be 10:00. At 12:00 noon, if the area appears quiet, 31 will re-cross the Ho Chi Minh Trail at a point of his own choosing, pick up the three CH-3E helicopters, call sign Knife, orbiting at 6,000 feet just west of point Foxtrot, and proceed to Ban Latthon. Descent will be made at this point down to 1,000 feet and it is then the responsibility of 31 to lead the three Knives to the LZ area at an altitude of his own choosing, over the previously flown approach route to the target. Upon arrival at the LZ, Nail 31 will circle into a higher orbit and talk the landing Knife into position. This Knife will be 51. Knife 52 and 53 will hold south of the LZ, 1 klick, at 1,000 feet, and be prepared for any eventuality. The escort A-1s, Hobo 23 and 24, will sweep the area ahead of the advancing FAC and Knives in orbital circles at 5,000 feet. Once Knife 51 is in position over the LZ, he will descend to grass-top level and discharge his insert team. Once the team is on the ground, Knife 51, 52, and 53 will withdraw and begin a departure by way of the original entry route. This route will provide screening cover because of the hills on either side. The only chance for ground fire will be from isolated foot patrols if you or they should fly directly over one. Nail 31 will climb to altitude and remain in the general area for one hour after the inserted team is on the ground. His remaining in the area will act as a safeguard in the event the insert team runs into trouble and a fire fight. As you all know, the first two hours on the ground are the most critical. A second FAC, Nail 20, the backup pilot and aircraft, will relieve Nail 31 on station. If Nail 31 fails to get airborne or aborts for any reason at all, the number two FAC will assume 31's duties. In other words, the FACs will reverse roles."

The briefing droned on and on. I glanced around the room and took another look at the players. There was Sergeant Sweeny, my Green Beret observer. Only this time I knew he was not going along. Sitting beside him was a grunt second looie for this special mission. Looking around some more, I spied the backup FAC. "Triple Shooter," we called him. He was good—none better. Nobody would have suspected that he and I were officers in the USAF. There was no rank or insignia on our camouflaged jungle fatigues, draw-tied over the top of plain green jungle boots. Only on our camouflaged hats was there evidence of rank. The front of mine held a small, single gold leaf. His had a plain pair of tiny silver bars. The fronts of both hats were turned back and up, pinned in place with a long twenty-penny nail.

Triple Shooter looked at me and made a face. I knew what his animation meant. The area where the briefing was centered was anything but a piece of cake. He and I both had been into and out of the area daily for a week. We had been flying three different routes to possible LZs. We had been sneaking up and down river valleys, over hills and down dales, taking color photographs of all features in the areas. The helicopter pilots who would fly the insert missions would never see the actual route until the day of the real mission. The color transparencies that we turned in were used in briefings for the chopper pilots to familiarize them with what to expect. None of us FACs that flew the Prairie Fire missions ever selected an LZ. We simply turned in the film, along with our debriefing information, and made recommendations. Somewhere down the line, in the halls of the upper echelon at Da Nang, somebody made a selection as to the exact coordinates for an intelligence team insert. We FACs often questioned the wisdom of the selection, but since the decision was not ours to make—and maybe the chief grunts knew something we didn't—we never raised any real row over it. One place was about as good as any other, we thought—that is, none were good. It was always a damn turkey shoot wherever we went.

I was a little uneasy with the second lieutenant going along. I was superstitious. Sweeny would have made me feel better. I knew how he acted under fire and knew I could depend upon him in a clutch. I think he felt the same way. We never said anything to each other about the relationship, but I felt it. I had picked Sweeny up by way of default. My first Green Beret observer, Sgt. Herb Winters, was killed on just such a mission as we were about to undertake.

While I was back in the States for a short leave over Thanksgiving, Sergeant Winters and another FAC, Capt. Jay Cobb, flew their mission. They had been leading a trio of Knives up the same river valley where we were going. Altitude for the CH-3Es and the FAC was low, apparently just over 100 feet above the grass. The FAC had partial flaps down in order to keep his aircraft from running off and leaving the choppers. Scuttlebutt among some of the pilots was that Jay and Herb had taken ground fire through, and in, the cockpit area of the O-2. Someone else came up with their own conclusion that a sudden updraft caught the O-2 and caused it to roll inverted, stagger on over to a generally upright, straight-in position, and strike the ground in a flat, near wings-level attitude. Nobody was really talking much. However, the rear engine of the O-2 came out of its mounts and crashed through the cockpit upon ground impact, killing both men.

A packette on the mission had been aboard, so a considerable amount of effort was made to retrieve that packette. An effort was made to recover the bodies, too, but groundfire had become so intense that repeated tries were driven off. The mission packette was retrieved, but not all of the material. It seems that some of the documents were taken out and were being used as the mission progressed, which was normal. The recovery team could not withstand the groundfire in its intensifying amount and retreated before the bodies could be extracted from the wreck. Therefore, a satchel charge was thrown into the aircraft, which was also a standard action used by rescue teams to destroy as much of a downed aircraft as possible and make parts of aircraft unusable by the enemy, whether there were unrecoverable bodies inside or not.

However, the satchel charge did not explode. Consequently, with air cover from A-1s always being handy anytime a rescue team was working on a crashed aircraft, the FAC did what was always done—he directed an airstrike on the wreck to insure destruction of both the highly sensitive mission documents and the wreck itself.

As my mind returned to the briefing, I heard an Air Force sergeant talking about antiaircraft fire on The Trail and saw his pointer moving from point to point as he talked. But I really didn't pay too much attention to him. The area of The Trail that we had to cross was so infested with antiaircraft guns, and they moved so frequently, that it was sheer madness to think that any portion of The Trail was safe. The Knives knew it, and I knew it. I saw the helio CH-3E aircraft commanders roll their eyes and look at me and Triple Shooter.

The briefing broke up with a call for questions. Nobody had any. There was a hearty "Atten-hut!" and everybody filed out. I watched the grunt with the black tape on his legs get up and go out. He was team leader according to the briefing officer. He would lead ten Cambodians into the extreme western DMZ area in an attempt to gather information on the strength of the NVA that were known to be streaming south for a buildup along the DMZ. He was also to look for bridges and anything else of military value, and to keep his eyes peeled for a Caucasian that had been seen several times wearing black pajamas, leading about forty North Vietnamese regulars. It had been rumored that this guy was either an American defector or a Russian. Nobody knew for sure, but they sure did want to capture him.

There was a small room just off the hallway, near the main entrance to intelligence building, that had been set up as a chapel. A lot of the crews stopped in to say whatever it is that they say in a chapel. We had many different faiths in our squadron and on the base. The little room saw a lot of various denominations pass through. For some it was a good idea that they stopped on the way out—they never got another opportunity. I hesitated on this day. Something tugged at me. I went in and stood silent for a few moments, hat in hand. Then I picked up my machine gun and walked out the door and down the dusty red dirt road.

My mind was racing as I walked to the aircrew personal equipment building. I had been in Southeast Asia for six months and had flown a considerable number of missions over North and South Vietnam and over Laos—and I had heard of only two U.S. soldiers being on the ground in Laos on armed combat missions. Whatever we were doing as part of Prairie Fire and whatever we had done as part of Heavy Hook were top drawer.

I pulled my survival vest off the peg with a grunt. It was heavy. Early in the war, I had learned that the Pathet Lao did not take American prisoners—or any prisoners at all if they could help it—and it was no secret that FAC pilots were considered a prize catch. We had seen what happened to pilots who were caught; we had recovered their mutilated bodies. Pilots were machine-gunned while hanging from trees in their parachute harnesses and while they stood with their hands up, ready to surrender. They were tied to trees and tortured—or worse.

So we FACs traded our olive and green Air Force flying suits for straight-leg grunt fatigues with mottled green and brown tiger-stripe camouflage. I traded my Smith and Wesson .38 Combat Masterpiece for a 9mm Browning pistol with a thirteen-shot clip. I had also talked my buddies in the 5th Special Forces into giving me a 9mm Swedish K submachine gun, which cost me two fifths of V.O. cognac.

The O-2 was sitting ready in the hot sun when I drove up beside her. The *Pink Panther,* as we called her, was a dirty little bird. Her gray paint job was smudged with grease and red dirt here and there. But she was ready and ran top-notch according to the chief. We were fully armed with two pods—fourteen—of 2.75-inch Willie Pete white phosphorus rockets. This was not much in the way of munitions, to be sure, but it would suffice for our needs. We did not intend to shoot any rockets, which made one hell of a cloud when they exploded, since we did not want to draw attention to ourselves. We would save the rockets for targets of opportunity on the return, fuel permitting.

I was sweating up a storm as the chief held the harness of the chute open for me. The heavy flak vest, with its overlapping plates of steel, was no lightweight—about 20 pounds of metal for upper torso protection, front and back. There was no armor plate in the O-2. A .30-caliber AK-47 submachine-gun slug could cut through the thin aluminum skin of the little bird like a hot knife through butter. Normally, on regular FAC strike and reconnaissance missions at higher altitudes, I sat on the damn flak vest, but today we would be in the bushes, and I was wearing the thing.

My observer was apprehensive as hell. He had never been on a mission with me, and never one of these insert missions before. He was new to the game and told me he had come up from Monkey Mountain down in South Vietnam for this exercise. But he had been well briefed and knew all the radio codes and rules of the game. He looked ridiculous in his fiberglass flak vest, with its big lifesaver collar.

The *Pink Panther* gathered speed as I pushed both throttles up against the stop. She lifted her nose a bit, grumbled a tad at all the weight, and soared into the blue Thai sky. I waited until I had safe flying speed and altitude and flipped the gear lever to the up position. The O-2 had retractable gears on it, but once the retract lever was tripped, the big gull-wing doors on the aft fuselage opened wide like doors on a house. The main gear struts unlocked, dropped down like a duck lifting off a lake, rotated backwards, and tucked up inside in the trail position. To throw the gear lever into the up position too soon, if the bird was not flying well, and open those big barn doors would be like throwing out an anchor.

Nakhon Phanom Royal Thai Air Force Base lay only about 6 miles from the Mekong River. The Mekong was the dividing line between the "good guys" and the "bad guys," and a fully loaded O-2 required about five minutes to get above 3,000 feet. Some of the other pilots had encountered occasional small-arms fire as we crossed the river on climbout. Therefore, I had changed my own tactics to allow for a long straight-out climb after lifting off, then begin a slow circle to come back close to the base on a parallel line to takeoff, climbing all the time, with another reverse of course before crossing into Laos. This maneuver would put several thousand feet of altitude under me and get me out of most of harm's way, rather than the usual tactic of most of the "young" pilots of simply climbing out on a gradually increasing line and crossing the Mekong at 500 to 1,000 feet—down where just about anyone could knock you out of the air with a lucky single shot out of anything. And at 500 feet or so, an AK-47 Russian assault rifle could stitch you from eyeball to toenail in the blink of an eye with a thirty-round burst, and the assailant would be gone on his samlar (three-wheeled bicycle) before anybody would know who did it.

The main portion of the famous Ho Chi Minh Trail lay some 80 nautical miles from the Mekong—or about forty-five minutes of flying time in the *Pink Panther.* There was no need for us to do anything except get on across The Trail and into the target area. Rather than run the risk of getting shot down before the mission even started, I let the bird continue to climb once we crossed into Laos. Seven thousand feet was a good altitude to cross the really bad portion of The Trail ahead, down around what we called "the chokes" at Alpha, Bravo, Charlie, and Foxtrot. That whole 30-mile stretch of trails and sideroads was crawling with antiaircraft guns, mostly the deadly ZPU .60-caliber heavy machine guns and 37mm five- and seven-shot antiaircraft cannons. The 37s normally had a shell bursting altitude of 9,000 to 10,000 feet. I wanted to be below that altitude because it was far easier to duck a single shell or string of shells than it was to get away from a sky full of shrapnel. The 37s were no real problem if you could see the projectiles coming. They seemed to travel rather slowly and looked exactly like glowing orange beer cans floating up.

I selected the 105 degree TACAN radial of NKP to track outbound on. That heading would take us across The Trail and into the general target area, but I wanted to stay clear of the old Tchepone airfield and the Xe Banghiang River crossing. Tchepone was a really "bad" place. Our other squadron pilots had reported SAM missles on the "Banana Karst" just across the river. I wanted no part of the SAMs, not today.

The green jungle that slid beneath the wings of the O-2 lied about the peaceful looking country below. Towering teak trees climbed for 200 feet into the hot sun. Now and then a glistening patch of flat green spoke of a rice paddy where a village or family scratched out a living in the primitive land. There were no roads of any kind along our course. A few trails and tracks, but the only hard surface road, Lao 136, was left behind as soon as we had crossed the Mekong. The land was like a place time had forgotten.

As we approached the main artery of The Trail, the lieutenant began to come alive. The beautiful greenery of the landscape was giving way to isolated pocks of red here and there— bomb craters. As we neared the Nam Kok River and the village of Ban Nammi, the whole world below seemed to turn red and unearthed, as though some giant farmer had plowed everything.

"What's all that?" my observer asked.

"That," I said, "is the Ho Chi Minh Trail. Never seen it before?"

"Naw, never," he replied. "Gee whiz, I thought I would be looking at some sort of a road or town or something. Nothing like this."

The Trail had been bombed so many times at this point, near Foxtrot, that it looked like the face of the moon. There was hardly a tree or bush standing for several miles in any direction. The place was devoid of any life except the enemy soldiers and vehicles that passed along the track or were stationed there.

Once across the Nam Kok and the Xe Namkok Rivers, I swung the bird around to the left to intercept the 085 degree radial off of the Savannakhet TACAN and began a slow descent from 7,000 feet to 4,000 feet. The countryside below was changing. The teak forests of the west had given way to a mixture of karst cliffs, small rivers, and more frequent rice paddies, with more banana trees. As we approached the border between South Vietnam and Laos, all that changed again and became rolling high hills covered with 15-foot-tall elephant cane.

"Well, we are here," I told the lieutenant.

"Huh?" he said. "How do you know? I can't tell a thing from where I sit."

"You just trust me," I said. "The Xe Banghiang River valley is right there on the left. It runs straight into the DMZ about 15 miles ahead at Ban Tchepone and at Ban Co Bai. Quang Tri, South Vietnam, is only about 35 miles away on a heading of 095. Our insert LZ is right there on top of that ridge at Ban Chay. The Houay Namxe River is tight up against the cliff under Ban Chay village. See it?"

"Yeah, I think I do."

My watch showed almost 11:00. "We got about an hour before we have to go back and get the choppers," I told him. "Let's take a look around and see what we see. Dig out the gyro-stabilized binoculars and plug them into that outlet there."

The binoculars looked like a shoebox. Under good conditions, you could see someone eating his lunch on the ground from 4,000 feet.

"We'll stay up here and reckie-teck around," I said as I swung the bird around in a slow turn toward the North Vietnamese border barely 5 miles away.

There was nothing moving on the ground below, absolutely nothing. It was very quiet. I could hear some fighter-bombers talking excitedly on the UHF, over around Xa Dong. But that was across the ridge and on the coast of the South China Sea of North Vietnam. It seems somebody had spotted a MiG. The clock ticked.

"Better get started back," I told the lieutenant. "It will take us about thirty minutes to re-cross The Trail and pick-up the Knives."

We swung around and headed back toward The Trail at a point I felt was relatively safe, for the sake of the CH-3Es. It was just below the "Chokes" and above "Foxtrot." Ban Thai was my selected crossing point. I knew the heavy helicopters had little maneuverability should Charlie decide to start taking pot shots at them with 37s. And you just don't hide three machines the size of CH-3Es in thin air.

I tuned in the strike frequencies on the Fox Mike radio and gave a shout. "Knife 51, Knife 51. This is Nail 31. How do you read?"

There was silence.

"Knife 51, 52, or 53. This is Nail 31. How do you read, over?"

Static.

"Howdy, Nail, this is Knife leader."

"Loud and clear, Knife lead," I answered. "What's your position and angels?"

"Uh, we are at angels 5, 115 degrees at 65 miles off of NKP."

"Knife 51, you are entering hostile airspace. Orbit your force in a right circle and climb to angels 7, over," I instructed.

"Gotcha, Nail."

"Let's go get 'em," I told the lieutenant, "They will be sitting ducks if they try to cross without help."

I pushed both mixtures up to rich, both props to the stop and both throttles up to 25 inches of manifold pressure. Airspeed climbed on the *Pink Panther* from 90 knots to a roaring 110 knots. Time was running out, and I wanted to get to the helicopters and get them across the trail. The actual insert of the team was scheduled for 12:30.

"Gotcha in sight, Knife," I said.

We were drumming along at 4,000 feet, 120 knots, and I had spotted the big CH-3E's up on top of the ridge in front of me. All were in a trail formation. The two Hobos, in the A-1 Skyraiders, were orbiting around like two pelicans over the flock.

"Turn to 065 degrees off of Savannakhet and proceed," I instructed the lead Knife. "I am right with you."

"Make smoke, Nail," said leader. "We don't have you in sight."

I punched the smoke generator button for one second.

"Gotcha, Nail," said number three. "He is at the two o'clock position, lead, and low."

I struggled on up to get on an even keel with them. "Follow me, Knives," I said. They fell in behind in a ragged line. I had my fingers crossed.

"Flak! Flak!" somebody shouted.

"Give a clock position," a Hobo shouted.

"Forget it, Hobo, forget it. We have no time," I hollered. "Push it up, Knife. Push it up. Shove it over a little." I wanted them to get more power on the rotors and pick up a change of airspeed to screw up the gunners tracking them. One way was to dive a little. Looking over my shoulder I spotted a few white puffs in the air way off to the port of the formation.

"37s," I said to the observer. "It is a good way away. It sure got everyone up on their toes though." Then I instructed the flight: "Coming up on IP. Ban Talouay dead ahead."

I had previously selected that point from whence to begin our run to target because it was a place easily spotted on the ground and would provide high hill cover to the right and left once we got down inside the little river valley. It was doubtful, too, that there would be any hostiles at that small, out of the way village, tucked up into a deadend stream valley. I throttled back and began a slight zig-zag approach down into the river valley. Unlike the FAC that had been shot down earlier, I liked to keep my airspeed and flaps up, and kill time by cutting back and forth across the flight path, rather than a slow straight path. The helicopters fell in behind me.

"Watch 'em," I told my observer. "I can't keep an eye on them and clear the way, too."

We swung hard left at Ban Coh and let on down to below the tops of the hills on either side, which were at about 300 feet. We were following the Xe Banghiang River in a twisting flight, around one curve and across another. Some guy riding a water buffalo whizzed past on the right and looked up in complete shock as I sped by.

"Watch careful, Knives," I said into the boom mike. "Coming up on cross-over point." By "cross-over" I meant a slight climb up the ridge on the south of the river to get on the backside of the 500-foot ridge that led to Ban Chay. I figured that if we played our cards right we could sneak up toward the top of that ridge and discharge the team without anybody spotting us from the valley below.

"Up and over," I said to the flight, and swung the *Panther* around in a hard right turn. We zipped over the tall grass in a flash, blowing the cane down behind us. "Starting a climb, Knife, your LZ is at your nine o'clock position by the white rocks."

"In sight," came the terse reply.

I could sense the tension in the cockpit of the lead helicopter. "Two and Three, hold at one click to the south," I instructed the other two Knives.

We swung around in a slow circle, climbing for altitude. I spotted the two A-1s overhead, circling—waiting. Knife 51 came around in a hard-over turn once he was on top of the ridge and went straight for the white rocks I had told him about. We climbed. Knife 51 went into a hover. The tailgate on the CH-3E was down. I could see the team leader jump. Then another man. Then another.

"We are taking ground fire," screamed Knife 51. "We are taking fire!"

"Oh, God!" I shouted. "Hobo leader, the LZ is under fire, give me cover. Give me a clock position, Knife."

"Don't know. Don't know," he replied.

By then the team leader, the GI, was up on his radio. "I'm taking hits, I'm taking hits," he screamed. "Get us out. Get us out."

"I'm hit and over-heating," the LZ helicopter was yelling.

"Pull off," I said. "Pull off. Knife 52, get in here quick. Stand-by for recovery."

I was standing the O-2 onto her wingtips trying my damnedest to locate the source of the smallarms, to no avail.

The GI was back on the air. "I've got one man wounded, two with a broken leg and two with punctures."

"Strafe to the North, Hobo," I shouted. "Hit the ridge top. Hit the ridge top." I swung around and talked number two Knife in on the LZ. His door came down in the rear. "You are too high, 52. Get down. Get down."

"I'm taking hits," he yelled. I saw an A-1 sweep the ridge with 20mm cannon slugs and roar off, with his wingman rolling in for a pass.

"Knife 52 is taking small-arms fire, FAC. There he is. I see him," yelled the copilot of 52. "Damn, he's right on top of the rock. . . . I've got four on board. . . . I'm pulling out."

"Oh, shit," someone said. "Get in here, 53. Get in here."

Another voice was yelling, "I'm hit, I'm hit!"

"Take my goddamned machine gun and shoot that little dink bastard off of that rock when I go past," I told the lieutenant.

He fumbled around, got my Swedish K, got the window open, and—*brrrrrr!* We got him as I swooped over the rocks and pulled up in a rocket-firing pass for a mark. The jig was up by then. Secrecy was gone. The only thing that mattered was to try to get the team out and all aircraft back home safely. The A-1s were yelling for a position to fire at. The helicopters were yelling that they were overheating and were pulling out. It was a rout.

"Hold on, 53," I said. "Hold on a minute longer. 51 and 52, you can head out." I flipped over in a half-ass rocket run and pressed the fire button for a pair release. "Hit the smoke," I told the Skyraiders. "Hit the smoke."

They rolled in. Knife 53 was yelling that he had everyone on board—he thought—and was departing.

"Count noses, count noses," I kept telling him, "Then RTB."

I gutted the O-2 out and went straight for the grass tops to get away. Sweat was running into my eyes. The lieutenant was bug-eyed but pouring 9mm slugs out the window all over the white rocks. He emptied both clips that I had in the gun.

I could see the helicopters flopping along ahead of me. It was nip and tuck to catch up. They had had it. One and Two had bullet holes. So did Three. We were clean—no damage to us. The A-1s were in good shape.

"Okay, gang," I said. "Sorry about the trouble. Let's RTB."

I followed the choppers and watched for problems.

The mission was a flop. Whether it was sheer coincidence that the NVA troops were on the LZ or had planned the ambush, we never found out. But since we had been showing a good bit of interest in that particular area, we suspected that patrols had been increased. I put another team into the same area, 1 klick farther east about a week later, consisting of three GIs and five Cambodians. They got on the ground safely and remained for two days. Then they ran into the white guy in the black pajamas with thirty NVA Regulars. There was one hell of a firefight. The GIs called in an air strike right on top of their own position. Nobody got out. We inserted a team to take a look after it was all over. There were bodies all over the place. The three Americans were dead. The Caucasian was dead. One Cambodian was severely wounded, but he died en route back to base.

The area was a total disaster. No team could stay on the ground more than a few days without running into trouble. On another mission, one Cambodian traded clothes with a dead NVA and walked right past a Pathet Lao patrol. The LZs became like shooting galleries. The NVA would build hides right on top of them and shoot the hell out of any helicopters that went in for a team drop. It became so hostile that we finally gave it up and moved the operation.

One thing we did learn was that North Vietnam had a hell of a lot of people in and around the DMZ area, with light armor. Maybe we accomplished something. I don't know. I had gotten the LRRP team in to try to catch the unknown Caucasian, but unfortunately their luck ran out. It was evident the team had fought like devils to try and save themselves, but perhaps realized it was a lost cause and made a last stand like George Custer, taking as many as they could with them when they called the fighters in on themselves.

In January 1969 I flew ten Cricket West missions, five Igloo White sensor-insert missions, two Knife transmitter-insert missions, two normal Trail missions, and seven Prairie Fire missions for MACV-SOG and the 5th Special Forces. Twenty-six missions in thirty-one days wasn't a bad record. But the night FAC missions were looking more and more attractive. I was tired, having been at the game since late summer. I felt I needed a change of pace, and becoming a plain old night pilot was just what I needed.

As luck would have it, a senior major got promoted to lieutenant colonel, and he needed a job with more responsibility. I was asked to check him out as squadron scheduling officer. One of my last duties as scheduling officer was to schedule myself into the night program starting February 1. I'd be flying under Maj. Carl Flemming, "Major Night Fighter" himself.

In mid-February, the new scheduling officer got himself into the "Scatback" program flying T-39s out of Thailand and left the squadron. Not long after, I ran into the ops officer at the O Club while I was having a late breakfast after sleeping until ten, running a mile, taking a long shower, shaving, getting into my clean tiger stripes, and just generally taking my time.

"Reggie," the ops officer began, "when you coming back to do the scheduling job? We sure could use you now that Al is gone."

I sat my tall glass of iced tea down and answered him, "Sir, I do appreciate your need, and ordinarily I'd be really pleased to re-do the job for you, but I am now a night fighter. The squadron now only has four night FAC pilots including me, and you know as well as I do that every night we have to have four missions over The Trail at minimum. Sir, I just don't see how I am going to be able to help. And, besides, Major Flemming runs the night program. Thank you, anyway."

I snickered. This was the guy who made only two missions per month across the Mekong into Indian Country so he could get combat pay. And rocket range got invented by him and built under his supervision on the Thai side of the Mekong River so that he wouldn't have to fly across the Mekong any more than twice a month. This was the guy who wanted us FACs to bring rockets back from a mission, then fly to his rocket range and practice shooting Willie Petes. He never had many takers flying on his rocket range. It seems like everyone always had to shoot all of their Willie Petes on their missions and came home with empty pods.

CHAPTER 12

Go Get the POWs!

Opening the door to the briefing room for a premission rundown was always a thrill. You never knew what was in store for you. This day was no exception. The minute I walked in, I had that queasy feeling I always got in my ankles when things were not quite right. It was already hot outside at six o'clock. I had my slouch hat pulled down low over my eyes to shade them from the glare of the rising sun. My tiger-striped fatigues were already wet with sweat. I had a cold, clammy feeling where the top stuck to my backbone in the cold air conditioning of the sterile room; my sleeves were rolled up to above the elbows. The Swedish K submachine gun felt cold, too— deadly so. I hesitated in the white illumination of the fluorescent lights in the ceiling, staring at the room of people. Every seat was full. The drapes on the briefing board were closed.

"Come in, major," said a gentleman in starched bush shorts and jacket. I had never seen him before. Sitting in the front row was a trio of men I had never seen before either. They wore those funny long-billed caps, like the kind sport fishermen wear when out after marlin and sailfish, the kind Ernest Hemingway liked. Then it struck me. I had seen a Pilotus Porter aircraft come sneaking onto the base just after daylight. That kind of aircraft belonged to but one variety of people: the CIA. The Porters and the German Dorniers belonged to them—the James Bond types, as we called them. From time to time, we would see them coming and going to and from the base. We did not know too much about these people, except that they usually "operated" way upcountry in the mountains on the PDJ and fiddled around near the North Vietnamese, Chinese, and Burmese borders. They flew around in "funny" aircraft, the kind painted dark gray with no markings; they came and went like will-o'-the-wisps. Now we had three of these Steve Canyon types in the flesh and a fourth one telling me to "come in." Indeed, this was to be no ordinary mission. These kind of guys carried the power of God. They did whatever they felt like in the scheme of war, overthrowing governments and setting events into motion.

I took a seat in the back row. There was no room left for me to sit anywhere else. I saw a lot of Army Top Kicks and O-6s scattered around. Another Nail FAC came in, the second one fragged for the day's mission. His reaction was about like mine—startled. Normally, the only personnel in a briefing for a mission would be the FAC, the briefing officer, weather officer, and any passenger who would be going along, such as a photographer. On the larger missions, there were always a few extra people present to know the whole picture, but nothing like this—a room full of thirty people. Any day that we went into the briefing room at TUOC (Intelligence) and found an entourage of strange people, we knew something unusual was up.

For months we had been hearing rumors that there was a POW camp in Laos—supposedly not too far from us, up on Route 8 in Cricket West. It was also supposed to be moved from time to time, and the POWs were shuffled around. The information seemed to be creeping in from one of the "road watch" teams that we had put out in that area as well as from paid informers. One time we heard there were Americans being held at Ban Loy, then Ban Phon Dou. It was scuttlebutt. Each day, one or the other of the six Cricket West Squadron pilots was in those areas. We could never spot anything unusual. Of course, all of the buildings up there looked pretty much the same from 4,000 feet. We couldn't get much lower than that. The 37mm antiaircraft guns were intense in the areas along Route 8, 12, and 13, even though it was all a peaceful-looking piece of real estate with gray karst mountains, bright velvet-green trees, diamond streams, rice paddies, and lush banana groves.

Through our gyro-stabilized 20-, 40-, and 60-power binoculars, we could see people and animals. We also spotted gun emplacements, which we skirted like a pointer around a rattler.

If you got too close, they would hose you if they thought they could get you. Any pilot who came sauntering by with his head up his ass was dead meat. One such 37mm at the foot of Mu Ghia Pass picked off one F-4 a day, for eight days in a row, before we figured out his hiding place.

I had been in the area of Ban Loy the day before. I had worked that area all along the Nam Don River to Ban Lao, all along Route 12 and Route 8, then up to Ban Thami, out to the Mekong, and back again. I had seen nothing on four hours of reccie. It was uneventful, except for some 37mm fire along Route 12 when I put in a string of mines for the road. So it was a huge surprise to learn that Ban Louang was the target.

The room grew very quiet when the rear door was locked and an armed guard stood there at parade rest with a loaded M-16. An Air Force major whom I did not know assumed the role of briefer for the day. He was highly professional. He had short, clipped black hair, a neatly trimmed mustache, and starched and pressed green fatigues—which in itself was a rarity. You never saw any of the troops at NKP running around in starched and pressed fatigues. Usually, the fatigues of base personnel looked exactly like where they had been washed—in the Mekong, where the hooch girls did laundry.

The major pulled on a cord at the side of the briefing curtains. The dull-green canvas drapes slid open to reveal a map of Laos, the Steel Tiger portion, about 7 feet high and 10 feet in length. It was covered in red and blue circles that represent known antiaircraft gun positions as well as suspected gun positions. Red was for known—or hot—positions. There were the radials of the NKP TACAN jutting like spokes on a bicycle wheel, with each spoke representing 5 degrees of the compass rose. Each spoke marked 2 mile increments in ever-widening rings spreading out from the center. Therefore, it was fairly easy for anyone to immediately obtain a fix on a particular small area. The amazing part of this operation was that Ban Louang was practically under our noses, located about the 053 degree radial of Channel 99 TACAN at 24 nautical miles. We would have suspected a POW camp to have been much farther to the east, closer to the North Vietnamese border. But there it was, big as day, circled in bright orange.

The major used a long, standard-issue wooden pointer with the black rubber tip. "Gentlemen," he said slowly and precisely, to let his shocking words sink in, "our mission for the day is to make an attempt to retake seven American POW pilots. We have information leading us to believe they are located here, at the Lao village of Ban Louang." He jabbed the board, then droned on. "The only other village in the area is Ban Yiang, approximately 1 klick to the west, southwest. Both are unfriendly. I repeat, unfriendly. To the northwest of Ban Louang you will see a cluster of typical Lao huts. They have no name. We have further reason to believe the prisoners are moved from village to village periodically under the cover of darkness. Why, we don't know. How long they will remain at this present location is unknown. They were there yesterday."

A murmur crept through the crowd in the room. I was then thinking of 1st Lt. Jimmy Short. Was he there? Jimmy had been my next door roomie. I thought of the Justin cowboy boots left where he had set them several weeks ago. The hooch girls still shined them. Jimmy had committed an unpardonable sin for a FAC. He had allowed himself to fly around a "sucker hole" in heavy overcast. Any enemy gunner on the ground below would have been watching that sucker hole like an ice fisherman watching a cork on a frozen lake. Jimmy knew that. He forgot. The sky was thick clouds when Jimmy took off from NKP. The clouds were beginning to lighten some by the time that he got to the Ho Chi Minh Trail. At approximately the 046 degree radial of NKP, Channel 99, 82 nautical miles out, he spotted a break in the overcast and began circling it. On board with him was a senior master sergeant who had been a crew member in World War II on a B-17 that had been shot down in Germany. As Jimmy and the sarge circled the hole in the clouds, a burst of 37mm antiaircraft fire met them, cutting the left wing off their O-2A aircraft and sending it into unmanageable flight. Jimmy tried to get the sarge out. They had some difficulty with the side door, the only way out. Finally, they both got it unlatched and jettisoned. Jimmy kicked the sarge out and followed. As the sarge went out, he hit the bottom of the spinning aircraft and bounced over the whirling rear prop, his chute opening immediately. And Jimmy's chute opened a few seconds later. But those few seconds saved the sergeant from capture by the NVA. The drift of Jimmy's chute took him over NVA troops.

The sergeant had only one survival radio with him in his vest since he was along for a one-time ride as a passenger to see The Trail. He took it out as he floated down, pulled out the antenna to call for help, remembered that the radio was not tied to him, pushed the antenna back down into the radio, and put the thing away. He could see Jimmy coming down in his own chute a mile away. There were many North Vietnamese soldiers running around on the ground below as the pair descended. All were running toward Jimmy firing their AK-47 assault rifles at him in his descent. The sarge hit the ground—fracturing a leg—rolled his chute up into a ball, and ran up the hill on which he had landed. Finding a pile of thick brush, and a downed tree, he crawled in under the thankful cover. Up the road he could hear much shooting and yelling. He did not know what was happening to Jimmy. He could have been dead for all he knew.

Then the NVA soldiers came looking for the sergeant. They sprayed the brush with AK slugs, but the sarge remained quiet and still, like a rabbit in a brushtop. When they finally passed, he pulled out the survival radio and began calling for help. A 23rd TASS FAC heard him, and a SAR mission was launched. The sergeant was rescued successfully. We later learned that Jimmy had been in Ban Louang.

The major continued, "Nail 31 will lead the mission with four A-1 Sky Raiders to the rendezvous point for the helicopters, Bobcat One and Bobcat Two. Nail 33 will direct and escort the choppers."

He looked at me. I nodded in understanding. I was writing on the back of my hand the call signs, times, and coordinates.

He stood with the stick pointing at us and said, "These choppers are Buffs, the CH-53E." We all understood. The 53s were the big boys, the long-range kind that could be refueled in flight. We wondered where they were coming from. There were none at NKP, only the somewhat smaller CH-3Es.

The major jabbed his pointer at me. "Nail 31, you will lead the flight of four A-1s to the rendezvous point and set up air cover in orbit. The rendezvous point is the 050 degree radial of Channel 99 at 20 nautical miles. Time of rendezvous is 0900. Everyone check their watches."

We did, pulling out the stems and punching them back in after the major counted down.

The briefing went on. "The choppers will be coming from the west. Their time on station at the rendezvous point will be precisely at 0905. Upon arrival of Bobcat One and Bobcat Two, Nail 33 will lead the two CH-53s down into the Houay Naphong valley behind the cover of the hill there and follow the creek channel straight into Ban Louang. Once the air crews come around the hill, the target will be dead ahead, 1 klick, and should be in sight. The choppers are depending on you. The element here is surprise. The enemy would expect us to make a try at dawn. Instead, we go at midmorning to try to catch all our POWs in the field, outside of the buildings, working. The approach must be fast and sure. In and out quick. There is a fair-sized NVA force in the area. The Bobcats will proceed straight to the edge of the village, land, and disgorge their troops. Each Bobcat will be carrying ten heavily armed 5th Special Forces personnel. Nail 33 will direct the landing and circle the LZ maintaining airborne communications with Blue Chip Control, Smoky Control, and Invert Control. Nail 31 will lead the A-1s in on cover fire and mop up if we run into resistance. Is that clear?"

Everyone nodded. I felt a few butterflies zooming around inside my belly. I did not think the NVA guards would take too kindly to an unfriendly force attempting to take their prisoners from them. It had all the makings for a real turkey shoot—with all of us as the turkeys.

There were other details to the mission to be briefed on, like the weather. It promised to be a typical dry-season Lao day—

bright and sunny with the hateful smoky haze obscuring everything farther away than 2 miles. I was to have a Green Beret
observer on board. He would handle the radios for the ground
communications if the force were on the ground awhile. I would
handle all the aircraft calls and direct the A-1s onto the target,
and in and out during a fire fight.

People began to drift out of the room. Some stopped to talk
in hushed tones in little groups. I looked at the mission pouch,
the black leatherette flip folder with its maps and charts and
instructions. The newspapers back home would have a red-let-
ter field day if they knew what was going on here. Not only were
we not supposed to be here, all of the POWs and MIAs were
supposed to be in Hanoi. There were supposed to be talks
going on to get them released and accounted for. And here we
are going in on a raid for seven of the guys that no one will
even acknowledge are in Laos. It could be a wild day—and an
even wilder finish if we succeeded. I was sure somebody already
had a story cooked up to explain where the POWs came from if
we successfully rescued them.

On the way out the door to TUOC, I stopped in the little
room set up by the front door that served as a chapel. It was for
all denominations and faiths. I set the submachine gun down
outside the door, bowed my head inside, and said what I had to
say to "The Man." I was not sure whether I would be coming
back this way again or not. Then I picked up the olive-drab
Swedish K and walked away into the bright glare of the growing day. Troops were moving here and there. Jeeps and trucks
were going about their business, just as if everything was normal. It was normal to them. Only a very small handful of people knew what was about to take place.

The dark-blue Air Force TUOC crew bus came cruising by. I
hitched a short ride down to the personal equipment building.
The corrugated dull-silver building where all of the aircrews
kept their flight equipment stored. Everything hung neatly on
wooden pegs and in racks. A pair of sergeants looked up at me
from behind the counter where they sat. "Uh, oh," I heard one
murmur. They had seen me before—the Nail major who never

told them where he went, who usually had a Lao lieutenant with him, and who carried the machine gun. I shot a glance at them. They snapped salutes.

"Good morning to you, major," the skinny black one said.

"And a good morning to you, Jim," I returned.

I sauntered on back to my rack, hung the K on a peg, and pulled down my survival vest. I went through all of its pockets, checked the identical pair of survival radios out, and got fresh batteries for them. I felt the edges of the two knives tied to the vest, the dagger and the hunting knife. They were razor sharp. Satisfied, I put both back into their sheaths and lashed them down tight with shroud line in case of a bailout. The four hand grenades were where I had left them yesterday. There were 300 rounds of spare 9mm ammo in side pockets for the Browning high-power and the Swedish K sub. The whole thing was heavy as I slid into it.

The skinny black sergeant came walking back. "Can I help you, major?" he asked.

"Yeah, please take my chute to the counter," I said. I jerked the heavy, metal-plated chest armor from its own peg, followed by the 6-pound fiberglass helmet. I tossed all of it on the counter and cracked, "Gimme a CAR-15 and about ten clips."

The other sarge laid it all out, looking at me. I gathered everything up and headed for the door not saying a word as usual, trying to stuff my blood chit packet down into a pocket on my tiger stripes.

"Have a good shoot, maj," I heard one say as the door closed behind me. I knew their curiosity was killing them. Where does this guy go?

The *Little Major* was squatting on the PSP parking ramp like an old tired pelican when the van rolled up to it. Two ground crewmen without shirts were running around it. The black umbilical cord running into the side of the bird from the APU was giving it life. Lights were on in the cockpit. I could smell the heat of burned oil.

"You ran 'er up, sarge?" I asked as I stepped in under the right wing and dumped my gear on the cockpit floor.

"Roger, sir," he snapped back smartly. "Sergeant Sweeny was here a moment ago. He went off toward the operations building I think." Sweeny was my 5th Special Forces observer, an old friend and MACV-SOG covey rider who had flown often with me.

I had to give the good ground crews of the 23rd credit; they kept the birds in top shape despite the long and frequent missions each aircraft flew. Each sortie out of the squadron was between three and five hours in length. The gray and white and black birds often came back shot full of holes. But they were always patched and ready to go when it came mission time again. There were really not that many birds in the squadron. About twenty total were all we had. We had no luxury of spares. Aircraft were in short supply. With an around-the-clock mission, day in and day out, it was a terrible load and strain to place on maintenance to meet the sortie requirements.

As I inspected the Form One, Sergeant Sweeny came strolling back. In his arms was a load of 4-inch-thick black tubes. Around and around his neck and waist were loops and loops of shiny, gold-colored 7.62 M60 ammunition. Another Green Beret sergeant was bringing up the rear carrying Sweeny's M60, the one with the grapefruit can soldered to the side so the belted ammunition would not hang on feeding. I raised up and looked at him.

"What in the hell?" I said, surprised.

"Oh, no problem, maj. Me and the boys just wanted to be sure we didn't go away undergunned on this trip."

"Yeah, I'll bet," I said, knowing Sweeny's taste for shooting at somebody. "What's in the tubes?"

"Oh, them, sir?" he said, loading the stuff in behind the seat.

"Yeah, them," I snapped.

"Uhh, them is grenades," he smiled.

"Goddamn, Sweeny," I said, "Just how many do you need anyhow?"

"Oh, maybe a full dozen. Thought we might need them if we have to get on the ground, maj." he replied.

I shrugged my shoulders and pointed a gloved finger at him. "Now, you listen to me, Sergeant Sweeny. If you play with those goddamned things, you be damn sure you hold them out the window, and put the rubber band on the spoon before you pull the goddamned pin. Do you understand me?"

"Sir, I do. I do," he shot back, smiling.

I was remembering the Raven FAC who dropped a smoke grenade in between his legs in an O-1F. The smoke grenade rolled back under his seat and into the tail of the aircraft. He burned himself right out of the sky. I wanted none of that—a live plastic B grenade rolling around loose in the cockpit would be totally fatal.

From my left seat I leaned over and hollered out the door at him, "Come on, Sweeny, get your butt in here. We gotta go find us a war."

"Rog, maj, rog," he said, and jumped in.

"Clear!" I shouted out the little side window, looking at the front engine guard.

He gave me a thumbs up signal, shouted back, "Clear!"

I hit the starter. The engine whined with the starter's pull. The yellow-tipped black prop cranked over slowly. With a puff of gray smoke, the engine caught, coughed, then roared to life. I jockeyed the throttle. I watched the gauges for a moment. "Clear on two," I yelled.

"Clear," came the reply.

Number two caught immediately. The gauges on the instrument panel all settled down. I had a lump behind my back. There was always a lump somewhere in all of that damn gear. I shuffled and wiggled around in the seat, trying to get comfortable. It was barely eight o'clock, and sweat was pouring off me. I could feel it running down my sides. The steel-plated chest armor was crushing me, all 20 pounds of it. It was very uncomfortable and hot.

I thumbed the UHF and spoke firmly, "Hobo 24 Flight, this is Nail 31, over."

There was static.

"Roger, Nail 31. This is Hobo 24 Lead, over."

"Check your flight in, Hobo Leader," I replied.

A pause.

"Hobo 24 Flight, check in," Hobo Lead said. "Hobo 25. Hobo 26. Hobo 27. Hobo 24 flight is ready to taxi, 31."

"Roger. NKP tower, Nail 31, taxi with a flight of four Hobos."

The tower replied, "Nail 31, with a flight of Hobos, you are cleared to taxi runway 27. Winds are 250 at 10 knots. Your altimeter is three-zero, zero five, over."

I thumbed the button on the yoke and said, "Nail 31, taxiing with a flight of Hobos."

The *Little Major* pitched and rolled in slow motion on the PSP steel matting, like a ship at sea. He was heavy with fuel, all we could get on board. We rocked along at slow idle. I glanced up the ramp. Here came the Hobos. I saw them pulling out of their parking area—fat green and brown birds as big as a World War II B-17. Their single-engine, four-bladed props ticked over and the heavy aircraft rolled slowly back and forth under their load. All were E models. Each wing of each bird was wall-to-wall hard bombs, 500-pound frags, fourteen each. I could see the barrels of their 20 mike-mike wing cannons sticking out at me, like tongues of death.

The armament sergeant ducked in under our wings left and right, in a flash, pulling the safety pins from the rocket pods. I let him get out front and show me all of the pins with their long red streamers. I nodded when I was satisfied he had them all pulled. Gently, I eased the *Little Major* up to the number one position on the taxiway and waited for my Hobos to go through their armament check and then their runup. The big 2,700-horsepower radial engines shook the ground at full power. My O-2 was dwarfed by the sheer size of the ugly old A-1s.

I pressed the black mike button and said clearly, "Nail 31 is number one for takeoff, NKP tower."

"Nail 31, you are cleared for takeoff. Surface winds are now light and variable."

I ran the pair of throttles up smoothly, coming around onto the runway in a rolling start. The throttles were pushed up to their stops for full military power. Airspeed was building. Slowly, The *Little Major* shuffled along like a drunk with too much of a load in his belly. Faster and faster and faster the little wheels turned. I felt the wings begin to take the load. Back on the yoke. The nose came up about 5 degrees. Faster and faster we rolled. I held the bird down until I saw 90 knots, made a quick pull on the yoke, and the machine sprang into the air. Clear of the PSP, positive rate of climb, up with the handle for the gear. The gull-winged doors opened behind me on the sides and the main gears tucked back, the doors snapping shut. Three green lights. Then all were out. We were on our way.

I flicked the UHF radio dial. "Invert Control, Nail 31, airborne NKP, leading a flight of Hobos."

Invert shot back, "Good morning, Nail 31, we have a contact, turn right to a heading of three-four-zero degrees and climb to angels five."

I acknowledged. The *Little Major* hummed along seeming to grow peppier as we climbed. I flipped open the side window, leaned back, took out a Camel, and lit up, watching the smoky haze grow thicker ahead of me. Rice straw burnoff was what it really was. The Mekong was off to the right, a brown ribbon of slick quiet water. Sandbars were lined with black dots that were really water buffalo. A long, engine-powered boat with a big wake was chugging its way down the center of the river.

"Sweeny," I said, "take a look at that. Good target, huh?"

He had his seat pushed way back. "Yeah, maj, why don't we go for a shot?"

"Naww, that one is friendly," I replied. "I guess." You never knew who was friendly and who wasn't until they shot at you.

The Hobos were airborne behind me. I could hear them talking to Invert. They had the power and speed on me. I glanced over to the left and spotted all four in their climb, outclimbing and out-distancing me and coming up fast. They were brown against the green of the trees along the river. The sun sparkled on their canopies.

"Hobos coming up on the left," I told Sweeny.

"Got 'em," he answered, leaning forward and craning his neck. His helmet looked too tight for him. At 5,000, I let the bird accelerate to 110 knots, before pulling the throttles back slowly, adjusting them and the EGT gauges, then the mixtures, and then the props. I readjusted the throttles once more to get optimum EGT difference. Laos and its gray karst mountains were coming up ahead.

The Hobos out-climbed me and began to circle slowly overhead to stay with us. I felt good, knowing that they were there with their immense firepower in reserve if we needed it. These A-1 pilots were good. I knew that. I knew each one of them. More than once we had bent our elbows together at the club with drinks and cried in our beer, counting the days until "wake up." That is the way we counted for going home: "fifty-one and a wake up" meant fifty-two calendar days until departure for the States. You could tell how long a guy had to go by simply looking at his hat. Everyone had markings on their cap like they were keeping score at a tic-tac-toe game. All the markings were clusters of four little marks with a fifth mark drawn diagonal through the four. Old timers, also known as short timers, had rows and rows of marks on their hats. These four Hobo pilots had a lot of marks among them.

I settled back again in the seat and felt comfortable with the crew I saw circling overhead—all tough-stuff, all seasoned by many dives onto The Trail dropping Dragon's Teeth and gravel mines, all seasoned by terrifying dive bombing runs on The Trail in the black of night. I felt confident with these guys circling me.

We had a little time to kill before rendezvous. I continued on up the Mekong on the Lao side of the river, leading my force. Don Don Island and Ban Natat fell behind us. I felt it would be a good idea to come in from the northwest, over the karst at Pha Kabok and hold over the mountain top at Pha Nangdoy with the Hobos. That would put us within an easy dive distance onto any problem that might pop at Ban Louang. Nail 33 was airborne. He had gone on ahead of us to intercept Bobcat One and Two. We could hear him talking off and on. The UHF, HF, and FM radios were all checked out at altitude, likewise the single sideband. We knew a lot of big people would be listening to this fiasco. Smokey checked in, then Blue Chip. Blue Chip was Saigon—a *long* way away. Smokey was an airborne

C-130 command post controlling activities and strikes within Cricket West operations and was somewhere nearby at 30,000 feet overhead. Invert, the NKP radar post, had us in sight at all times.

"I'm gonna crawl over in the back, maj," Sweeny said to me, "and get my stuff ready." His "stuff" as he called it was his grenades and the deadly-looking M60.

"Okay," I said. "But be careful, okay?"

He nodded. Actually, there was no need for me to be so concerned with him. He was a real veteran. The NVA called him "Mad Dog." He had a price on his head, too, a big one. He had been on the ground in North Vietnam more than one time. He, like all the 5th Special Forces people, were experts at what they do best—killing people. Everyone of them had a "trade" as we called it. Some were knife men; some were explosive experts; most were experts at something that had to do with hurting the other side. I was positively glad they were on my side.

Sweeny and one other soldier had once shadowed some 200 NVA regulars all day in North Vietnam on a "little mission." They waited until the NVA settled down at dusk to begin their cooking fires and then waded in on them with grenades and automatic weapons. While Sweeny and his compadre made a good dent in the size of the force, two men against 200 was a bit one-sided. After the initial surprise of Sweeny's attack, it didn't take the NVA long to get their shit together and come along in hot pursuit. Sweeny and his buddy got pinned against a karst cliff and began hollering loudly on their radio for help. The black of night was the only thing that saved them. Sending in Hueys to pluck the pair from the very hands of the riled NVA was not anyone's idea of fun, not in the inky murk of the North Vietnamese river valley where they were holed up.

Clack! I heard the cold rattle of metal behind me. Turning my head, I saw Sweeny had put a belt of ammo into the M60. He had laid out the extra belts in a neat little row one on top of the other. His grenade tubes were stacked in a pile back under the radio rack. Though I did not tell him so, I was frankly glad to have him with me. I knew that if we had to smash the bird onto the ground and had to walk away, Sweeny and his personal arsenal would come in mighty handy. Neither of us might survive in the end, but somebody would be hurting real bad before we cashed in our chips. Neither of us wanted to be taken alive. We had hurt them too bad, too often. They knew us. The PL used to call in the blind: "Mad Dog, we know you there."

The hands crawled around on the black face of the issue watch. The old, dirty, sweat-stained nylon band on it was wet again, as it always was from the sweat that crept out from under my kid leather flight gloves. Suddenly, I heard it. The call. Loud and clear. Bobcat Leader was checking in.

"Nail 33, this is Bobcat One, over."

A chill ran up my spine. This was it.

Then I heard the reply: "Bobcat One, this is Nail 33, over."

I shivered. It was 90 degrees outside the window, yet I shivered with excitement. The two Lycoming engines in the O-2 were growling loudly. Wind was whistling in the little side window to my left. Sweeny looked at me. Our eyes met for an instant. It was time for us to earn our pay. We both knew the time was at hand. Like the professional he was, Sweeny went back to his weapons. If I needed him on the radio, I knew he'd be back over in the front seat in a flash. He was that kind of a guy—joking and seemingly carefree, but when things turned sour, he was all business.

"Heads up, Sweeny," I said. "We gotta open the store."

He nodded. I swung the *Little Major* over in a tight right bank and picked up the 20-mile arc of Channel 99, following it back to the 050 radial. I looked up at the white, oil-streaked bellies of the Skyraiders circling overhead, like cruising sharks in the sea.

"Push 'em up, Hobo 24 flight," I said. "Set 'em up."

"Rog, 31," he replied nonchalantly. But I knew their hearts were racing a mile a minute, just like mine.

Hobo 24 lead cut in, "Got the Bobcats in sight, 31, bearing three-five-zero, high."

I squinted up through the roof of the bird. There they were. God, they were big, like huge green grasshoppers whirling along, one stacked up behind the other, their long refueling probes sticking out like snouts. I could see the rotors spinning like spokes on a wagon wheel. Seeming to turn backwards, then forward again. Nail 33 was at the rendezvous point. He was talking his choppers down, coaxing them. We did not know where they had come from, but we guessed Udorn Royal Thai Air Force Base.

I held my A-1s out to the west a little, giving Nail 33 time to get his Bobcats down, reassuring them. He was circling tightly over the rendezvous point. The white topside of the O-2's wings was glistening in the early morning sun. The CH-53s were slowly settling in on him, falling in behind his bird. He made his call to Blue Chip.

"The jig is up," he said. "The game is on, Blue Chip."

A pause in the transmission.

"Copy, Nail 33. The umpire requests a score when you play your game, over."

"Roger," said 33.

Nail 33 made his turn back toward the northwest and started his descent for the Houay Naphong Valley. We watched them descend right on down, heading for the grass tops and the cover behind the Ban Viang hill.

"Chop, chop, Hobo 24," I called. "Follow me over to the Pha Nangdoy karst."

No acknowledgement. Instead, the four A-1s pulled in over me, tight. We wanted to keep the radio chatter down to a minimum.

"Hobo 24 flight, go tactical freq," I called.

"Roger, 31."

I whirled the UHF dial, the HF, too.

"Hobo 24 flight, check in," I said.

The call back was crisp and clear. We circled, like a flight of buzzards eyeing a meal below. We hoped we would not be needed. I dropped the *Little Major* down to 2,500 feet so I could get a better look at the happenings without having to use the binoculars. I did not want them in my way.

"Initial point," I heard Nail 33 say. "Beginning the run."

I had a lump in my throat, a dry taste in my mouth. Far below I could see the white wingtops of 33. He was skimming along the deck, leading the show. Bobcat One and Two were just behind him, in trail. I inched the *Major* closer to the area, straining hard to see better. The birds below me banked sharply to the right as they came into the clear from behind the hill. Then Nail 33 was up and over Ban Louang, starting his circle to altitude to control them and give radio cover. The Bobcats went in straight, both settling down in a huge cloud of orange dust that their rotors kicked up. Then I heard it, what we didn't want—

"We are taking fire, we are taking fire," Bobcat One was calling.

Nail 33 asked, "You copy, 31?"

"31 copies, 33. Give me a clock position," I replied.

"Right out of Ban Viang, 31. Give us some help."

"I'm on my way, buddy," I yelled.

Ban Viang was an easy shot.

"Get set, Hobo 24 flight. Hit my smoke. Nail 31 is in hot," I hollered.

I yanked the *Little Major* over in a steep dive and made a run for the center of Ban Viang. Wing rockets were set for a pair of Willie Petes. I saw Sweeny open the door window on his side and stick the M60 out. The thatch huts were growing bigger in the yellow rings of the gunsight. I picked one big hooch and punched the shoot button—both rockets whooshed away in their corkscrew pattern. From 2,500 feet to less than 1,000 happened in the blink of eye almost. Then I was pulling back on the yoke, hard, right into my gut, and stomping right rudder. We went over the big hooch just as the pair of rockets exploded. Some guy in a green uniform came running out the front door. Sweeny was in an excellent position for him to fire. The bird was up on its right side in a steep bank.

The big M60 began thundering in my ears. Spent brass was flying out the side of it. Sweeny was up on his knees, hosing the running guy. I saw him fall.

I hollered, "For Christ's sake! Don't shoot the goddamned struts off, Sweeny."

He didn't hear me. I saw green tracers go past my window and over the nose. I kept The Little Major in its shuddering tight bank and moved out of the way for the A-1s. I heard Lead call in. His 500-pounders were shaking the Plexiglas windows in the *Major* as the bombs burst below. We were that low.

The radios became a wild melee of yelling and chatter. From what I could hear, Bobcat One had taken hits and was overheating. His troops were out and running into the near hooches in Ban Louang. Bobcat Two was hit with small arms also. NVA troops were in the edge of that village. Nail 33 was hollering at me to give him covering fire. I cranked the *Major* over in a streaking run for the edge of the village, centering a low building on the yellow pipper.

"Hit my smoke, Hobo 25," I called.

Sweeny was yelling, "There's one of those son-of-a-bitches on the roof!"

A figure was standing on the roof aiming a weapon. I could see his tracers coming up the gunsight as he fired at us. The 60 was thundering again. The cockpit reeked of burned gunpowder. Sweeny's orange tracers laced around all over the roof. I heard the *whumps* on the *Major* like somebody was outside with a hammer. The guy on the roof fell, dropped his weapon, and rolled off over the edge of the roof. The pair of Willie Pete rockets flashed and exploded right at the base of the wall of the building. I pulled back hard. We went up and over the building. The guy that had been on the roof was a heap on the ground.

"31's hit," I called. "31's hit."

The M60 was still roaring in my ears. Its ejected brass was a steady stream, going out the window, flying back against the radio rack.

"Pull up, Bobcat One," I heard Nail 33 yelling. "Pull up. Don't hover there. See if some flight will cool you down. . . . Hobo 26 is in, 31."

Then the whole world began to explode as he salvoed his wing loads of 500 pounders off to the side of the village and onto the hooch where my rockets had hit. I quickly scanned all of the engine gauges. We were running okay. I came back around for another run. I was now the low bird; 33 was top cover. I didn't have the time nor power to take the bird back to altitude. We had to stay where we were.

Then I heard the ground commander calling Nail 33. "There is no one here, 33. The team is gone."

My heart sank. We all knew what that meant: no POWs. They had been moved in the night.

Hobo 24 and 25 were yelling. "We are taking Zepe fire, 31. We are taking Zepe fire."

That meant .60-cal heavy caliber machine-gun fire.

"Strike at will, Hobo 24 and 25," I told him.

Figures were running across the ground in front of us. I saw tiger stripes—they were friendly. The team was running back to Bobcat Two. One man fell, rolling on the ground, and then was still. Another began dragging him to the chopper. I saw little spurts of dust among the figures as they were running—bullet strikes. Orange flashes were coming from a ditch just outside of the village. The Major was low, less than 1,000 feet. I cranked it around, hard, dropped the nose, and stitched a line of 2.75-inch rockets through the ditch. The 60 was stuttering again. We flashed over the ditch. Four figures in green uniforms were stretched out on their bellies and sides motionless.

Sweeny was peeking over the side, yelling out the window, "You bastards won't do that again soon." He shook his fist.

Smoke was pouring from the burning thatch hooches. Some of it was white; some of it was black. The Hobos were working the damn place over but good. There was a series of flashes and explosions at Ban Viang.

I heard one Hobo yell, "We got the gun, we got the gun."

Nail 33 was coaching his Bobcats back to life and altitude. Bobcat One was trailing smoke lightly. Bobcat Two was calling he had daylight showing through the sides of the bird. "Full of holes," he said. Our bird was running okay, but we did not know how much damage we had taken. It looked like the show was over.

I punched the mike and told the Hobos, "Head 'em up, Hobo. Head 'em up, the game is over."

"Rog, 31."

I could see the Bobcats climbing away from the smoke with 33 leading, all heading west.

Sweeny was talking, "Well, goddamn, maj, I'm butt deep in cases back here," he was.

"Okay, put that thing away. Clear it," I told him.

"Gotcha, maj," he said slowly.

The front engine stuttered a little, shook, coughed.

"You hear that, maj?" he said, his eyes big, looking straight ahead.

"Put that shit away, Sweeny, and get up here," I told him. I did not have to tell him twice. Suddenly, he was sitting right beside me, listening very intently.

The engine coughed again and began to lose power. Revs were going up despite power loss. It looked like a runaway prop.

"We got a problem, Sweet, ol' boy," I told him.

"No shit, maj," he remarked solemnly.

"Nail 31, this is Nail 33, over," came a call.

"Go ahead, 33, this is Nail 31." I answered.

"You got a problem, buddy?" he asked. "I see you are trailing a little white smoke, okay?"

"Uh, that's a roger, 33. Nail 31 has failing power on number one engine. Suggest you call the umpire and report the game status. We are still flying. I don't think it is necessary to alert Jolly, over."

The answer was slow and questioning. "Roger, 31, understand. But we will shadow you until you are back across the fence, over." Jolly was the boys in the SAR unit with the rescue chopper, which we affectionately called the Jolly Green Giant.

The Hobos had cleared the area. All were safe. The Bobcats were making it to Channel 99 to nurse their wounds and rest. It seemed I was the only casualty in the aircraft force with a questionable future. Even though the Bobcats had taken hits, they were already back across the fence, the Mekong, and were starting on their approach to the field. Number one engine was now running rough.

Sweeny was sticking his helmeted head out the side window, looking. Then he was back in, looking at me, saying, "We got a few holes out there, maj. Pulling a nice white trail, okay?"

"Well, shit, Sweeny. We are still flying, aren't we? No sweat ol' buddy." I did not want to worry him unduly—I knew he just might jump the hell out on me. One Green Beret had almost done that to me once and we were not even hit, just thumped around a bit by some exploding 57mms. I did not want Sweeny having to walk back. I was fond of him and didn't want to lose him.

The *Little Major* was plowing along gallantly, but airspeed was only some 90 knots, about 20 knots lower than what it should have been. But we were still in the air, and we were making headway. The muddy Mekong slid slowly under the wings.

I thumbed the mike. "NKP tower, this is Nail 31, over."

"Roger, Nail 31, we have you in sight to the east. Your winds are 260 degrees at 10 knots. You are cleared to land. Do you require assistance, over?"

"Ah, NKP tower, that is a roger. 31 requests that you alert crash. 31 requests a straight-in approach. 31 will make a full stop landing on the active and vacate the aircraft. Request you advise Nail operations, over." I jettisoned the rocket pods, then briefed Sweeny. "As soon as we touch down, I'll cut both engines, throw the switches. You get the hell out, okay?"

He nodded. The end of the runway was coming up. I waited, kept the gear up, let down about half flaps. The bird shuddered some. When the end of the runway went under us, I threw down the gear handle and pushed the rear engine power up, reducing the front one a little. When I did, the damn engine quit cold. I snatched it to feather. It didn't go. We staggered in like a crippled duck. Just before the main gears touched, I pulled the rear engine throttle back to idle. The *Major* thudded to the PSP runway and rolled along bumpily. The front tire was flat, too. I got on the binders and cut both throttles off, threw all switches to their off positions, and jumped out.

Sweeny was gone. He was 100 yards ahead. I was right behind him, running hard. There he stood, out in the grass. I came huffing up to him carrying about 30 pounds of flight gear on me. He held out a pack of cigarettes to me, saying, in his usual, on the ground, carefree manner, "Well, maj, looks like we walked away from another one. Piece of cake, huh?"

I just looked at him with a withering smile and said, "Yeah, Sweeny, a piece of cake."

CHAPTER 13

Christening of a Night Fighter

The February night was as bright as I had ever seen. It was cold at 4,000 feet above The Trail, even for tropical Laos. Outside air temperature read 40 degrees. I had been hanging my head out the windowless right door of the O-2 for nearly an hour. I was chilled, and my right eye hurt from the strain of looking through the greenish-yellow glare of the Starlight scope.

I took a deep breath, leaned back in the right seat, snuggling deeper into my flight jacket, and lit up a Camel. "Head on up to Delta 35, Carl," I told my check pilot. "We'll work our way back down to the chokes and maybe pick up a straggler."

This was my last ride before being turned loose on the Ho Chi Minh Trail as a night forward air controller. It was a check ride. Carl Flemming, my instructor pilot, ruddered the ugly little black O-2 around, and pushed mixtures, props, and throttle forward. Like a great pregnant bat, we clawed for a few precious feet of altitude. Having just come "on station," the aircraft was heavy with fuel and a full load of ordnance.

When Cessna designed the twin-engined, twin-boomed aircraft, they called the Skymaster. I am sure they never dreamed it would be put to the supreme aerial test—combat. My confidence in the aircraft is limitless. The Air Force designated the Skymaster as the O-2 (observational aircraft, second model) and used it as a spotter airplane. At Nakhon Phanom, we had further modified the O-2A to suit a very special need of ours— the need for night forward air controlling and reconnaissance. A standard daylight O-2 had been modified by painting it a flat black color with blood-red numbers. The right window was removed so that a navigator could lean out over the side to scan the terrain below with a light-gathering scope. A floor mike had been installed on the navigator's side so that he could talk while using both hands to manipulate the bulky Starlight scope. Anticollision beacons had been covered with large metal cones so that the blinking red beacons could be seen only from above the O-2s. There were no country-of-origin markings.

While the daytime O-2 FAC aircraft were usually armed with only two pods of 2.75-inch smoke rockets, nighttime O-2s mostly carried only one pod of seven rockets. Also, the black night birds carried four air-burning parachute flares and two ground-burning wood and magnesium markers. The 2.75-inch smoke rockets were the Air Force's standard white phosphorous marking rockets. The air-burning flares were also standard type, set to ignite and burn with a blinding white light seconds after dropped from the aircraft. A small parachute allowed several minutes of illumination over the ground below before the flare either burned up its parachute and fell to the ground or burned itself out and floated lifelessly to the ground.

The ground-burning markers, which we called "logs," were actually a 6 x 6 x 18-inch wooden block with a magnesium core and igniter. The logs burned with a dull yellow glow for several hours on the ground. They looked like a campfire.

The stretch of The Trail we were patrolling ran from about the 085 degree radial of the Nakhon Phanom Tacan at 63 miles distance to the 100 degree radial at 70 miles, covering about a 15-mile stretch of the trail along the Nam Phanang River. We were hunting trucks. Any traffic we'd likely see would have to come through Mu Ghia Pass, 25 miles to the north, directly out of North Vietnam. Our section of the road led in a wiggly fashion toward that border.

It was a seemingly lifeless stretch. Not just one road passed through the sector, but a whole network of tracks, roads, and interconnecting trails—all for vehicular traffic. And it all led to Cambodia, far to the south. During daylight, a person had the impression he might be looking at a section of the moon. The areas along the roads had been bombed, naped, rocketed, and machine-gunned so much that there was mile after mile of craters, burned jungle, and dust. There had been villages along the Xe Bangfai River, the Se Bangfai, Nam Panang and Nam Ngo. But long ago the villagers had been used up by the invading North Vietnamese to build and repair the road network. The villages could still be seen, but Pathet Lao and NVA regulars used the villages and structures for refuge. Natives were gone. Few of the villages were intact. All had some damage. A great many had been burned down. The only way we pilots could strike a village was if we were taking ground fire and had seen vehicles go into it. Villages were a taboo to hit—normally. It galled the hell out of us, but there was always the chance there could be civilians in them. But even if there were, you could bet your bottom dollar they were not "innocent civilians." They'd kill you just as quick as an NVA soldier. Anyway, the political implications were too great and we were advised against hitting them—even though we knew the NVA and Pathet Lao were hiding men and equipment in them during the day and moving it at night.

Most activity along The Trail was under cover of darkness. A few workers were out fixing the roads during the day, a few antiaircraft gun crews were ready to fire, but mostly the men were sleeping, the trucks hidden, and supplies were stacked in the jungle. Night was the time for activity. It often looked like the Los Angeles freeway.

At just about dusk the first cooking fires would appear in villages. Some trucks would start moving slowly out of caves and others from truck parks deeper in the jungle. Antiaircraft guns would come to life, fully manned.

Night over the Lao jungle was an awful place. It was full of death. The ground below along the trails and roads was teeming with soldiers and hostile civilians. There were few lights to see until napalm fires and bomb fires started something burning. There was no horizon, just blackness, miles and miles of velvet blackness filled with airplane-smashing mountains and stinking jungle below. It was eerie. The night was so thick you often felt like you could reach out the window and grab a handful of it. For hours at a time there were only the lifeless red and green eyes of the instruments staring back at you and the low growl of the engines as you circled and circled and circled over The Trail. And then the night would retreat a little bit when the flash of a bomb went off below. Or a flare hung swaying on its chute, casting weird and dancing shadows onto canyon walls, spitting and spewing sparks, trailing a small thread of rancid white smoke along behind it.

The night could be a friend, too. It hid your flight. It telegraphed a shooting. Any spark of light in the inky gloom was instantly spotted. Neon-red strings of 37mm shells stood out as if etched on a painter's canvas. The dazzling white, winking lights on the sides of the karsts you knew, without a doubt, were heavy .60-caliber ZPUs. The speeding thin streaks of green and yellow you saw before your eyes were not fireflies, but hails of heavy-caliber machine-gun slugs tearing past.

Carl and I flew steadily on up to the beginning of our search area, Delta 35. It was merely a set of coordinates on a map. To us it meant the intersection of three roads. Vegetation was sparse here and any trucks moving would be easy to spot. Trucks were "movers" to us. Ordinarily, this particular spot—Delta 35—belonged to the flare-dropping C-123 flare ships out of NKP, called Candlestick. We had the area to ourselves tonight. Candlestick, as usual, was late getting on station.

As we swung through the intersection of D-35, I stuck the Starlight scope out the window and started scanning. Carl throttled back to 23 inches MP and 2,200 rpm and leaned the engines out. Since our navigators had to lean out the right side of the aircraft to look, we always made right-handed circles along our routes of patrol.

The green light field of the scope was filled with a clear picture of the road below. In fact, it was outstanding. There was good moonlight. I felt sure I could see anything that moved. On such a bright night, I knew the NVA would be driving minus headlights. This night was an exception to the usual inside-of-a-cat darkness.

"See anything?" Carl asked.

"Naaa, nothing," I said. "I can follow the main road all the way down to the white water crossing on the river."

I looked up and down the roads and trails as we circled. It was quiet. We hit the "Y" where the Xe Bangfai and Nam Phanang met and started south. About every two or three minutes, Carl would ask the same question, whether I saw anything.

Suddenly, I saw something. "I think I see a mover way down the road."

"Just one?" Carl asked.

"Yeah, just one. But that's good for openers. Swing around that karst behind us and cross the road at right angles so I can look up it."

Just south of the village of Ban Pakphanang, the main road ran fairly straight. Here I thought I'd seen a single vehicle driving without lights. It could have been a shadow on the road, but when we crossed the road, I was looking almost straight down. I had definitely seen a truck.

"Hey, Carl. I got a mover. Looks like a small truck of some sort."

"Okay, we'll see if we can get him. Which way is he going?"

"Down the road toward the boot." The boot was a lump of big rock. I twisted the radio to Channel 15 and thumbed the mike: "Alley Cat, Alley Cat, this is Nail 31."

"Nail 31, Alley Cat. Go ahead," came the reply from the C-121 orbiting high overhead.

"I have one mover headed south. Request ordinance."

"Ah, roger, 31, I have Nimrod 25. Where do you want him?"

"Send him to 090 at 62 miles of NKP," I replied.

Nimrod 25 was a A-26 bomber of World War II vintage. They flew out of Nakhon Phanom, the same as we Nail FACs did. The "Nims," as we affectionately called these fellow pilots in their vintage aircraft, were the best night-fighter pilots in Southeast Asia. They were the real dragon killers. When you wanted a night job done right, you called for the Nimrods. Why? Well, these guys were seasoned pilots, high timers, and all they ever flew were night missions. The morale of the crews of the A-26s was superb. Their aircraft were good. The A-26s had plenty of power for a reasonable getaway speed. They could stay on station in excess of four hours, and they carried a real shopping load of munitions to drop. The FAC could take his pick of what he wanted expended on pass after pass after pass on a truck convoy or a firing gun. A look at the wicked black and green A-26s was a look at death itself. With eight forward-firing .50-caliber machine guns, the 26s could stutter a hail of oblivion onto any vehicle. External wing racks could unload 750-, 500-, or 250-pound napalm bomb canisters, frag bombs, CBU canisters, or mines onto vehicles, guns, stores, or troops. From her slightly bulging belly, the old bastard bomber could drop the weapon all us night FACs loved—the funny bomb. Shaped like a hot water heater, it was effective, even though it was a hangover from World War II. The bombs ignited after leaving the plane's bomb bay; the log-shaped case split open and spewed boiling white-hot burning oxides and metal and phosphorous over an area as big as one football field. For dropping on vehicles and troops in the open, it was our favorite.

Because of the limited quantity of the funny bombs, we had agreed with the Nim pilots to use them only if we had six or more trucks in a close convoy or if troops were bunched up. The bomb had some bad traits, too. Both the Nim pilots and night Nails knew them. The bomb was useless if dropped from too high. The killing pattern would have holes in it. Wind played hell with it and could scatter the phosphorous. If used over thick jungle, it wouldn't stop a line of june bugs. The foliage would stop the phosphorus from reaching the ground. But catch a close-traveling truck convoy bumper to bumper in the open, and it was a disaster for them. Dropped from a proper height and speed along a road, the bomb went off with a blinding white light and created total destruction. The rectangular pattern it covered looked like the ground had turned to boiling lead.

The Nim reported in at the TACAN coordinates I had passed along. "Nail 31, Nimrod 25 on station, whatchagot for me?"

"Nim, ole boddy," I said, "I have a nice fat little staff vehicle of some kind. Wanna try for him?"

"You got anything else?" he questioned.

"No, Nim," I told him. "It has been a slow night and only the pros are driving tonight. We can follow this boy a ways and see what turns up."

"Na, let's have a go, Nail," he answered back. "My butt's killing me from sitting so long. I've been up here three hours with no action."

We had two kinds of truck drivers on the Ho Chi Minh Trail—the pro and the rookie. There was no in-between. The rookies would jump out of their trucks and take to their heels, leaving the trucks where they stopped with doors open—easy prey for us. On the other hand, the pro would drive like blazes when we got after him. He had learned that his best chance to stay alive, if caught on a road, was to make a run for it. A speeding truck on a jungle road is one hell of a target to hit at anytime, much less at night.

This guy was a pro. I watched him creeping along in the road shadows. When he came to an open moonlighted stretch, he really poured on the coal, but he gave an easy dust trail to follow. He didn't think about that. We played cat and mouse for 2 miles. I am sure he could hear our engines in the night sky above him.

"How you want to take him, Nail?" the Nim asked.

"Well, he's coming up on a good crossroads soon," I told the circling A-26. "I'll go on ahead and drop a single ground-burning mark, then talk you into position for a strike with CBUs."

We had no ground fires at all. I knew the small light put off by the log flare would be ideal for the Nim pilot to spot. I could run him east to west, and a single drop of CBU would likely destroy the truck. The CBUs were deadly if used right. The canisters the CBUs were carried in had numerous tubes packed with round, softball-sized, whirling, finned bomblets. The individual bomblets would fall like hail around the target and explode, sending thousands of small steel ball bearings tearing through men, machine, and jungle. I knew I couldn't be guaranteed a fire, but if I could stop that truck in the right place, I'd attract road workers and soldiers who would have to move it and pick up the dead. If I were lucky, I just might get a couple of other trucks stopped until the mess was cleaned up. Then we'd get them, too.

The Nim blew my idea. "Hey, 31!" he called. "I got a plan."

"Okay, tell me, Nim," I replied.

"Well, I can see the main road. If you can talk me in on him, I'll machine-gun the bastard!"

I looked over at Carl. His eyes were shining wickedly, and he was grinning from ear to ear. I suppose the dull glow from the dimly lit instrument panel made me look as weird and sinister, too. Here we were about the kill the enemy, and we were actually ready and willing to go—and we enjoyed it. We had been in Southeast Asia too long. But that is what we got paid for. That is why he and I sat there together in that cramped little airplane, half a world away from our families and friends and country. With thirty years of professional service and 8,000 hours of flying time between us, we had come to fight. We meant to kill or stop every enemy soldier, truck driver, gunner, road worker, or vehicle we could. Every truck we stopped here, in mid-Laos, meant fewer men and supplies, less equipment, that would reach Cambodia and South Vietnam to be used against our soldiers.

"Head down the road," I told Carl. "Keep me right over the road and give me a 30-degree right bank turn when I ask you, okay?" I then began briefing the Nim: "Nimrod 25, this is Nail 31. Your target is the one vehicle. He's headed south toward Delta 57 at about 4 knots. Your road runs north-south generally; the terrain is 528 feet at target strike point. Highest terrain in a 4 klick area, to the east, is 2,040 feet; northwest is 2 klicks at 2007 feet. You have heavy troop concentrations all along the main trail. There are many known 37mm and ZPU antiaircraft guns in the immediate area. None have fired tonight. Your best area, if hit, is due west at least 10 miles. Your run-in winds are 140 at 10 knots, your FAC is at 4,000 feet. Suggest you run from south to north, below me, and pull off west."

"Gotcha, Nail!"

"You have my beacon in sight, Nimrod 25?" I asked. He said he did. "Good, then can you see the straight stretch of main road coming south? It makes a 15-degree left turn and is a straight segment for about 1 klick, then makes another slight left bend?"

"Roger, Nail, I have it," he replied.

"Okay, Nim, get on your downwind leg; he's coming into the first turn in about two minutes."

"Ready, Nail!"

"Okay, Nim, turn crosswind; in one minute he'll be coming out of the turn—ready, ready, 30 sec, Nim. He's in the middle of the road; he's coming in, Nim—now! Start your run!" I yelled.

"I'm in hot, Nail!" he yelled back.

I couldn't see the howling A-26 swooping like a killer hawk on a mouse, but I could see hundreds of tiny, winking diamond flashes walking up the road to the truck. The high-explosive incendiary hail of .50-caliber slugs were plowing up the road. The truck driver saw them as well—but too late. White spots spattered all around the truck. Then like a shadow, I saw the A-26 flash through the view of my Starlight scope.

Before I could call any instructions, the Nimrod informed me he had seen the truck and was coming back for a reverse run. Again the .50-caliber slugs went marching down the road. I had the truck in sight. The slugs danced all over it. The Nimrod was calling off target, going "high and dry."

"You got him, Nim! You got him!" I called. "He's starting to burn."

The small truck lay dead in the road. I could sort of imagine what two strafing passes had done to it—low, fast, and close in on it. A yellow glow had started on the truck's right side—from spilled gas, I was sure. Then the yellow turned orange and black smoke started to roll—oil and gas fire—and soon, the truck was a glowing red ball of fire and smoke. Scratch one mover.

We continued to work our section of The Trail until well past 2100. Nothing was moving. We hadn't expected much. Moonlight nights are not the best for killing trucks. Charlie wasn't stupid. He knew we could see too well. Dawn and dusk and on the darkest of nights were when the trucks moved. Carl was satisfied with my progress and ended my night check-out. He and I laboriously shucked our parachutes and switched seats. I had to get us home, which was more than forty minutes away, due west out of Laos.

I got all settled into the left seat, pushed the mixtures full rich, full increase on the props, full throttles, and inched the ugly old Skymaster up to 5,000 feet. As a parting salute to the sixteen antiaircraft sites at Delta-18 and on the Pistol Karst, I swung the bird over on her side in a tight circle and triggered the whole rack of air burning flares. Then, a little back pressure on the yoke, and we clawed for altitude. The airspeed went from 100 to 90 to 80 to 70—we were hanging on the props. The flares went off with a brilliant glare. The Pistol Karst came into view. I ruddered hard to the left, twisted the controls over and roared in on a long dive at the side of the gun-invested piece of rock. As the pipper in the illuminated gunsight settled down, I squeezed a rocket off. The *whoosh* of the rocket going off 10 feet from my left ear was startling. Sparks fluttered around the windshield.

"They're shooting! They're shooting!" Carl was hollering. He was delighted. "To the right! To the right!"

"Yeah, I see him," I drawled.

A little right rudder and the yellow pipper slid right. I punched the red button under my right forefinger—a rocket away. The wink, wink, wink below wasn't fireflies. Down with the finger again. Little green and blue streaks were floating up at me through the gunsight. The Willie Pete rockets were spattering all over the side of the karst with great billowing belches of fire. Twin muzzles of a ZPU were really spitting at us. A twin stream of burning red beer cans floated up at us from farther right. Each string had seven neon-red cans in it. A 37mm antiaircraft gun had opened up on us.

I had had enough. I pulled the yoke back in my gut, twisted right aileron in, and squeezed out the rest of the rocket pod at the 37mm. The shells were still headed our way. I watched the evenly spaced glowing "beer cans" floating up at us as if in slow motion, knowing full well each one was death for us if we were hit by one. I turned the yoke left, pushed forward on the stick, kicked bottom rudder, and slid the dirty old bird down to the left—letting her fall sideways. The 37mm shells started going out. Then in seconds came their explosions. Each of the fourteen shells began exploding behind us, to our right—bushel-basket-sized puffs of white smoke with brilliant orange bursts and thousands of little sparks shooting off in all directions.

"Kind of slow tonight," my instructor said, matter of factly, as we headed home. Then he snuggled down in his flight jacket and said, "Wake me up when we turn on final. You are cleared to be a night fighter. I'll brief the head nav and you will be scheduled every night from now on to fly with us."

I smiled and replied, "Gee, thanks, boss." But inside, I knew that unless Carl cleared me to be a night FAC, I would not be flying in the night 23rd FAC program. Carl was "Mr. Night FAC Instructor." That was his sole job and as a high-flying-time major with 1,000 hours on The Trail at night, in two back-to-back tours. He was Mr. Perfection and would accept nothing but safe and precise control of all situations by the night FACs of the 23rd. Night forward air controlling on The Trail was a very, very dangerous job. The quantity of antiaircraft guns stationed along the main stretches of the Ho Chi Minh Trail was unbelievable, like twenty to thirty to the mile in places. They were mostly 37mm guns.

Night FACing on The Trail was high adventure in itself. Some people claimed that it was insanity, that we were all crazy men. The pilots and navs had great confidence in each other and were professional killers of the enemy. Time and time again, as we would climb out from NKP, then cross the Mekong and head for The Trail, we could spot sixty to eighty strings of 37mm red-orange shell strings in the air from 25 miles away. We had losses. Although I checked out in February as a night FAC, I alternated with day missions through March, after which I flew only nights on The Trail until my last mission on June 22, 1969.

CHAPTER 14

A Finale

Intelligence had not warned us that there could be NVA helicopters in Steel Tiger. They seemed to be turning up more frequently these days, and I seemed to be the only one finding any. It was like there was some sort of a voodoo curse pinned upon me, the Curse of the Vanishing Helicopters. No one else saw them. It was eerie. Intelligence was starting to look at me real funny.

Take the case of the Russian flying crane. There were no Russian aircraft, including helicopters, in Laos—or so Intelligence claimed. However, the big light-gray Russian Mi-8/17 Hip helicopter I saw sitting on the ground at Ban LaBoy Ford late one afternoon was not a figment of my imagination. The only problem was that I was solo when I encountered it. It was late in the afternoon, almost dusk, as I came wheeling and diving and jinking along. I had been over near Bat Lake Road up on the North Vietnamese border near the DMZ. We had had a Prairie Fire team—eight Cambodians with one GI leading them—on the ground there for fourteen days. The monsoon rains had been heavy, and we hadn't been able to get the team out on time. Therefore, we had been making drops everyday— food, candy, cigarettes, *Playboy* magazines, the works.

Coming back from one of these drop missions, I happened to swing by Ban LaBoy Ford. There it sat, right out in the open. A helicopter? For a second I thought I was seeing a mirage. I made a wide swing around to the north and slipped in behind a little cloud cover. Like a jack-in-the-box, I popped out from behind a layer of clouds, took a quick look with the 20-power binoculars, and ducked back into the clouds before someone on the ground saw me. The huge gray machine was just sitting there, with its rotor whirling at idle. Two large six-by-six trucks were backed up to the side of it, either loading or unloading something, probably medicine, food, and ammunition.

Thinking I could catch myself a big helicopter like a sitting duck, I called for air support. Invert wouldn't give me any fighters. Instead, the controller said he had to check with Blue Chip—that is, Saigon—since shooting at helicopters in Laos was a no-no. Then he started querying me: What is the helicopter doing? What does it look like? Is it friendly? What color is it? This question-and-answer crap went back and forth for at least fifteen minutes while I circled the area. The light was fading with each passing minute. I toyed with the idea of making a rocket pass myself, but my better judgment ruled that out. It would've been a death plunge. Ban LaBoy Ford was a bad place, with lots of guns. I might have slipped in and fired a couple rockets, but there's no way I could have gotten away. Instead, I kept begging Invert to send me some fighters to dump on this guy. I still couldn't get anything, even though I kept telling Invert that the chopper was Russian—not NVA, not Chinese, not ours. It was unfriendly. Finally, it became too dark for me to see anything, and I had to leave.

On another occasion, early one morning, Sergeant Sweeny and I were coming back from Xom Khe, North Vietnam. We had been over into the Rao Nay River valley to check on a clandestine operative we had dropped a few days earlier. Coming back, we popped up over the ridge between Laos and North Vietnam at Phou Katang and caught a white H-19 helicopter sitting on top of the ridge like a roosting turkey. A pilot on the left side stared at me. He was Caucasian, wearing green glasses, a bush jacket, and a headset. I don't know whether we or he were more surprised, but I came out of the valley with the throttles against the stop, trying to get over the ridge as fast as I could, away from Vietnam, keeping to the brush and cover as closely as I could. There were MiG 21s in the area, and we weren't sure whether the NVA radar had picked us up or not. I turned back to get one more look, and in those few seconds, the helicopter was in the air and heading down the valley on the Lao side of the border. Once again, I tried to get Invert to send me fighters. When I described the machine, I was told to "Forget you saw that object, Nail 31."

＊＋ ⊠◊⊠ ＋＊

One of my "chores" late in my tour in Laos in 1969 was to check out the new navigators as they came into the squadron. By June 1969 the war was going to hell as far as we were concerned. The paperwork was beginning to catch up. There were always more and more reports to fill out and more flying safety meetings to attend.

There was even time to give pilots "check rides" to see if they measured up to Air Force standards. That really just galled the hell out of us old timers in the squadron. We had been around for a year and flown through the thick and thin of it all, and for us to have to be evaluated on procedures by a young upstart of a pilot who hadn't flown any real combat rides in Laos was galling. One such pilot told me I was "pressing too close" to the target for safety and should have fired my marking rockets from 5,000 feet rather than 2,500.

I just looked at him and said, "Captain, if you don't like the way I am flying this airplane, fail me so I can get the hell out of here. I have been doing this for a year. It is impossible to get a Willie Pete rocket on the ground within 50 meters of the target from 5,000 feet. And 50 meters is the maximum amount of error we are allowed to make when we are marking for these sensor runs. If you can hit a 50-meter bulls-eye from 5,000 feet, here, I'll get out of the seat and you do it, okay?"

He shut his mouth. A rocket range was even dreamed up by our new ops officer on the Thai Mekong side. We called them "strap hangers," all the support staff that were beginning to overrun us at NKP and dream up all these self-justifying, job-justifying things to do. Our rocket range officer crossed the Mekong only twice a month—to get his combat pay. By June

1969 we were having more and more young pilots and navigators come into the squadron. When I first arrived in the 23rd
TASS in mid 1968, most of the pilots were at least of the rank
of major, along with a few lieutenant colonels.

With five new navigators in the squadron itching for action,
it was my job as an instructor pilot in the squadron, with the
night experience to back me up, to check these guys out, to
make them "combat ready" so they could go out on The Trail.
It was my standard procedure to take these new night navigators just across the river into Laos and work them along the
main road where they had some lights to see by. The possibility
of getting our butts blown out of the sky on a training mission
was low to nil. Usually, I would take off when it became real
dark, about nine o'clock, fly across the Mekong at the village of
Thakhek, and let the new navigator look at the town with his
Starlight scope. I'd let him see the bright lights of the town,
then begin to work farther and farther into the interior with
fewer and fewer lights to see. Gradually, as each of the new
guys became more and more experienced, I would take them
farther afield, out into the real black of Laos, but still not on
The Trail yet.

In early June 1969, two weeks before I was to rotate back to
the States, I had been training a young navigator by the name
of Capt. Earl Summers. Earl was an eager and capable young
officer, sharp and alert. He and I had made three missions
across the Mekong in his training for Trail life. Most people
had never even heard of a Starlight scope, much less used one,
and Earl was no exception. It required hours of use to get
acquainted with it and even more hours to be able to interpret
what you were looking at, especially if the light was really dim
or the night totally black. Earl had picked up the weird charac-
teristics of the scope immediately. We had "killed" countless
vehicles along Lao Routes 13 and 136, next to the Mekong.

As we worked farther inland, we even flushed a helicopter on
two consecutive nights over by the village of Mahaxai. Mahaxai
was no pansy of a place for sure. It was the hangout for an NVA
regiment. The only problem was, they were playing it cool and

not giving us FACs any trouble. As long as they didn't shoot at us, we had to leave them alone; they knew it, and we knew it. I figured the helicopter meant the NVA in Mahaxai had something big in the works.

Earl had seen the choppers take off from about the same place each night—the "Doughnut" Karst, as we called it, which was a pile of volcanic rocks that looked just like a doughnut from the air. We had been working slowly east out of Maxhaxi, following Route 121 out to the intersection of Route 126, and then swinging back west to work along the Bangfai River, following it up to Route 120. On this particular night, as we came abreast of the Doughnut Karst, I dropped a ground-burning log flare to give Earl something to look at through his scope. I then circled off to the east to let it start to burn hot. When we came back over the Doughnut Karst, the flare was gone.

"That's odd," I said. "The log should be burning. Take a look with your scope."

He did and reported nothing but black below.

"Hmm, let's try a flare then and see what's going on," I said. I tripped off a parachute flare. It popped, the chute opened, and the flare began to burn with its eerie yellow glow, swinging back and forth as it descended. It was trailing its usual line of sparks and melting flare case.

Earl was looking at the ground with the scope and suddenly exclaimed, "There goes one!"

Taken by surprise, I asked, "One what?"

"A helicopter!" he shouted, with his head sticking out the window on his side.

"What?"

"Yep, there he goes."

I was going to try to get this guy if I could. "Give me a verbal turn instruction," I told Earl.

"Turn right," he replied. "I'll tell you when to roll out."

"What's he look like?" I asked him.

"Can't tell for sure. Can't make out anybody, only the rotor in the moonlight. Turn right more. Now roll out," he instructed me.

I was doing precisely what the man was telling me.

"He's headed for the karst again," he said. "Turn right again."

I did. This went on for ten minutes. Then the chopper was right back to where it had come from.

"Let's drop another log," I told Earl.

"Okay," he answered, still peering out the window with his scope. This boy was doing well. The log fell and ignited. We made a big circle and came back. We could see the flare. Suddenly, it was gone.

"Earl," I said, "I think somebody is down there putting our flares out. Let's drop another parachute flare." We did.

No sooner had the flare begun to burn than Earl was hollering, "There he goes again! And we are taking ground fire! I can see muzzle flashes in the scope."

"Gimme directions, Earl, and we will see if we can get a shot at this guy, okay?" I told him.

"Roger, I gotcha, turn left. Roll out now. Turn right."

While he was instructing me, I was on the horn to Invert telling Invert Control what we had.

"Are you taking ground fire?" Invert asked.

"Affirmative, affirmative," I was telling him.

"Turn right. Roll out now," Earl was saying, in a calm voice. "He's making it for Maxhaxi," my young nav was telling me.

Then, as if someone had flashed a light, I caught the gleam of the whirling rotor on the helicopter. Instantly, I flipped the rocket fire buttons to the fire position and rolled in on the scampering helicopter from 4,000 feet. I did not have time to alert Earl to what I was doing. The *whoosh, whoosh* of the twin-fired rockets caught him completely by surprise. He snapped up off the scope like a ground squirrel looking out of its den.

"Sorry, old boy," I told him. "There he goes." I whipped The Restless One over in a quick turn, leveled out, and popped at the dodging, darting helicopter again. He got the message when the first pair of rockets passed him on the right side. Both of them were misses on him. While I still had him visually in the gun sight, I gave him a fourth rocket. I saw it streak past the chopper on the left side. The chopper whipped over to the right. I whipped with him, popping a fifth rocket at him—another miss. I could not get this boy to stand still long enough for me to center him in the pipper.

"Altitude," Earl yelled.

I looked. I was down to 2,000 and still dropping, twisting and turning with this guy. "He's trying to sucker us into the karst there by Mahaxai," I told Earl.

The chopper was straight away now, and streaking for the deck. I gave him a sixth and seventh rocket, with the both of them behind and a little high. Then he was gone, swallowed by the night, and we were rocketless.

"Well," I told Earl, "that was our chance to be a hero. One NVA helicopter shot down by one Nail FAC at night. Some headline, huh?"

"I guess so," he replied.

We swung around. I pushed the power up and we climbed back up to our 4,000 feet of working altitude. Then I told Earl, "Let's go on back to the Doughnut Karst and see what we see, okay?"

"Yeah, sure," he answered, beginning to look outside again. About halfway back to the karst I heard him yell, "By God! There he is again. He's headed straight back to the karst."

"Watch him," I said, "let me know what he does."

"He just landed!" my nav exclaimed loudly.

"Nail 31, this is Invert, over," came a crisp voice in the helmet. "You still got that chopper, 31?" the voice asked.

"That is a roger, Invert," I told him.

"Uh, 31, then I have a Nimrod 25 coming to you. He is just taking off at NKP and should be with you in about five minutes. Can you use him, over?" the voice asked.

"Send him, buddy, send him. To the 100 degree radial of Channel 99 at 30 miles," I said.

In about three minutes I heard the radio rattle. "Nail 31, this is Nim 25, over."

"Roger, Nimrod 25, this is Nail 31. I have a helicopter for you. He is on the ground at the Doughnut Karst. What kind of ordinance do you have?" I asked.

The Nim pilot shot back, "I have 2,500 rounds of .50-caliber in the nose, Nail, four 750-pound napes and four 750-pound hard bombs, over."

"Roger, Nimrod 25, this is Nail 31. We will dispense with the normal target information since you are familiar with the Doughnut Karst. Your target is an unfriendly helicopter that just landed on the north side of the karst. He is within 100 meters of the side of the karst. I want you to make a run from north to south, dropping all four napes in a salvo 200 meters north of the north side of the karst. You copy?"

The A-26 pilot said he had enough moonlight to make the drop without me popping a flare.

"Then it is your target, Nim 25. Nail 31 is pulling off to the east, over," I told him.

"Understand, 31," came the answer.

"Watch it now, Earl," I said. "The Nim will be in any second." We orbited well out of the way. I was not sure in which direction the A-26 would pull off the target. I would have bet he would go straight through, but you never could tell. So I wanted to be well clear of him and any antiaircraft fire that might just pop up.

Suddenly, the whole side of the karst lit up like a Halloween bonfire at a wiener roast. The four 750-pounder napalm bombs threw a streak of fire almost 300 meters long and 150 meters wide. It looked like the whole world was on fire down there. Just as the string of fire reached the side of the karst, back in the middle of it, there was a tremendous explosion.

"You got him, Nim," I was yelling into the boom. "You got him."

"Yeah, well, just to be sure, 31, here I come again with the guns."

We could not see the striking black and green A-26 in the murk, but we sure as hell could see the eight .50-caliber heavy machine guns lacing the ground in the fire with high-explosive incendiary slugs. They danced all over the area.

"Take it high and dry, Nim," I was calling.

"Roger, 31," the Nimrod acknowledged, "and good show little buddy."

The attacking A-26 swung off into the night, heading for The Trail. He still had some ordinance remaining, and he wanted to drop it on some trucks out there. We could hear another Nail calling for air cover.

I asked Invert if he could get me a reccy bird down for some photos of the place. He said he could. In some twenty minutes, Invert had me a photo bird on the scene, an F-101 VooDoo. The 101 made two passes over the area, running his highspeed cameras. I wanted this to confirm the kill. I knew that the Nim had gotten the helicopter. The explosion that had come from the center of the nape fire was not coconuts blowing up.

Earl looked at me in the glare of the dim cockpit lights and remarked, "I think this has been one hell of a night. How about we adjourn to the bar?"

"I second the motion," I told him. "You pass, Earl. From now on you can go on out to The Trail and play with the big boys!"

On the way back to the field, Earl asked me, "Aren't you about ready to rotate back to the States?"

"Yes," I responded. "As a matter of fact, I felt if you passed your ride tonight, I would make this my last night flight. I'm tired, Earl. I have been at it out here almost every night for three months solid. I feel I'm on the edge of my luck. I figure it is time to hang it up. In four months I have killed seventy-five trucks and forty-one guns and five elephants. And tonight the chopper. I quit. I think this was the grand finale. My luck is sort of shot full of holes, Earl."

He mused, "Whatcha gonna do now before you go?"

"Well," I told him, "I have about ten days before my port call. Probably do another couple of day missions. Then I think

I will take it easy. Leave it all up to you young guys. About a year of this will make an old man out of you fast. And I have been flying in Laos and on The Trail ten months. It is time to quit, Earl. And I intend to do just that real soon."

The runway lights of Nakhom Phanom seemed particularly bright, like friendly beacons winking at me. I did not linger when I stepped from The Restless One. It was just about all over for me. I knew there would be no more nights of zooming in under those confounded flares on The Trail. No more nights of diving into the bowels of the dragon, wondering if I'd come out the other side in one piece. No more nights of watching the A-1s of the Hobos, the Zoros, going inverted in their pull off after a dive bomb run. No more slipping and dodging the strings of red beer cans that floated up at you in slow motion. Those seemingly harmless, euphoric balls of red floating up to meet you. No, I would not miss it at all.

Earl gathered his chute and his survival vest and began to walk away. I said to him, "Earl, I have seen the elephant and beat him. Night after night, day after day."

He turned to me, looking at me funny. "Huh?"

"Oh, never mind. You will understand what I am saying in about a year."

Earl was shaking his head as he climbed onto the blue bus. I watched in amazement as the Lao driver dashed from the driver's seat and took off into the glare of a street light to catch a huge rice bug. I continued to watch in equal amazement as the man bit the bug in half, letting the hard part fly way into the night.

I climbed onto the old dusty bus, sat on the hard board seats, shifted the ugly little submachine gun some so it would not catch on my leg, and said to the driver, "Take me home, James."

The little guy turned and hollered at me excitedly, "Me not James. Me Thai boy. Me Nakthang."

I looked at him out of the darkness from the back of the bus, then stretched out on the board seat, pulling my slouch

Nail hat down over my eyes, and said to him, "Aww, go to hell, you stupid shit, but you stop bus at airmen mess so I can eat."

"Okay, I stop you eat airman's mess," the driver sing-songed back at me. I looked skyward and thanked my angel. "Thank you, Lady, two more, I think, and we will end this insanity. Without your help I couldn't have made it. Thank you. Amen."

Earl snickered.

APPENDIX

Laos Background

To appreciate what was going on in the turmoil of Laos, some additional information is necessary.

MR I - Commander & Staff
Cmdr, Brig. Gen. Tiao Sayavong
Dep Cmdr (Ops), Col. Bounchan Savathphayphane
Dep Cmdr (QW), Col. Tiao Vannaseng

MR I - Subdivision
Phong Saly - Cmdr, Col. Vannaseng
Houa Khong - Col. Khamphay Sayasith
Sayaboury - Lt. Col. Vikon Bilavaron

MR II - Commander & Staff
Cmdr, Maj. Gen. Vang Pao - Leader of Meo Tribesmen and Guerrillas CIA-Trained and Financed. Established Long Thien city as secret base-camp.
Dep (Ops), Col. Chansom Pakdymonivong
Dep (Logs) Col. Bounnoi Phaophongsavath

MR II - Subdivision
Sam Nuea - Lt. Col Phanh Siharath
Xieng Khouang - Lt. Col. Neng Cheu

MR III - Commander & Staff
Cmdr, Maj. Gen. Bounpon Makthepharaks
Dep, Brig. Gen. Kot Venevongsos
Dep (GW), Col. Bounteng

MR III - Subdivision
Khamkeut - Lt. Col. Vannivong Soumpholphakdy
Khammouana - Col. Lattanabanlang
Tchepone - Col. Savath
Savannakhet - Col. Nouphet

MR IV - Commander & Staff
Comdr, Maj. Gen. Phasouk Samly
Dep (Ops), Brig. Gen. Kane Insisiengmay
Dep (Log), Col. Khammay Vannavong

MR IV - Subdivision
Saravane - Col. Vang Thanadabouth
Sedone - Col. Khampheth Thousavath
Attopey - Col. Khong Vongnarath
Khong Sedone - Col. Koka Phomspha
Champassak - Col. Somsack
Sithandone - Col. Moly Siphanthong

MR V - Commander & Staff
Cmdr, Maj. Gen. Kouprasith Abhay
Dep (Ops), Col. Thonglith Chokbengboun
Dep (Psyops & Logs), Col. Onh Sananikone

MR V - Subdivision
Vientiane - Col. Inpanh Louangrath
Paksane - Col. Atsaphanthong Pathammavong

Neuts
Cmdr, Mong Soui Subject - Colsing Lt. Col. Pong

Key U.S. Officials to the Lao Government
Chief of Mission (Vientiane): Ambassador William H. Sullivan
Army Attache (Vientiane): Colonel Kurtz J. Miller, Jr.
Navy Attache (Bangkok, Thailand): Capt. Charles A. Barton, USN
Air Attache (Vientiane): Col. Robert L. F. Tyrrell

LAOS, JULY 1968

PART I. GOVERNMENT

A. Key Civilian Officials:
Chief of State: King Avang Vatthana
Prime Minister, Minister of Foreign Affairs, Minister of National Defense: Souvanna Phouma (Neutralist)
Deputy Prime Minister, Minister of National Economy, Minister of Planning: Prince Souphanaouvong (Communist-Neo Lak Hak Xat)
Deputy Prime Minister, Minister of Education: Leuam Insisiengmay (Conservative)
Minister of Finance, Minister of National Economy (Acting): Sisouk na Champassak
Minister of Planning (Acting): Inpeng Suryadhay

B. Type and Stability of Government:
Constitutional monarchy with parliamentary government in which Cabinet theoretically responsible to elected National Assembly. Souvanna Phouma's Government of National Union, formed in 1962 by coalition of Conservative, Neutralist, and Communist Neo Lao Hak Xat (NLHX) factions, remained legal government despite rightist coup attempts and withdrawal of Communist elements from active participation in government. Tripartite coalition government never effective throughout Laos; Neo Lao Hak Xat continued to administer areas under its control. Souvanna's Cabinet strengthened by influx of vigorous young administrators as result of reorganization. The 59-member National Assembly, elected 1 January 1967, was more competent and disciplined than its predecessor. The Government's progress was impeded by factional, family, and regional loyalties which played predominant roles in domestic politics. Stability in non-Communist areas of Laos depended on maintenance of cooperation between Souvanna, the Royal Laotian Army, and the King. Souvanna, though personally aware that the security of Laos depended on U. S. support,

maintained posture of neutrality and commitment to tripartite governmental facade in order to retain international acceptance.

C. Insurgency

Estimated 29,500 Pathet Lao troops were supported by 19,500 North Vietnamese cadre and regular troops as well as by 2,500 Dissident Neutralists. Pathet Lao was the name given to the military arm of the NLHX (New Lak Hak Xat) political party. It has been renamed the Lao People's Liberation Army, but the latter name is not in common usage.

In addition, about 15,000 NVN personnel, consisting of an undetermined mixture of regular troops and civilian laborers, were estimated to be in Laos for the purpose of building, maintaining, and securing the infiltration routes between North Vietnam and South Vietnam. That force was normally not involved in the North Vietnam Army/Pathet Lao effort against the Royal Laotian Government forces.

D. Communist Influence

The Neo Lak Hak Xat (NLHX), the Lao Communist political organization, remained increasingly dependent on North Vietnam for direction and support. Despite NLHX withdrawal from active roles in government in 1963, Lao Communists continued to regard tripartite concept as the source of legitimacy locally and abroad and as a framework for rejoining the government when situations opportune for suspension of hostilities and adoption of political tactics were at hand. Cabinet posts held by the NLHX were filled by Neutralists or Conservatives but remained earmarked for the Communist should they elect to rejoin the government. Conservative elements in the government determined to permanently bar Communists from these seats but failed in their attempts.

PART II. MILITARY, GENERAL

A. Key Military Officials

Armed Forces: Commander in Chief of the Royal Laotian Army (Forces Armees Royales, FAR), Maj Gen Ouan Rathikoun;

Navy Commander of FAR River Flotilla, Lt. Col. Sinthavavong Kindavong

Air Force: Brig. Gen. Sourith Don Sasorith

B. Position of the Armed Forces

The Armed Forces were relatively stable, and remained in support of Prime Minister Souvanna Phouma's Government at that time.

C. Military Budget

For fiscal year ending 30 June 1968, $34,414,666; 51% of total budget, and 210 of estimated GNP. Dollar values converted from KIP at the official exchange rate of 240 KIP equal $1.00.

D. Military Alliances and Agreements

Agreement signed at Geneva, 23 July 1962, prohibited any military alliance inconsistent with neutrality of Laos, including SEATO.

E. Manpower Resources:

1. Population: 2,801,000 as of 1 January 1968. Males (ages 15-49: 672,000; physically fit, 360,000. Major components: Lao—50%; Phouteng (Kha)—27%; Thai—16%; Others—7%. Illiteracy (1968) 70-75%.

2. Conscription: Under provisions of 1950 decree, all able-bodied males subject to 18 months compulsory military service. However, the FAR is actually maintained by volunteers, since the pay compares favorably to that of the few civilian jobs.

3. Reserves: No organized reserve system.

4. Mobilization Capacity: The various military factions in Laos were currently at or near maximum mobilization with available reserves in 1968.

PART III. MISSION and CAPABILITIES of FORCES

A. Army

(Forces Armees Royales (FAR) and Forces Armes Neutralistes (FAN)

1. Mission: Territorial defense and counterinsurgency.

2. Capabilities and Limitations: Although FAR and FAN were able to oppose Pathet Lao on relatively equal terms, they usually could stand up to North Vietnamese Forces (North Vietnamese Army—NVA). FAR, organized for internal defense, it was little more than an early warning system against North Vietnamese or Chinese incursion.

The enemy dry season offensive which began early in 1968 was the most intensive of recent years. In January 1968, the FAR suffered a costly defeat at Nam Bac, where it lost a force which represented most of its tactical reserve. The Pathet Lao-North Vietnamese forces made significant inroads into government territory, and have succeeded in tying down FAR units in static defense positions. The Communists were in a position to harass towns and lines of communication almost at will.

Laotian troops were physically strong and agile, familiar with local terrain and social conditions. However, they suffered from inadequate training and education, dependence on foreign assistance to train and maintain forces, lack of will to fight, and lack of logistical capacity for sustained field operations. They were also inclined to be indolent, fatalistic, and non-aggressive.

3. Status of Arms and Equipment: Sufficient stocks of small arms and individual equipment were available to equip existing forces in Laos. Vehicle and equipment maintenance at the organizational level was poor because of a general lack of technical skills on the part of the Lao. Attrition of material was high, even allowing for the adverse climate. Warehouse space was critically short.

B. Navy

(FAR River Flotilla)

(C) The Laotian River Flotilla, under the control of FAR, was a small river force with a fair capability to patrol the Mekong River and provide troop transport. The Flotilla's effectiveness and its river convoy escort capability were increased by the addition of six 60-foot diesel-powered river craft.

C. Royal Laotian Air Force

(RLAF) an element of FAR

1. Mission: To provide logistical support, tactical air support, armed and visual reconnaissance, medical evacuation, and airlift for the Royal Laotian Army (FAR).

2. Capabilities and Limitations: RLAF was capable of providing transport and aerial resupply support and had an effective tactical air support capability, utilizing T-28 trainer aircraft as fighter/bombers. The RLAF was solely dependent on foreign sources for material and logistic support.

3. (C) Status of Arms and Equipment: All aircraft were conventional, of U. S. design, and considered in good condition. Maintenance was rated satisfactory; was generally performed by non-Lao personnel.

D. Paramilitary Forces

All paramilitary forces were under the control of the FAR.

PART IV. MILITARY STRENGTH and ORGANIZATION

A. Army

(Forces Armees Royales (FAR), Forces Armees Neutralistes (FAN), and ADC (Guerrilla) forces.

1. Personnel Strength: FAR—45,000; FAN—9,500; Auto Defense du Choc (ADC)—5,000; Total—59,500.

2. Organization: FAR ground forces were organized into 61 infantry battalions, 1 artillery regiment (4 battalions), and 1 armored "regiment" (4 company-size groups). Royal Army Forces were deployed throughout the western half of the country. Although FAN forces were moved toward incorporation into the FAR, they retained a nominally separate status. These forces were organized into 14 infantry battalions, 1 armored battalion, and 1 artillery battalion. The FAN forces were concentrated in the Vang Vieng, Muong Soui, Lao Ngam, and Souvanna Khili areas. In addition, there were 50 separate company-size guerrilla units of the Auto Defense du Choc (ADC), under FAR control, which were directly responsive to local

regional FAR commanders. A reorganization of the FAR was approved which would standardize battalion strengths and improve operational control of the five Military Region commanders by removing intermediate command echelons.

B. Royal Laotian Air Force

(an element of FAR)

1. Personnel Strength: 1,500 personnel (total includes 102 pilots)

2. Aircraft Strength: Total 67 (56 prop; 11 hel) In operational units: 61 (50 prop; (16 trans; 25 tnr; 9 other; 11 hel; 11 piston)

3. Organization: Consisted of 5 major commande: Tactical, Air Training, Air Transport, Air Material, and Air Communications.

A reorganization plan had been approved but had not been fully implemented. Under this plan, the air force was composed of 4 composite squadrons located at Vientiane, Savannakhet, Luang Prabang, and Pakse.

C. Total Military Personnel Strength

Royal Laotian Army (FAR)		51,950
Army	(45,000)	
Air Force (RLAF)	(1,500)	
River Flotilla	(450)	
ADC	(5,000)	
Neutralists (FAN)		9,500
Army	(9,500)	
TOTAL		61,450

COMMUNIST FORCES IN LAOS

1. Mission: To win support of the people, overthrow the government, and establish a Communist regime.

2. Capabilities and Limitations: Were capable of effective guerrila operations and of mounting conventional attacks of battalion size. Spearheaded by NVA cadres, Pathet Lao were generally effective in offensive actions against the FAR and Neutralist forces. Without such cadres, Pathet Lao suffered

from generally the same deficiencies as FAR: low level of basic education, inadequate training, lack of will to fight, and ethnic diversity (40% of Pathet Lao troops were drawn from ethnic minority groups). NVA/PL troops could have overrun Laos with little difficulty, but without the NVA presence, the Pathet Lao would have probably collapsed both politically and militarily. Logistic support entirely depended on maintenance of existing roads and trails between Laos and North Vietnam (NVN).

3. Status of Arms and Equipment: A variety of small arms, automatic weapons, mortars, and light recoilless rifles, some artillery and light antiaircraft artillery obtained from numerous sources were present. Formerly supplied by USSR, in 1968 by NVN and ChiComs. In addition, weapons of U. S. manufacture captured from Neutralists and FAR and others of French origin were utilized. Maintenance of weapons and supplies received from North Vietnam was generally adequate.

4. Personal Strength and Units:

	Strength	Infantry Battalions	Combat Support Battalions
Pathet Lao (PL)	13,350	27	29
Pathet Lao with NVA Advisors (PL/A)	10,300	35	
Pathet Lao/North Vietnamese Army (PL/NVA)	12,500	36	
North Vietnamese Army (NVA)	12,850	32	1
Dissident Neutralists	2,500	14	3
Total Communist Forces	51,500	144	33

5. Organization: Communist forces were loosely organized into 144 infantry battalions concentrated in northern, northeastern, and eastern Laos. These battalions included pure Pathet Lao units, Pathet Lao units with North Vietnamese Army advisors (Approximately 20 per bn), mixed Pathet Lao/North Vietnamese Army battalions (approximately 1-1 ratio, PL to NVA) and regular North Vietnamese Army battalions. All battalions

were relatively small, varying between 200-400 men each. Two dissident Neutralist groups allied themselves with Pathet Lao: Khamouane dissidents (1,300 troops) operating in Phong Saly Province, Northern Laos, and the Deuane dissidents (1,200 troops) operating in the Plaine des Jarres.

At a later point I will tell of missions over the North; then into Laos. Both conducted and executed by 23 TASS FAC's and 5th SF forces. These were called Heavy Hook missions where Long Range Reconnaissance Patrol Teams, called "LRRP's," were inserted into North Vietnam on fact-finding forays for a period of four to seven days to survey road traffic, monitor ground force activity and numbers of enemy troops present in the area where the teams were inserted. Team insertion was made by U.S. helicopters. Personnel used on these intelligence-gathering efforts were trained Cambodians, South Vietnamese, Meo Tribesmen, some North Vietnamese who had defected to South Vietnam, and paid mercenaries of French background. No U.S. military personnel. Initially.

Prairie Fire Missions came into being when Johnson halted bombing of the North and abolished the MACVSOG team insertions into North Vietnam. All teams that had been on the ground in North Vietnam were simply extracted and new teams were then inserted into Laos. Here, though, as intelligence-gathering teams were inserted into Laos the use of U.S. Army 5th Special Forces personnel came into being. In the autumn of 1968.

During December and January of 1968 and 1969 I inserted various LRRP teams into Laos. All in the Song Ben Hai River Valley west of the DMZ. The first team I inserted from two CH-3E helicopters, call sign of "Knife" had one SF G.I. on it as team leader. A team of eleven members. The G. I. as leader, with ten Cambodian team members with him. We were shot off the Landing Zone with that team getting two wounded, two sustaining broken legs, one impaled on elephant grass stalks, and both helicopters taking damage from automatic weapons. Another team had three 5th Special Forces personnel with five Cambodians. And this team tried to catch a Caucasian leading

North Vietnamese Regular Army personnel, but the total team was lost as it got into a fire fight and called in an air strike on themselves.

NAIL PROCEDURAL GUIDE FOR HEAVY
HOOK/PRAIRIE FIRE MISSIONS (ACTUAL INSERT)

The following is intended as a guide for FAC's conducting MACVSOG 5th SF Heavy Hook and Prairie Fire Missions. Prairie Fire missions executed in Laos only (BOTH AS DIRECTED AND LAID ON BY HIGHER HEADQUARTERS)

    1. Three types of missions can be encountered:

       a. Visual Reconnaissance (re-supply)

       b. Insertion

       c. Extraction

    2. The FAC will be the mission commander and is responsible for the conduct of the flight during all three type missions.

    3. An U. S. Army observer will fly on all HH and PF missions.

    4. FAC Responsibilities

       a. Visual Reconnaissance (re-supply)

          (1) The pilot and observer will agree on the target area prior to take-off.

          (2) The observer will recommend ground sites as potential helicopter landing zones (LZ) or hover sites for ladder of hoist use (ladder will extend approximately 60 feet, hoist 100 feet). The FAC will also observe such sites and recommend for or against the site.

          (3) When sites are selected and agreed upon the FAC will select a rendezvous point and the best route to the LZ, considering terrain and known hostile defenses. The FAC should fly this route during the VR mission.

          (4) Occasionally FAC's will be called upon to re-supply ground teams. The present method is for the Army observer to drop the supplies out the right window. This has proven to be inaccurate; however, it is

hoped in the near future rocket pods can be modified for re-supply purposes. Another method that
might be used is the use of VNAF A-1E's. In these
instances an English speaking VN officer or an
American will be in one of the aircraft. The FAC
will direct the A-1E's to the re-supply area and if
necessary instruct the ground team to lay out the
appropriate panels or provide smoke signals. The
FAC should be scheduled to be in the re-supply
area 'a minimum of 30 minutes prior to the A-1E's
arrival.

(5) Occasionally a ground team will become disori-
ented and request the FAC to locate and provide
their ground location. In these instances the Army
observer will contact the ground team on FM and
request them to emit an FM signal of DF. The FAC
will then home in on the signal. Once an approxi-
mate location is determined the observer relays
the information to the ground team and other
interested agencies.

b. Insertion/Extraction

(1) Normally two FAC's will be scheduled on day of
insertion/extraction. One FAC will be primary for
the mission, the second FAC will be scheduled for
a VR mission plus backup for the insertion/extrac-
tion. Both FAC's will attend the TUOC briefing
although scheduled for different take-off times.

(2) During the briefing the FAC scheduled to make
the insertion/extraction will brief the helicopter
and escort pilots on the best route to the target
area, rendezvous point, and approach to the LZ.
The FAC also designates where he wants the high
helicopter to hold and where the escort aircraft
should work during the insertion/extraction. Frequencies are agreed upon and all air assets
should be knowledgeable of the mission.

(3) Generally, the primary FAC will launch 30 minutes prior to the helicopters and escort aircraft.

He will immediately proceed to the target area and determine whether the mission is a GO or NO GO based on weather and hostile action. If the air assets are being held on the ground for the FAC's decision they will be notified through Deer Trail or through Cricket. If the air assets have been launched they will be notified of the FAC's decision on the appropriate agreed frequency.

(4) If the weather appears favorable the FAC should send a GO signal. If he is doubtful about the weather he should relay a weather hold until he is sure or marginally sure the mission can be accomplished. If the weather is inclement the FAC should send a NO GO signal.

(5) If a weather delay is imposed or a mechanical problem develops aboard the air assets, and the first FAC becomes low on fuel, the second FAC will be scheduled to launch two hours after the first FAC and if it become necessary relieve the first FAC on or near the target area.

(6) During the insertion/extraction the FAC, from previous VR experience, knows the routes, LZ hover sites, terrain, etc. The FAC guides the low helicopter into the LZ for the insertion/extraction (usually by providing no-gyro headings). The FAC is continually observing and looking for hostile actions that may influence the success of the mission.

(7) In the event hostile defenses are encountered the FAC must determine whether or not the mission should be continued. The FAC is responsible for directing fighter strikes against hostile actions in the target area.

(8) The FAC should keep in mind during an insertion mission that continually circling the LZ could compromise the LZ. Therefore, it is best to off-set from the LZ when directing the helicopter to the target area.

(9) During an extraction mission the U. S. Army observer will coordinate with the ground team, generally on FM. The use of smoke, mirrors, or pin-lite flares by the ground team can be used and will aid the helicopter in locating the LZ. Aircraft smoke rockets will not be used unless specifically requested by the Army or helicopter personnel.

(10) The FAC will keep the low helicopter in sight at all times and should be aware of the location of the other air assets.

(11) On occasion, a multiple insertion/extraction will occur. The FAC, in this situation, is responsible for moving the air assets from one location to another and repeating the insertion/extraction process.

These Top Secret missions flown by the 23rd TASS FAC pilots with, for, and in direct support of the U.S. Army's 5th Special Forces, under MACVSOG (Military Assistance Command, Vietnam, Special Operations Ground), while politically name-covered by the innocent-sounding term of "Studies and Observation Group," are absolutely the best trained, most motivated, most capable, professional soldiers, meanest bad asses the United States Army possesses. They are the GREEN BERETS. The skills at war these troopers possess goes beyond words, their persistence and dedication to job accomplishment is of extreme caliber and honor.

Also, the FAC pilots of the 23rd TASS who flew and operated in Laos in direct support of the Lao Armed Forces, especially the Army, under the Secret Cricket West Program. The geographic area of Laos in which, and over which, this program covered and FAC sorties were flown by the "Nail" Fac's, consisted of a 200 mile stretch of Lao soil from the Lao side of the Mekong inland for a 20 miles depth. That strip of land the Lao Army tried to keep free of the Pathet Lao and NVA forces extended from the town of Vientiane in MR V, through MR III and all the way along the Mekong into the edge of MR IV below Savannakhet. Every day Monday through Friday from

0800 until 1700 the FAC's of the 23rd TASS "fought" the Lao war in that strip of land with a Royal Lao Army Lieutenant on board, using a Lao call sign. Eagle Red was the author's.

The 23rd's pilots who flew the Cricket West Program, just as those who flew for the 5th Special Forces under MACVSOG, were the most experienced pilots the 23rd had. Never, at any one time, were there more than five or six pilots checked out and qualified to fly "Cricket West." The pilots who flew these two Secret and Top Secret missions guarded who was permitted to be checked out to become qualified to fly each program. As the old, experienced FACs who flew the various programs rotated back to "the world," as we used to say, or on an emergency basis when a pilot was lost, a meeting would be held among the pilots flying either, or both programs, and a replacement pilot would be selected and voted upon to become one of "the brothers" to fly in these special mission programs. Only level-headed, cool, professional, high-flying-time pilots were selected. Especially so, where the 5th Special Forces insert and extraction LRRP missions were involved, as possibilities of engagement with NVA forces was certain to be 100% over time. Lives were at stake on each and every mission. The lives of the Special Force personnel, the indige personnel used so often, the helicopter crews who had to insert and extract the teams, and more often than not, also the lives of the FAC's and the fighter/bomber pilots and crews who had to give cover fire and support to the 5th's mission if the shit hit the fan.

In the cases where the 23rd TASS FAC pilots flew in Cricket West's area, with a Royal Lao Army observer on board, there were also direct engagements with Pathet Lao and North Vietnamese regular troops as the PL and NVA personnel tried to overrun or to capture Lao outposts, villages, or take whole sections of land that was under free Lao control. Therefore, it was imperative that the 23rd FAC be a mature, highly experienced pilot and Forward Air Controller. Almost on a daily basis battles would erupt somewhere within the Cricket West's geographical area where enemy and friendly forces would be engaged in a shoot-out within measured feet of each other, near hand-to-hand. And, in such circumstance, where the FAC was required to call in "fast-movers," jet fighter-bombers, or Lao F-28 fighters, the difference between who the FAC ordered ordinance dropped on was the pure experience of the FAC and his cool-headed control of the situation. In any engagement, the absolute worst thing in the world that a FAC could do was, become excited, lose control, and drop ordinance upon "friendly" personnel. We called it, a "short round." Where the FAC made a mistake and hit friendly force personnel with bombs, napalm, machine gun fire, that was an unforgivable mistake and the FAC would no longer be a FAC. Therefore, when the necessity of dropping ordinance in close proximity to friendly troops became a reality, often live or die for survival, the experience and deliberate, calm, actions of a FAC was an absolute must. Consequently, to avoid a political nightmare, even though the U.S. was not officially in Laos conducting war activities, the political scene was not a place for a green, young, inexperienced Forward Air Controller to be flying in the Cricket West Program and, by accident or otherwise, drop ordinance upon Lao soldiers and forces friendly to the Lao military who could be working with them.

However, no matter how hard we tried, no matter how much ordinance we expended onto the North Vietnamese army, the Pathet Lao, and no matter how hard and how much effort the Nail and Raven FAC's worked to support the Lao military forces, our CIA and Air America, the handwriting was on the wall even in 1969 when I left Laos, left Nakhon Phanom; that handwriting simply said, "there are too many of the enemy, the supply line to this part of the world is too long and too thin, and our efforts, like those of the French would end in tragedy. The French's ended with the fall of Dien Bien Phu. Officially, our's ended upon August 15, 1973. Laos was won by the communist forces. But, before the end came in 1973, during 1968 and 1969, us pilots of the 23rd TASS flew daily in Cricket West and Laos on Prairie Fire missions and day and night strike missions. There was constant enemy activity. By mid-1969 the area to the west of the DMZ contained some 70,000 NVA Army personnel. Landing Zone watchers were employed by the NVA to alert NVA special forces teams to kill or catch the U.S. 5th SF teams inserted into Laos. Activity by both sides was heavy and kill and be killed activity was on-going all over Laos by 1969 in ever increasing magnitudes.

Laos was broken up into geographic areas for command and control purposes, for communications and battle priorities. Pilots and aircraft out of NKP operated in and over all of Laos. Primarily 23rd TASS FAC's flew Steel Tiger, Tiger Hound and the D,E,F and G areas of steel Tiger and Tiger Hound. Plus CW.

BRIEFING GUIDE CRICKET WEST OPERATION
From take-off until landing, the sortie is basically under the direction and control of the Lao observer. On take-off he will first ask you to fly to GT 109 which is in the outer northern limits of Thakhek, right on the river. A line drawn from the Thakhek airport to the west, right off the end of the runway, will put you right over GT 109. The observer will make contact with the Army unit stationed there who will, in turn, give you the area of assignment.

From GT 109, you will sometimes proceed to the eastern end of the Thakhet runway where you will find another Army camp. This one is the basic artillery camp called GM 19. Observer will again make contact for any further targeting in case GT 109 does not have anything.

From GM 19, you will normally proceed to C-1 which is in the second valley north, and has two outposts; one marked by an orange letter as determined by the day and code. The other final outpost, which is by a small piece of karst and shows a ten foot letter "T". C-1 will normally have a target for you if you are working in Cricket West. If not, a heading of approximately 150 degrees will take you over two karst ridges to a gentle slope heavily wooded, with a small slashed out area, and a small camp in the middle of it guarding the arroyo. This camp is B-2. The observer will again talk to the ground for lucrative targets. If there is no news from B-2, then head about 120 degrees and go to another little slash camp, called B-1, which is very close to the little river and is supposed to be in friendly hands again. In the present state of confusion, you may be asked to go directly from GF 109 to B-36 which is part way down route Thirteen, south from Thakhek. Your observer will tell you when you are there.

If, when you finish the check-out with GT 109, the observer says to go to B-34. Get Invert to give you steers to the 340 degree radial at about 43 miles. B-34 is located in the narrow gorge along the river and will be contacted on the same FM frequencies, 47.6. All locations are using these frequencies and you should have no problems. Prior to leaving the briefing, the briefing officer will tell you whether you will have Eagles or not. The Eagles are F-28s flown by Laos and are from Savannakhet. Normally you will be briefed by your observer before we go as to general target area. The normal rendezvous for the Lao F-28s is at Ban Penang, the little town just on the edge of the river, south of Mahaxai, or whatever other coordinates you decide upon with the observer. Once you are airborne, you should contact Smoky control on 255.1 and ask them what time you will have Eagles. After you have checked all the rendezvous points previously mentioned you will tell Smoky where you will be working and where you want his Eagles to meet you. Smoky control will usually give you Eagles at Alpha time (0830), Bravo time (1030), or Charlie time, which is (1430) in the afternoon. He may give you an oddball time later on depending on resources. Smoky will also give you the ordinance carried by the Eagles.

You must speak very slowly to the Eagles; Eagle lead usually speaks good English. If you have Seri or Sohn or Konchan with you you can tell him to have lead hit your smoke or make corrections. Mark first and verify with the observer that this is the proper location.

As I told you, the area of BV-34 is presently OK for strikes without getting further ambassadorial approval. Check on the ground to make certain that the area is still OK. The ground commander across the river, when in contact with the Lao observer, has blanket validation for targets of his own choosing. Villages must be validated by and of his own choosing. Villages must be validated by and through Smoky control. Very tight subject at present. Check with intel for validated areas prior to take off. If you want a particular area validated, bring the coordinates back and pass to Smoky and they will notify you in the air as to the target status. The normal Cricket report of strikes will be turned in on all sorties except the Eagles. The Eagle strike in the same strike format will be called to Smoky control after the Eagles clear the target area. When you go to BV-34 it is entirely possible that you may have to relay through a Raven FAC to pass the info to Smoky unless you are at seven thousand feet. Normal operation in the B-2 B-1 C-1 area should be 4500' MSL in Cricket North, 340/43/89, at 5000' MSL south of the Little Rooster Tail, and west of route Thirteen you can safely operate at 3500'. Always test 47.6 with Dullness Control prior to take off. If it is inoperative, no point in going across the river. Be very careful in the high karst area as the bastards will move .50 cal machine guns up on top of the 1800 foot karst peaks, along with 60 mm mortars, to harass the ground troops and the FAC's. Normally, you can arrange a rendezvous with the Zoro at the 090 radial at about 22 miles. This will put you in a good position to go either direction to targets.

The Senior CW FAC will fly a mission with you one of these days holding hands. He will have the observer with him and you can monitor the freqs mentioned above and he will take you on a guided tour to the various complexes and target areas and friendly troop locations.

We kept accounts of what we did in CW. We had a regular format for our own information. It went like this:

Mission Debriefing Guide
1. Date
2. Hours (take off and landing times)
3. Nail Numbers (Pilot and Observer)
4. Outposts Contacted
5. Information received from outposts
   a) Enemy activity
   b) Target coordinates and description

c) BDA from previous strikes

d) Ground fire

e) Miscellaneous

6. Targets struck with BDA and Strike A/C each target

7. Significant VR

8. Recommendations

   a. Target to strike at future date

   b. Areas of continued VR

   c. Sortie launch time for following day

9. Whether or not mission was thoroughly debriefed with chief observer

10. Any other remarks.

Here are some exact diary accounts of days, missions and results. This only a partial of the activity, but gives a fair idea of what happened.

1. 7 Dec 68

2. 1320 - 1800

3. Nail 31 & 97

4. GT-109, C-1 Hdqtrs, C-1, B-1

5. Hdqtrs C-1: Area east of C-1 still heavily occupied with NVA & PL Troops. C-1 gave us a 60 mm mortar position plus troops at #1: WE 027283; 82 mm mortar position at #2: WE 034278; rice/ammo storage at #3: WE 078278.

6. Targets #243 were struck by Tomcat, a flight of 2 - F4's, with CBU-24. Tomcat 2 dropped 600 meters short of Target #3 causing a fire and large secondary explosion at: WE 040273 in a foliated area. Hobo 24 & 25 were put in on this position with CBU-24. No further results. C-1 informed us we were being fired upon from the small valley south at: WE 027264. Valley was covered with CBU-25. A company of NVA is located there. No visual results. A large herd of buffalo were spotted at WE 062273. They were strafed and ran into a foliated area to the north.

7. Village on chart 6044 III at: We 255 538. 3 Hootches — many well traveled paths in village — large buffalo herd — 150-175 in adjoining fields to the north and east. Vil-

lages at WE 228585 & WE 228589 suspicious. Received ground fire at D-75. Could not spot anyone.

8. Recommend further VR of above mentioned villages. Recommend strike be put in on new bridge located on chart #6043 IV at: WE 073289. Also recommend strike around north and south side of karst located at that position for a distance of 1000 meters either side. Also recommend CBU be dumped in small valley east of C-1, WE 027264, to keep NVA out. Recommend sortie T.O. for Monday 9 Dec. 0700

9. Kongta did not debrief mission with Lt. Sery.

10. Recommend observers obtain info ASAP from outposts and cut extraneous chatter.

1. 9 Dec 68
2. 0625 - 1105
3. Nail 31 & 95
4. GT-109; hdqtrs C-1; C-1, B-2, B-1
5. No initial information from any outpost.
6. We struck recommended target from previous mission on 7 Dec. Put Bigot, flight of 2-F4's, on WE 074289. Bridge, troops and pack animals near the bridge to the north. CBU-24 and 20 mm was expended. 3 pack animals were destroyed with one sec fire on south side of karst. Put in Baracuda, 2-F105's on WE 0272725. Herd of pack buffalo/supplies near C-1 to the east. Expended 20 mm. NVR due to the foliage. Put in Eagle Red 2-F-28's on WE 074289 bridge—expended napalm and 4 250 lbs. Destroyed bridge. Put Eagles on company of NVA in valley east and south of C-1 at: WE 027264. Received ground fire from WE 024282. Put in Firefly 24 on troops at this position with LAU-3 and 2 M-17's NUR to smoke and foliage.
7. The buffalo mesa still has herds totaling 1200 to 1500 head.

Bunkers in Vee shape (three in number) are located on south bank of D-75.

The two suspicious villages mentioned in previous mission at WE 228585 & WE 228589, which are fenced, are more than likely Meo villages—not hostile fortified villages.

At WE 300341 a large boat approximately 25 feet in length was spotted—heavily loaded with rice. I wanted to strike but the observer didn't want to, even though it wasn't in a friendly area. Observer wanted to depart area to see if boat would change location to prove unfriendly. I complied. Upon return could not locate boat.

Upon our return we contacted GT-109. We were informed that a full regiment of NVA (12 comp) or 3 battalions, are located in a two click square area. Also located with the regiment are multiple artillery pieces—unknown at this time other than .50 cal and .30 cal and possible 105 howitzers—plus 60 mm and 80 mm mortar.

Coordination and planning has been set up through TFA for a full scale bombing attack to commence at 0630 local on the 10th of Dec.

Stackpole Military History Series

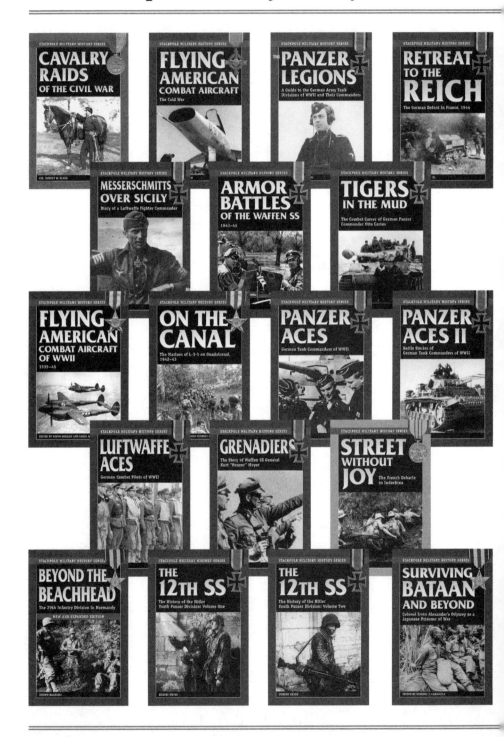

Real battles. Real soldiers. Real stories.

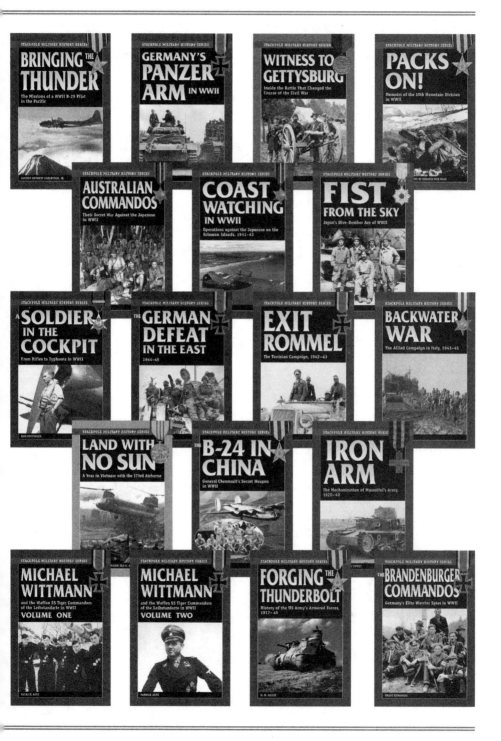

Stackpole Military History Series

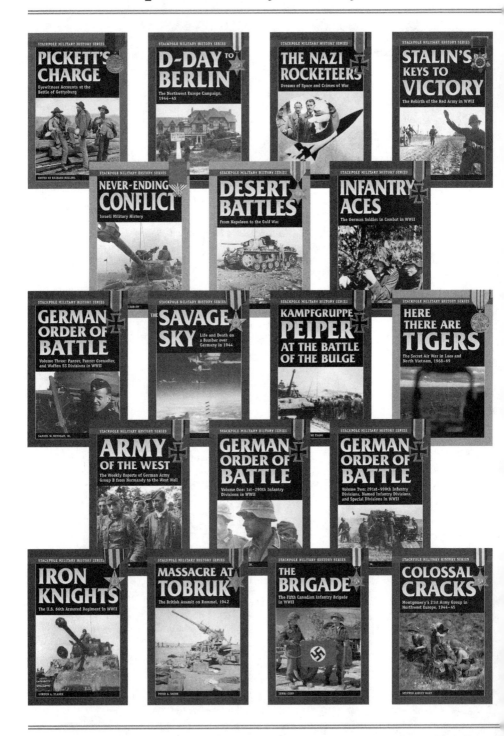

Real battles. Real soldiers. Real stories.

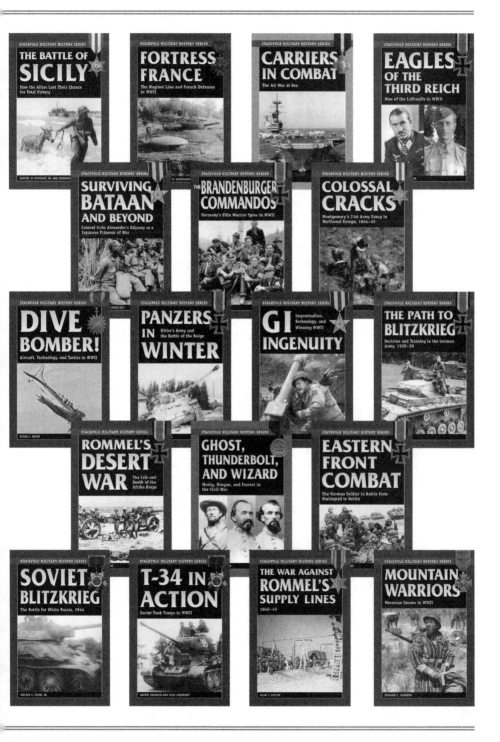

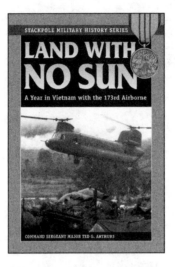

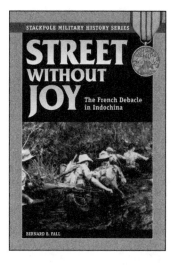

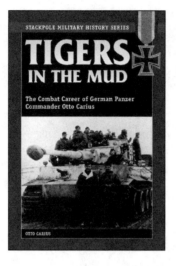

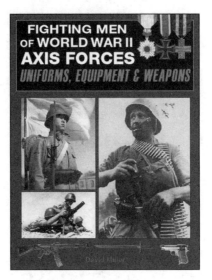